A·GUIDE·TO
Scriptural Symbols

A·GUIDE·TO

Scriptural Symbols

Joseph Fielding McConkie & Donald W. Parry

BOOKCRAFT
Salt Lake City, Utah

Library of Congress Catalog Card Number: 89-82332

ISBN 0-88494-726-2

First Printing, 1990

Printed in the United States of America

Contents

Shortened Citations for Nonscriptural Sources

Shortened Citation	Source
Doctrinal New Testament Commentary	Bruce R. McConkie, *Doctrinal New Testament Commentary*
Doctrines of Salvation	Joseph Fielding Smith, *Doctrines of Salvation*
Gospel Symbolism	Joseph Fielding McConkie, *Gospel Symbolism*
Millennial Messiah	Bruce R. McConkie, *The Millennial Messiah*
Mormon Doctrine	Bruce R. McConkie, *Mormon Doctrine*
Promised Messiah	Bruce R. McConkie, *The Promised Messiah*
Teachings	Joseph Smith, *Teachings of the Prophet Joseph Smith*

Introduction

A simple definition of *symbol* is recorded in *Webster's New World Dictionary of the American Language*. A symbol is "something that stands for or represents another thing" (p. 1442). Bullinger, in *Figures of Speech Used in the Bible*, explains that a symbol is "a material object substituted for a moral or spiritual truth" (p. 769). *The Interpreter's Dictionary of the Bible* defines a symbol as "a representation, visual or conceptual, of that which is unseen and invisible" (4:472).

Why Symbols?

Symbols are the most articulate of all languages. Indeed, symbols are the universal tongue. Birth and death, night and day, the sun and clouds, the moon and stars—these are known to all, as is the need for water, the taste of salt, and the warmth of fire. Thus these and countless things like them become symbols of timeless truths. Symbols bring color and strength to language, while deepening and enriching our understandings. Symbols enable us to give conceptual form to ideas and emotions that may otherwise defy the power of words. They take us beyond words and grant us eloquence in the expression of feelings. Symbolic language conceals certain doctrinal truths from the wicked and thereby protects sacred things from possible ridicule. At the same time, symbols reveal truth to the spiritually alert.

Symbols are teaching devices. Symbols are the language in which all gospel covenants and all ordinances of salvation have been revealed. From the time we are immersed in the waters of baptism to the time we kneel at the altar of the temple with the companion of our choice in the ordinance of eternal marriage, every covenant we make will be written in the language of symbolism. Some are uncomfortable with the temple experience because they are not familiar with the language of symbolism. The better we understand the language, or ritual, or symbol, the richer the experience we have in the mountain of the Lord's house.

As some are uncomfortable with the ceremony and ritual of the temple, so some are uncomfortable with the language of scripture. The language of both is foreign to them. Learning that language is richly rewarding. Let us illustrate: Joseph Smith received a revelation which is a prophetic description of the events of the last days and which begins with the injunction "Be ye clean that bear the vessels of the Lord" (D&C 133:5). The language is that of Isaiah (Isa. 52:11) and the imagery, that of the temple. Those who bore the "vessels of the Lord" were the priests who ministered in the holy place. Before they could bear the vessels, that is, before they could represent the Lord on his errand, it was necessary for them to be washed, anointed, and clothed in the garment of the priesthood. This ritual preparation was poignant with meaning; the washing obviously represented the necessity of their being clean both physically and spiritually in order to represent the Lord. The anointing with oil represented the outpouring of the Spirit. It naturally follows that if people are to properly represent the Lord, they must be filled with his Spirit, the requisite for which is that they be clean. Only then could they be clothed in the garments of the priesthood, for only then would they be worthy of the mantle or authority of the Lord.

Similarly, one might wonder why a bride and groom kneel facing each other across an altar when they are married in the temple. It carries great meaning to know that anciently the altar was always built on raised ground; thus, approaching the altar involved a ritual ascent. Further, the altar was the place of covenant, the place of sacrifice, and the place of the divine presence—each purpose being essential to an eternal marriage. Every gospel ordinance must answer the type; that is, symbolically it must reflect the principles it was ordained in heavenly councils to teach. Baptism must be by immersion because it is a type for the death and burial of the old man of sin and his coming forth from the grave in a newness of life in the morning of the resurrection. Joseph Smith taught: "Abel offered to God a sacrifice that was accepted, which was the firstlings of the flock. Cain offered of the fruit of the ground, and was not accepted, because he could not do it in faith, he could have no faith, or could not exercise faith contrary to the plan of heaven. It must be shedding the blood of the Only Begotten to atone for man; for this was the plan of redemption; and without the shedding of blood was no remission; and as the sacrifice was instituted for a type, by which man was to discern the great Sacrifice which God had prepared; to offer a sacrifice contrary to that, no faith could be exercised, because redemption was not purchased in that way, nor the power of atonement instituted after that order; consequently Cain could have no faith; and whatsoever is not of faith, is sin." (*Teachings*, p. 58.)

The Lord told Enoch that "all things have their likeness" and that "all things" were created and made to bear record of him (Moses 6:63). To understand the language of symbolism is to hear and comprehend that testimony.

PART 1

SCRIPTURAL SYMBOLS

Scriptural Symbols

Comprehending the usage and application of seven principal figures of speech is essential for the interpreter of scriptural symbols. Those who possess the knowledge of these figures are able to unlock the door to symbolic and figural language. A brief definition of the seven figures of speech, followed by simple examples, will illustrate their usefulness in determining and defining scriptural symbols:

1. *Metaphors.* A metaphor is defined as "a declaration that one thing is (or represents) another; or comparison by representation" (Bullinger, *Figures of Speech Used in the Bible*, p. 735). Followers of Jesus are like sheep:

"Ye are my sheep" (3 Ne. 15:24).
And Jesus is the guide of the sheep, the Shepherd:

"The Lord is my shepherd" (Ps. 23:1).

In the following three metaphoric expressions, humanity is compared to the grass of the field, the righteous are like the "salt of the earth," and Christ is the light of the world.

"All flesh is grass" (Isa. 40:6).
"Ye are the salt of the earth" (Matt. 5:13).
"Behold I am the light" (3 Ne. 18:16).

2. *Similes.* A simile is "a declaration that one thing resembles another; or, comparison by resemblance" (Bullinger, *Figures of Speech Used in the Bible*, p. 726) through the employment of the words *like* or *as*. In the first three examples, the youthful Jesus resembles a "tender plant," the wicked are compared to useless dross, and the hearts of Nephi's brethren are as hard as flint (italics are added to emphasize the usage of the words *like* and *as*).

"He [Jesus] shall grow up . . . *as* a tender plant" (Mosiah 14:2).
"Ye are *as* dross" (Alma 34:29).
"They had hardened their hearts . . . , that they had become *like* unto a flint" (2 Ne. 5:21).

Other similes compare the wicked to goats, dogs, or the "dumb ass":

"[They] fled from the presence of Alma and Amulek even *as* a goat fleeth with her young from two lions" (Alma 14:29).

"The people had turned from their righteousness, *like* the dog to his vomit" (3 Ne. 7:8).

"They shall be driven before *like* a dumb ass" (Mosiah 12:5).

3. *Hypocatastasis, or implication.* This is "a declaration that implies the resemblance or representation; or comparison by implication" (Bullinger, *Figures of Speech Used in the Bible*, p. 744). As a metaphor states the resemblance in a direct manner, and a simile features the words *like* or *as* to make a comparison between two things, hypocatastasis implies the resemblance between two objects.

In the following well-known verse, the reader can discern that the words *dog* and *swine* have reference to unrighteous and unholy beings. Nowhere in the context is the symbolism so stated; it is known only by way of implication.

"Give not that which is holy unto the dogs, neither cast ye your pearls before swine" (Matt. 7:6).

Similarly, the symbolic meaning of the words *wolves, flock,* and *trees* is implied in the following verses (a wolf is a false prophet or enemy to the Church, the flock represents members of the Church, and the tree which "bringeth not forth good fruit" is a person who does not perform good works).

"I know this, that after my departing shall grievous wolves enter in among you, not sparing the flock" (Acts 20:29).

"The axe is laid unto the root of the trees: therefore every tree which bringeth not forth good fruit is hewn down" (Matt. 3:10).

4. *Symbols revealed in plain language.* Often scriptural symbols are manifested in distinct and unmistakable language. Such is the case with parts of Doctrine and Covenants, sections 77, 86, and 113, and with Lehi's dream and many other parts of holy writ. For instance, Joseph Smith received the following explanation concerning Revelation 4:6:

"What is the sea of glass . . . ? It is the earth, in its sanctified, immortal, and eternal state." (D&C 77:1–2.)

In Doctrine and Covenants, section 86, the Lord revealed the figural meaning of several symbols, including "field" and "sowers of the seed."

"Concerning the parable of the wheat and of the tares: . . . the field was the world, and the apostles were the sowers of the seed" (D&C 86:1-2).

Nephi revealed several symbols of Lehi's dream, including the interpretation of the "rod of iron."

"What meaneth the rod of iron . . . ? . . . It was the word of God." (1 Ne. 15:23-24.)

John, in his Revelation, introduced several symbols, and then gave their interpretation.

"The seven stars are the angels of the seven churches" (Rev. 1:20).

"The seven candlesticks which thou sawest are the seven churches" (Rev. 1:20).

5. *Metonymy*. This "is a figure by which one name or noun is used instead of another, to which it stands in a certain relation" (Bullinger, *Figures of Speech Used in the Bible*, p. 538). Note how *sword* is used instead of the thing it represents — war.

"Neither shall the sword [i.e., war] go through your land" (Lev. 26:6).

A mountain can represent an idolatrous temple, where false deities are worshipped. Note that through the use of metonymy in Jeremiah 3:23, the words *hills* and *mountains* are substituted for "idolatrous sanctuaries."

"Truly in vain is salvation hoped for from the hills, and from the multitude of mountains" (see also Ezek. 18:6, 11, 15).

6. *Synecdoche, or transfer*. This is "the exchange of one idea for another associated idea" (Bullinger, *Figures of Speech Used in the Bible*, p. 612). For instance, in many instances the word *blood* is used to represent a person's guilt, not his actual blood. This is the case in Leviticus 20:9. "His blood shall be upon him" means "His guilt shall be upon him." Speaking of those who keep the commandments of the Lord, Isaiah said:

"Even them will I bring to my holy mountain, and make them joyful in my house of prayer: their burnt offerings and their sacrifices shall be accepted upon mine altar; for mine house shall be called an house of prayer for all people" (Isa. 56:7; see also Ezek. 20:40).

The idea of a "holy mountain" is exchanged for the concept of a temple. Notwithstanding the fact that the Lord refers to the temple as his "holy mountain," other temple-related things are mentioned in this verse — "house of prayer," "burnt offerings," "sacrifices," and "altar."

7. *Scriptural parallelisms* (i.e. synonymous, synthetic, and antithetical forms; antimetabole; simple, extended, and repeated alternate structures; chiasms; and the like). A defini-

tion of each of the various types of parallelisms is beyond the
scope of this introduction. (For a detailed discussion, see Bullinger, *Figures of Speech Used in the Bible*; or Donald W. Parry,
"Hebrew Literary Patterns in the Book of Mormon," *Ensign*, October 1989, pp. 58–61.) While this method in and of itself may
not be considered the greatest vehicle in determining symbolic
meaning, it can verify or confirm the interpretations of scriptural symbols as applied in the preceding six models. By way of
example, note how the following parallelistic structures suggest
figural meanings:

> "Awake, awake, put on thy strength, O Zion;
> put on thy beautiful garments, O Jerusalem."

(2 Ne. 8:24)

This synonymous parallelism points out that the words *garments* and *Jerusalem* are symbolic parallels of the words
strength and *Zion*.

In the following example, the city of Jerusalem is put in
place of Judah, or the Jews.

> "For Jerusalem is ruined, and Judah is fallen."

(2 Ne. 13:8)

Sword is often put for *war*, as is shown in 2 Nephi 13:25:

> "Thy men shall fall by the sword
> and thy mighty in the war."

Another synonymous parallelism demonstrates that the
"mountain of the Lord" is another name for the "house of the
God of Jacob," or the temple.

> "Let us go up to the mountain of the Lord,
> to the house of the God of Jacob."

(2 Ne. 12:3)

A synthetic parallelism demonstrates the same concept,
that the word *mountain* is a symbol for *temple*:

> "Even them will I bring to my holy mountain,
> and make them joyful in my house of prayer."

(Isa. 56:7)

Far more important, and overshadowing all of these seven
keys to interpreting scriptural symbols, are two indispensable
kinds of understanding, the possession of which is essential for
those who wish to understand the meaning of symbolic and
spiritual things. First, it is essential that the interpreter be
guided in all instances by the Holy Ghost. All types, figures,
symbols, emblems, shadows, and signs, as found in the scriptures, were given by the gift and power of the Holy Ghost. If the
interpretations of symbols are revealed in the scriptures, and

often they are, the same Holy Ghost will be the revealer of such things.

Second, it is essential that the interpreter have a solid background of the plan of salvation, which is to possess a firm knowledge of gospel doctrines and truths. "Before we can understand the symbol, we must understand the truth it is to convey. Understanding the principle must precede understanding the symbol. There is no substitute for good gospel scholarship, and there is no gospel understanding that will not be enriched by an improved knowledge of symbols and their meaning." (*Gospel Symbolism*, p. xi.)

Aaron. Priesthood duties of Aaron, the son of Amram and Jochebed, prefigured the sacred responsibilities of Jesus Christ, making him a type of the Lord. For instance, both the Lord and Aaron were high priests (Heb. 5:4–5; 3:1). As high priest, Aaron entered into the Holy of Holies once a year, bearing the names of the twelve tribes on his shoulders (the names of the twelve tribes were engraven upon the twelve stones of the ephod, or shoulder dress), offering a sacrifice for the sins of the people (Heb. 9:7). Christ, "by the sacrifice of himself," carried upon his shoulders the sins of the whole world, and then entered into the heavenly Holy of Holies (Heb. 9:24–26). (See also *Prophet.*)

Both Jesus and Aaron were anointed to their respective callings (Lev. 21:10; Acts 10:38). Aaron acted as spokesman for Moses (Ex. 4:14–16, 27–31), and Jesus spoke on behalf of the Father. During the absence of Moses, Aaron became the judge of Israel (Ex. 24:14), as Jesus is the Judge of the world (John 5:22; Acts 10:42).

Abel. In four principal ways, Abel, the righteous son of Adam and Eve, was a type of Christ. Both were called "righteous" (Heb. 11:4; 1 John 3:12; Moses 7:47). Both were shepherds (Moses 5:17; John 10:11). Both offered sacrifices unto God. Abel's was called "a more excellent sacrifice," but Jesus' sacrifice was the most excellent because he offered himself (Heb. 9:26; 11:4). Both were killed by the hands of the wicked (Gen. 4:8; Luke 11:51; 23:33). (See also *Prophet.*)

Abinadi. Abinadi's death by fire was a type of the manner in which the seed of his persecutors (the priests of Noah) would be destroyed (Mosiah 13:10; Alma 25:9–12). (See also *Prophet.*)

Ablution. Ablutions, or ritual washings (D&C 124:37; Heb. 9:10), symbolize the cleansing of the soul from sins and iniquities. It is one method the Lord employs to symbolize the washing away the filth of his people (Isa. 4:4). A Psalm of David best demonstrates the purpose of ablutions: "Wash me throughly from mine iniquity, and cleanse me from my sin" (Ps. 51:2; see also Ps. 73:13; Isa. 1:16). (See also *Fountain*; *Water*.)

Abraham. 1) Abram (Hebrew for "exalted father"), whose name was changed to Abraham (Hebrew for "father of a multitude"), was a type of God the Father. As the Father offered up his Only Begotten Son, so Abraham "offered up Isaac . . . his only begotten son" (Heb. 11:17; Gen. 22:2, 12; John 3:16). Jacob explained, "It was accounted unto Abraham in the wilderness to be obedient unto the commands of God in offering up his son Isaac, which is a similitude of God and his Only Begotten Son" (Jacob 4:5). Associated with this, Jesus is considered "the son of Abraham" (Matt. 1:1). (See also *Isaac*; *Prophet*.)

2) Abraham, as "the father of all them that believe" (Rom. 4:11), represents all who strive for eternal life. In this connection, therefore, it is noteworthy that the righteous Saints become the "seed of Abraham" (D&C 84:34), and are commanded to do "the works of Abraham" (D&C 132:32). (See also *Prophet*.)

Abraham's Bosom. Represents paradise, or the world of spirits, where the spirits of the just await the resurrection (Luke 16:22–23). (See also *Bosom*.)

Adam. 1) Adam, a Hebrew name which means "man" or "mankind," is a type for all men and for all mankind (1 Cor. 15:21–22; Rom. 5:12–21). As a passage in the book of Genesis explains, God "called their name Adam" (Gen. 5:2), speaking of Adam and Eve, the persons who represented all mankind.

2) The Apostle Paul explained that Adam was "the figure of him that was to come" (Rom. 5:14), referring to Jesus Christ. Both Adam and Jesus performed important roles in the plan of salvation (Rom. 5:18–19; 1 Cor. 15:21–22)—one transgressed the law, the other made atonement for all transgressors. It is fitting, therefore, that Adam was a figure of the Son of God. Furthermore, in an inspired play on words, Paul designates Adam as the "first man Adam," and Jesus as the "last Adam" (1 Cor. 15:45–47). (See also *Michael*; part 2: *Adam*.)

3) Adam, as father of all mankind, is a figure for the Father. From Abraham we learn that the name Adam literally means "first father" (Abr. 1:3).

Adder. The adder, known as the horned viper, hides in the desert sands of the Middle East, frequently in the imprint made by the foot of a camel, and then strikes at passing creatures. (See also *Asp*; *Cockatrice*; *Serpent*.)

1) The tribe of Dan is described as being "a serpent by the way, an adder in the path, that biteth the horse heels, so that his rider shall fall backward" (Gen. 49:17).

2) Too much wine is like a poison, so that "at the last it biteth like a serpent, and stingeth like an adder" (Prov. 23:31–32).

3) When ill-mannered persons speak poisonous and lethal words, they are as the venomous adder (Ps. 40:3; 58:4–5).

Adultery. "In a spiritual sense, to emphasize how serious it is, the damning sin of idolatry is called *adultery.* When the Lord's people forsake him and worship false gods, their infidelity to Jehovah is described as whoredoms and adultery. (Jer. 3:8–9; Hosea 1:2; 3:1.) By forsaking the Lord, his people are unfaithful to their covenant vows, vows made to him who symbolically is their Husband." (*Mormon Doctrine*, p. 25.) (See also *Harlot*.)

Aholah. A Hebrew word meaning "a tent." It alludes to an idolatrous sanctuary at the time of Ezekiel. In Ezekiel 23:1–5, the word *Aholah* represents the city Samaria, which figuratively committed whoredoms by worshipping idols.

Aholibah. *Aholibah* is Hebrew for "my tent is in her." In a parable of Ezekiel, *Aholibah* represents the city Jerusalem, who, with her sister Samaria, committed wickedness and abominations before the Lord (Ezek. 23:1–5).

Alma. The persecutions endured by the Book of Mormon prophets Alma and Amulek were, in many ways, similar to the oppressions known to the Messiah during his final week of mortality. All three were smitten upon their cheeks. All "answered nothing" and kept silent before their oppressors. And all were as majestic lions before the lowly goats (Alma 14:15–29). (See also *Prophet*.)

Altar. The Hebrew word for altar, *mizbach*, means a "place of slaughter or sacrifice" and represents a place of worship, prayer, sacrifice, atonement, and divine theophany. Anciently, much symbolism was attached to the altar. For example, altars were anointed with oil (Ex. 40:9–10; Lev. 8:10–11), had the words of the Mosaic law written "plainly" upon their stones (Deut. 27:8), and had an eternal fire burnt upon them (Lev. 6:12–13).

Also, according to the Mosaic law, altars were to be elevated (Lev. 9:22). The administrant would then make a ceremonial ascent toward God, where he was then found "before the Lord" (1 Kgs. 9:25; Lev. 4:6–7; Alma 15:17). Altars were situated before the throne of God (Rev. 8:3; Ex. 30:6; 40:5). Many had four horns upon the four corners (Ex. 27:2), upon which the blood of sacrificial animals was solemnly sprinkled (Ex. 29:12; Lev. 8:15; 9:9; 4:24, 30, 34). (See also *Temple; Tabernacle.*)

Amulek. See *Alma.*

Anointing. The anointing of a person or thing with sacred olive oil represents the sanctification (Lev. 8:10-12) and consecration (Ex. 28:41) of that person or thing. Anointings have been used to prepare for burials (Matt. 26:7-12; John 12:3-7), for the healing of the sick and infirm (James 5:14-15; Mark 6:13), and for the tabernacle (Ex. 30:26-27; 40:9) and its altar (Ex. 29:36; 40:10). Prophets (D&C 124:56-57; 1 Kgs. 19:16), priests (D&C 68:20; Ex. 28:41), and kings (Jacob 1:9; Ether 6:22) are anointed in similitude of the Anointed One, who is Christ (Greek for "anointed one") and Messiah (Hebrew for "anointed one"). These anointed prophets, priests, and kings are protected by God (1 Chr. 6:22; Ps. 105:15; 89:20-23; D&C 121:16), are taught from on high (1 John 2:27), and gain salvation (Ps. 20:6; D&C 109:80). Luke taught that Jesus was anointed "with the Holy Ghost and with power" (Acts 10:38). (See also *Olive Oil*; part 2: *Anointed; Christ; Messiah.*)

Ants. These tiny creatures "are little upon the earth, but they are exceeding wise." And although they "are a people not strong," yet they prepare during the summer months for the famine and hardships of the winter season (Prov. 30:25; 6:6). Ants are symbols of wise, industrious people.

Apostle. The life and works of every worthy Apostle typify the life of the Savior. Jesus is the perfect prototype, the Apostles are the types; he is the great exemplar, they are the great examples. The scriptures indicate that the Apostles were set first and foremost in the Church (1 Cor. 12:28), under the divine head, who is Jesus. They, with Jesus, form the foundation stones of the Church, Christ being the "chief corner stone" (Eph. 2:20). Christ is the Judge of the world, and the Apostles will judge the righteous of the house of Israel (D&C 29:12; 1 Ne. 12:9).

Furthermore, the Apostles, like the Lord, have the gift of prophecy (D&C 29:10), reveal the word and law of God (D&C 52:9), preach the gospel, heal those who are sick, raise the dead, and cast out evil spirits (Matt. 10:8-10). Thus the Apostles (Greek *apostolos*, meaning "one sent forth") are ministers "sent forth" (Matt. 10:5) to be "special witnesses" (D&C 107:26; 27:12) of the Lord, through their teachings, writings, and very lives. (See also part 2: *Apostle.*)

Apron. By sewing fig leaves together and making aprons for themselves, Adam and Eve covered their nakedness (Moses 4:13). In so covering themselves with leaves, they became trees, as it were. (See also *Tree.*)

Ark of the Covenant. The description of the ark of the covenant is detailed in the book of Exodus (Ex. 25:9-16; 37:1-9). Also called the "ark of the testimony" (Ex. 25:22), "ark of the Lord . . . of all the earth" (Josh. 3:13), "ark of the God of Israel" (1 Sam. 5:7), and the "holy ark" (2 Chr. 35:3), this divine vessel was connected with the divine presence of God. Also symbolically connected with God and his presence were the three items deposited within the ark — the pot of manna, Aaron's rod, and the tablets of the law (Heb. 9:4).

The ark served as God's footstool (Ps. 99:5; 132:7-8) as it was situated under his throne. The ark, being associated with Deity, brought blessings to believers of the Israelite faith (Josh. 3-4; 1 Sam. 7:1; 2 Sam. 6:2-17) and cursings to the unbelievers (Josh. 6; 1 Sam. 5:1-7; 6:19-20).

Arm. 1) Revelations equate the arm of God with the power of God. Such phrases as "power of his holy arm" (Enos 1:13), "by the power of mine arm" (Jacob 2:25), and "by my great power and by my outstretched arm" (Jer. 27:5) are frequently attested throughout holy writ. Indeed, the Lord uses his "arm of mercy" (Jacob 6:5) and his "everlasting arms" (Deut. 33:27) to create both man and beast (Jer. 27:5), to redeem his people (Ps. 77:15), and to gather the nations (Isa. 40:11). With his "strong arm" he scatters the enemies of Israel (Ps. 89:10), governs his kingdom (Isa. 40:10), and judges the people (Isa. 51:5). (See also *Hand.*)

In contrast to the arm of God is the "puny arm" (D&C 121:33) of man. Unlike the "strong arm" of Deity, the "arm of flesh" (2 Chr. 32:8) is weak and vulnerable. A verse from Nephi's psalm (2 Ne. 4:34; see also D&C 1:19) best illustrates this:

> O Lord, I have trusted in thee,
> and I will trust in thee forever.
> I will not put my trust in the arm of flesh;
> for I know that
> cursed is he
> that putteth his trust in the arm of flesh.
> Yea, cursed is he
> that putteth his trust in man
> or maketh flesh his arm.

2) The Lord's servants are his arm or his appendage as Aaron and Hur were the arms of Moses (D&C 35:13-14; 1 Ne. 22:10-11).

Armageddon. Armageddon, a Hebrew name meaning "mount of destruction," is a place found in Israel where literally scores of battles have taken place throughout history. It is also, therefore, the prophetic name of the area where the final great religious battle will focus during the immediate period before Jesus Christ makes his appearance in power and great glory.

Armor. The "whole armour of God" consists of spiritual weapons employed by righteous individuals to assist them in their warfare "against principalities, against powers, against the rulers of the darkness of this world, against spiritual wickedness in high places" (Eph. 6:11-17; D&C 27:15-18). Referred to also as the "armour of light" (Rom. 13:12) and the "armour of righteousness" (2 Cor. 6:7; 2 Ne. 1:23), this protective armament includes the "breastplate of righteousness," the "shield of faith," the "helmet of salvation," and the "sword of the Spirit," as well as protection for the feet and loins. Paul explained, "For the weapons of our warfare are not carnal, but mighty through God to the pulling down of strong holds" (2 Cor. 10:4). (See also *Breastplate; Helmet; Shield; Sword.*)

Army. Many appellations associate Deity as the master of armies. He is a "captain" (2 Chr. 13:12), a "man of war" (Ex. 15:3), a "commander" (Isa. 55:4), a "leader" (Isa. 55:4), a "shield" (Gen. 15:1), and the "Lord of Sabaoth" (Rom. 9:29; D&C 87:7; 98:2). *Sabaoth* is the Hebrew word for "armies" or "hosts"; hence the English equivalent of Lord of Sabaoth is "Lord of armies" or "Lord of hosts." The army of God consists of the faithful of his Church, whether those of ancient Israel (1 Sam. 17:26, 36), those of his latter-day Church (D&C 5:14; 105:26, 30-31; 109:73), or the departed faithful who make up the "army of heaven" (Dan. 4:35; Rev. 19:14; D&C 88:112).

In opposition to "the armies of the living God" (1 Sam. 17:26) are the armies of Lucifer. It was against this diabolical host that the armies of Jehovah battled in the "war in heaven" during the premortal existence (Rev. 12:7-9). After the Millennium, "the devil [again] shall gather together his armies; even the hosts of hell, and shall come up to battle against Michael and his armies." The final outcome of this "battle of the great God" is recorded in scripture: "And the devil and his armies shall be cast away into their own place, that they shall not have power over the saints any more." (D&C 88:111-14.) (See also part 2: *Lord of Sabaoth.*)

Arrow. Anciently the arrow was used for two chief purposes: hunting beasts and wild animals, and as a weapon. Associated with these purposes are three distinct symbols.

1) As arrows are of considerable worth to the hunter, so children are of great value to their father. Such was the comparison made by the Psalmist: "As arrows are in the hand of a mighty man; so are children of the youth. Happy is the man that hath his quiver full of them." (Ps. 127:4-5.)

2) The wicked "shoot at the upright in heart" (Ps. 11:2) with their arrows, and a "man that beareth false witness against his neighbor is a . . . sharp arrow" (Prov. 25:18). In other words, actions of the iniquitous wound the hearts of the righteous, as an arrow strikes through the breast of a beast.

3) The "sharp" arrows of God (Ps. 45:5; Num. 24:8; Deut. 32:23, 42; Ps. 77:17-18; Hab. 3:11) serve two purposes. They are instruments employed to bring judgment against the wicked, and they are used to chasten the righteous (Ps. 38:2; 45:5; 144:6; Lam. 3:12-13; Ezek. 5:16). (See also *Bow.*)

Ashes. Ashes are illustrative of the lowly and humble state of mortal man. They also act as a cleansing and purifying agent.

1) The Mosaic system of sacrificial rites and ceremonies directed that the ashes of the burnt heifer were to be utilized for "the purifying of the flesh" (Num. 19:2-19; Heb. 9:13).

2) Sackcloth and ashes were regularly employed by mourners of the biblical period. It was a common practice for the griever to tear his clothing, place ashes on the head, and to wear sackcloth (2 Sam. 13:19; Esth. 4:1-3; Jer. 6:26; Ezek. 27:30-31).

3) Penitent souls demonstrated their desire to repent by fasting, prayer, and by wearing sackcloth while sitting in ashes (Jonah 3:5-9; Luke 10:13; Job 42:6; Mosiah 11:25).

4) When Christ returns in consuming fire, the wicked will be consumed and become stubble. In that time "they shall be ashes under the soles" of the feet of the righteous (3 Ne. 25:3).

Asp. The asp of the Bible is the Egyptian cobra. It is an extremely venomous reptile (Deut. 32:33; Job 20:14, 16) which dwells in a cavity of the ground. Symbolically, the poison of the asp is as the speech of the wicked (Rom. 3:13), and its venom is like the deadly effects of wine (Deut. 32:33; Prov. 23:32). (See also *Adder; Cockatrice; Serpent.*)

Ass. During the biblical period, the ass was a common but important animal used for transporting both man and goods (Gen. 22:3; 42:26–27; 45:23; Ex. 4:20; 1 Sam. 16:20) and for agricultural purposes (Isa. 32:20; Deut. 22:10). Symbolically, then, this beast of burden represents a man or group of people who are required to bear a heavy burden. For instance, Jacob said of one of his sons, "Issachar is a strong ass couching down between two burdens" (Gen. 49:14–15). Abinadi prophesied concerning the wicked people associated with King Noah, saying that "they shall have burdens lashed upon their backs; and they shall be driven before like a dumb ass" (Mosiah 12:5; 21:3). Also, Israel has been designated an "ass" (Hosea 8:8–9; Jer. 2:23–24).

In contrast to the lowly ass was the indomitable horse used by warriors. The scriptures depict Christ riding both an ass and a horse. During the Lord's mortal ministry, he entered into Jerusalem "lowly, and riding upon an ass" (Zech. 9:9; Matt. 21:5). In the future, when he returns in glory, he will ride a magnificent white horse, and he will "make war" against the wicked (Rev. 19:11–14). (See also *Horse.*)

Assyria. The great eastern empire of Assyria of biblical days, with its appallingly cruel monarchs and its seemingly invincible armies, is a type of the warring nations of the latter days who will fight against Israel. However, although they succeeded then in deporting the northern tribes of Israel from the Israelite homeland, the God of Israel will prevail against the modern Assyrian nations and they will be burned as "thorns and briers." (See Isa. 10.)

Axe. 1) The mighty nation of Israel was and will be as a battle axe for the Lord as they destroy the nations and kingdoms of the earth (Jer. 51:19–20).

2) The axe of a husbandman is used in a symbolic sense by several inspired writers to denote the manner in which barren trees (men) will be destroyed (Luke 3:9; D&C 97:7; Isa. 10:33–34). (See also *Tree.*)

Babe / Baby. Converts to the gospel of Jesus Christ are "as newborn babes" (1 Pet. 2:2) in their gospel understanding. They must be nurtured with milk, or the simple doctrines of the gospel, for "strong meat belongeth to them that are of full age" (Heb. 5:13–14; 1 Cor. 3:1–3).

Babylon. "In prophetic imagery, Babylon is the world with all its carnality and wickedness . . . it is every evil and wicked and ungodly thing in our whole social structure. Conditions in the world today are as they were in ancient Babylon. What, then, is more natural than for the prophets, aware of the sins and evils and final destruction of Babylon, to use her as a symbol of that which now is and which shall soon be." (*Millennial Messiah*, p. 424.) Thus, the destruction and fall of ancient Babylon typifies the judgments and destructions which will fall upon the world during the events of the last days (Isa. 13; D&C 1:16). (See also *Assyria; Edom; Egypt.*)

Baldness. 1) In ancient times, artificial or unnatural baldness was a sign of mourning (Amos 8:10; Isa. 22:12; Jer. 16:6; Ezek. 27:31; Micah 1:16).

2) Baldness, when caused by God, is a judgment. Many in the latter-days will experience baldness in place of "well set hair" (Isa. 3:24; Jer. 47:4-5; 48:37; Ezek. 7:18). (See also *Hair.*)

Baptism. "Baptism is in similitude of the death, burial, and resurrection of Christ" (Rom. 6, chapter heading). Moses referred to baptism as "the burial" (JST, Gen. 17:5). Paul added these expository remarks: "Know ye not, that so many of us as were baptized into Jesus Christ were baptized into his death? Therefore we are buried with him by baptism into death." In other words, the "old" sinful nature in man is figuratively "crucified" and "destroyed" and then buried in the waters of baptism (Rom. 6:3-4, 6).

Interestingly, the Prophet Joseph Smith wrote concerning the temple baptismal fonts: "The baptismal font was instituted as a similitude of the grave, and was commanded to be in a place underneath where the living are wont to assemble" (D&C 128:13).

Succeeding the death and the burial is the figurative resurrection when the candidate emerges from the waters of baptism. When the recipient of baptism comes "forth out of the water [it] is in the likeness of the resurrection of the dead in coming forth out of their graves" (D&C 128:12). In other words, the neophyte has become a new person, born again as a newborn babe, with a whole and perfect spiritual body. (See also *Font.*)

Baptismal Font. See *Font.*

Bear. 1) A bear is typical of mighty warriors (2 Sam. 17:8; 1 Sam. 17:36-37) or wicked and oppressive rulers (Prov. 28:15).

2) God is "as a bear that is bereaved of her whelps" (Hosea 13:8) unto those that remember not that he is their Lord and their Savior.

Beasts. 1) Concerning the beasts mentioned in the seventh chapter of Daniel, the Prophet Joseph Smith taught that the "beasts are spoken of to represent the kingdoms of the world, the inhabitants whereof were beastly and abominable characters; they were murderers, corrupt, carnivorous, and brutal in their dispositions. The lion, the bear, the leopard, and the ten-horned beast represented the kingdoms of the world, says Daniel." (*Teachings*, p. 289.)

2) Joseph Smith once inquired of the Lord, "What are we to understand by the four beasts, spoken of in [Rev. 4:6]?" The Lord answered, "They are figurative expressions, used by the Revelator, John, in describing heaven, the paradise of God, the happiness of man, and of beasts, and of creeping things, and of the fowls of the air; that which is spiritual being in the likeness of that which is temporal; and that which is temporal in the likeness of that which is spiritual; the spirit of man in the likeness of his person, as also the spirit of the beast, and every other creature which God has created." (D&C 77:2; see also *Teachings*, pp. 287–94.)

Bed. 1) A bed, where men are naturally wont to rest and slumber, is associated with death and the grave, where the bodies of the deceased are found to be sleeping (Gen. 49:33; 1 Sam. 19:15; 2 Kgs. 1:4, 6; 2 Chr. 16:14; 24:25; Job 17:13; Ezek. 32:25). Both the grave and the bed are temporary places of rest—from the bed the body awakens in the morning hours, and from the grave the body will awaken by the sound of the trump, which will announce the resurrection. (See also *Sleep*.)

2) In order to avoid explicit and straightforward expressions concerning immoral sexual relations, many biblical writers employed the word *bed* euphemistically. For example, it is written that Reuben defiled his "father's bed" (Gen. 49:4), that a harlot "decked" and "perfumed" her bed with various fine coverings and precious perfumes in the hopes of attracting impious customers (Prov. 7:16–17), and that the wicked person "deviseth mischief upon his bed" (Ps. 36:4; see also Micah 2:1).

Similarly, the bed represents the place of spiritual adultery, such as idolatry. Such was the case with the house of Israel, who bedded with the other nations when they chased after their gods and forsook their Husband and Bridegroom, who was Jehovah (Isa. 57:7–8; Ezek. 23:17; see also Rev. 2:22).

3) The bed is often associated with divine visions. The young prophet Samuel (1 Sam. 3), King Nebuchadnezzar (Dan. 2:28–29), Lehi (1 Ne. 1:7ff.), Jacob (Gen. 28:10–19), and Joseph Smith (JS–H 1:29) each experienced a heavenly manifestation while upon their beds.

Bishop. The ecclesiastical duties of a worthy bishop are similar to those of Jesus Christ, the perfect Bishop (1 Pet. 2:25). Like the Lord, a bishop "must be blameless" and possess all the qualities of a faithful member of God's kingdom (1 Tim. 3:1-7; Titus 1:7). The bishop is a steward, and has power to deliver goods unto those in need, to grant an inheritance to the righteous (D&C 90:30; 51:5), and to administer in the temporal affairs of the kingdom. He is a judge of Israel (D&C 64:40; 42:82-83). In short, the bishop is an overseer (in Greek, *episcopus* means "overseer") and, as such, oversees the Lord's sheep in a specific area of the vineyard. (See also *Apostle; High Priest; Priest;* part 2: *Bishop.*)

Bittern. Biblical scholars have difficulty identifying the bittern—one claims the bittern is a "hedgehog," another holds that it is a "tortoise." Yet another learned man believes the bittern is a "porcupine," and still another asserts that it is an "owl." Notwithstanding this disparity, the symbolism of this beast is clear. The bittern is a symbol of a desolate and forsaken land, of an area destroyed by the wrath of the Lord (Isa. 14:23; 34:11; Zeph. 2:13-14).

Blind/Blindness. The figurative usage of the terms *blind* and *blindness* in the scriptures refers to the spiritual blindness of men—the inability to see the truth. Thus King Limhi's words to Ammon refer to the blindness of mankind: "How blind and impenetrable are the understandings of the children of men" (Mosiah 8:20). Amulek spoke of those with blind eyes who "will not understand the words which are spoken" by the prophets (Alma 10:25). Nephi asked of his brothers, Laman and Lemuel, "How is it that ye are so hard in your hearts, and so blind in your minds?" (1 Ne. 7:8.)

According to the scriptures, the devil blinds the spiritual eyes of man (1 Ne. 12:17; 3 Ne. 2:1-2), as do the practices of wicked men (D&C 76:75; 123:12). (See also *Eyes.*)

Blood. 1) During all dispensations when animal sacrifice was practiced, the blood of sacrificial beasts represented and prefigured the blood of Christ's atonement. During the Mosaic era Jehovah said "I have given it [the blood] to you upon the altar to make an atonement for your souls: for it is the blood that maketh an atonement for the soul" (Lev. 17:11).

In a manner unknown to man, the blood of the Lord cleanses the repentant souls of men and allows them to gain salvation. Moses taught that "by the blood ye are sanctified," speaking of the blood of the "Only Begotten" (Moses 6:59–60), and Paul added, "And almost all things are by the law purged with blood; and without shedding of blood is no remission" (Heb. 9:22).

It is understood by all peoples that "the life of the flesh is in the blood" (Lev. 17:11; Deut. 12:23); that is, blood is the essence of physical life. Similarly, eternal life is found only through the blood of the Redeemer. Jesus said, "Except ye eat the flesh of the Son of man, and drink his blood, ye have no life in you. Whoso eateth my flesh, and drinketh my blood, hath eternal life" (John 6:53–54). Thus the blood which flows in our veins gives us physical life, and through the blood of the Redeemer we have eternal life.

2) *Blood* and *iniquity* are synonyms in many scriptural passages. For instance, Isaiah wrote, "For your hands are defiled with blood, and your fingers with iniquity" (Isa. 59:3). Micah wrote, "They build up Zion with blood, and Jerusalem with iniquity" (Micah 3:10; see also Hab. 2:12). And Paul taught, "For the bodies of those beasts, whose blood is brought into the sanctuary by the high priest for sin, are burned without the camp" (Heb. 13:11; see also 2 Ne. 9:44; Jacob 1:19). (See also *Sacrifice*.)

Boaz. The Hebrew word *goel* means "redeemer." During the Old Testament period, a *goel* was one whose right and duty it was to redeem the inheritance of a deceased male relative and marry his widow. The children of this marriage would take upon themselves the name of the dead husband so "that his name be not put out of Israel" (Deut. 25:5–10). It was for these purposes that Boaz accepted the responsibilities and duties of a redeemer and married Ruth the Moabite (Ruth 4:4–10). In this sense, Boaz served as a type and shadow for Jesus Christ, who is the Redeemer *par excellence* (Isa. 41:14; Alma 37:9; 3 Ne. 10:10). (See part 2: *Redeemer*.)

Body. 1) The "body of Christ" is the Church, both in the sense of a "body" being a congregation or assemblage and in a figurative sense. This can be illustrated from the epistles of Paul. "Now ye [the Church] are the body of Christ, and members in particular" (1 Cor. 12:27). "He [Christ] is the head of the body, the church" (Col. 1:18, 24; see also Rom. 12:4–5; Eph. 1:23).

2) The sacramental bread represents the body of Christ (Moro. 4:3); thus we hear Jesus explaining to the Saints, "He that eateth this bread eateth of my body to his soul" (3 Ne. 20:8).

3) Paul and others taught that our body is a temple (2 Cor. 5:1-5; 1 Cor. 3:16-17; 6:19; Hel. 4:24). "What? know ye not that your body is the temple of the Holy Ghost which is in you, which ye have of God . . . ?" (1 Cor. 6:19.) Similarly, the body of Christ is a holy temple (John 2:19-21; Rev. 21:22).

Bone. 1) The word *bone* is used to denote a familial relationship between two parties, both in a physical and in a spiritual sense. After the rib was taken from Adam, he said, referring to Eve, "This is now bone of my bones, and flesh of my flesh" (Gen. 2:23). Abimelech spoke to the family of his mother's household, saying, "Remember also that I am your bone and your flesh" (Judg. 9:2). It was the twelve tribes of Israel who made the claim to King David, "Behold, we are thy bone and thy flesh" (2 Sam. 5:1).

Concerning the usage of the word *bone* in describing a divine relationship, the Apostle Paul wrote, "For we are members of his body, of his flesh, and of his bones. . . . This is a great mystery: but I speak concerning Christ and the church." (Eph. 5:30, 32.)

2) The Hebrew word for bone is *etzam,* the root of which means "self" or "substance." Perhaps with this in mind, the prophets made figurative comparisons, equating the bones of a man with his true self, or the substance of which he was made. Thus the prophets often equated the actions of man with his bones. If a man's deeds were righteous, then his bones were said to be healthy or fruitful (Prov. 15:30); i.e., his inner spiritual self was healthy. (See also *Dust.*)

On the other hand, if a man's actions were sinful and wicked, then his bones were said to be rotten or dry (Prov. 12:4; 14:30; 17:22), "vexed" (Ps. 6:2), "out of joint" (Ps. 22:14), or "broken" (Ps. 51:8). Concerning the bones of the wicked, the prophet Job wrote, "His bones are full of the sin of his youth, which shall lie down with him in the dust" (Job 20:11); and according to Ezekiel, "Their iniquities shall be upon their bones" (Ezek. 32:27).

Book, Eating of. Ezekiel was commanded to eat a book (Ezek. 2:8-10; 3:1-4). Six centuries later the Apostle John was given a book by a heavenly messenger, who told him to "take it, and eat it up" (Rev. 10:2, 8-10; see also Jer. 15:16). "The little book which was eaten by John . . . was a mission, and an ordinance, for him to gather the tribes of Israel; behold, this is Elias, who, as it is written, must come and restore all things." (D&C 77:14.)

Elder Bruce R. McConkie has explained that "John's act of eating a book containing the word of God . . . signified that he was eating the bread of life, that he was partaking of the good word of God, that he was feasting upon the word of Christ— which was in his 'mouth sweet as honey.' But it made his 'belly bitter'; that is, the judgments and plagues promised those to whom the Lord's word was sent caused him to despair and have sorrow of soul. . . . Ezekiel had a similar experience. He was commanded to eat a roll (a book), which was in his mouth 'as honey for sweetness,' but in the writing itself there was 'lamentations, and mourning, and woe' (Ezek. 2:6–10; 3:1–3)." (*Doctrinal New Testament Commentary*, 3:507.)

Bosom. The place of embrace, nurture, and love, the bosom signifies a special hallowed intimacy. Jesus is said to be "in the bosom of the Father" (John 1:18; D&C 76:13), and the city of Enoch is in the bosom of God (D&C 38:4; Moses 7:31). (See also *Abraham's Bosom.*)

Bow. 1) The bow of the archer is figuratively associated with deceit and falsehood (Ps. 78:57; Jer. 9:3).

2) This weapon pertains to the judgments of God; the Lord will break the bow of the wicked and mighty (Hosea 1:5; Zech. 9:10; Ps. 46:9; 76:3).

3) Bows are employed by the wicked against the righteous: "The wicked have drawn out the sword, and have bent their bow, to cast down the poor and needy, and to slay such as be of upright conversation" (Ps. 37:14; 11:2). (See also *Arrow.*)

Bowels. The bowels are the inner parts of a person's body, such as the stomach or womb. The bowels are representative of two principal things.

1) King David, speaking metaphorically, told his servants, "Behold, my son, which came forth of my bowels" (2 Sam. 16:11). In a similar scripture, Abraham is told by the Lord, "He that shall come forth out of thine own bowels shall be thine heir" (Gen. 15:4). Therefore, bowels in these examples represent the seat of generation and reproduction.

2) When the Hebrew idiom states that a mother's "bowels yearned upon her son" (1 Kgs. 3:26), the expression indicates sympathy for a loved one. Other idioms express similar tender feelings, in phrases such as "my bowels are troubled for him" (Jer. 31:20) and "my bowels are filled with compassion towards you" (3 Ne. 17:6). Thus the word *bowels* often signifies the sympathy one has for another.

Branch. 1) In the scriptures, the twelve tribes of the house of Israel are represented as being "an olive-tree." In accordance with this, each of the twelve tribes is known to be one "branch of the house of Israel" (1 Ne. 15:12; Jacob 5; D&C 10:60). Thus the Nephites, who were of the tribe of Joseph, were called "a remnant of the house of Israel, a branch who have been broken off" the olive tree (1 Ne. 19:24). The remaining tribes are branches of the same tree (1 Ne. 10:12–14).

2) As a tree often represents a man, so a branch signifies one aspect of a man (Mal. 4:1; Job 29:19; Prov. 11:28; see also John 15:1-6). Therefore, figuratively, a man has roots, leaves, and branches. Concerning the final status of the wicked, it is said that "his roots shall be dried up beneath, and above shall his branch be cut off" (Job 18:16). (See also *Root; Tree.*)

3) Jesus is the "righteous Branch" (Jer. 23:5; Zech. 3:8). (See also part 2: *Branch.*)

Brass. Brass, an enduring substance which the revelations call "precious" (D&C 124:27), is a metal used in connection with holy things. Examples include the vessels, instruments, and materials of the Mosaic tabernacle (Ex. 27:2-19). The first temple of Jerusalem (2 Kgs. 25:7-17) and the temple of Nauvoo (D&C 124:27) had many parts composed of brass. Additionally, the scriptures refer to the "serpent of brass" made by Moses (Num. 21:9) and the plates of brass which "should never perish" (1 Ne. 5:19). A simile written by John describes the feet of the Son of God as being "like fine brass" (Rev. 2:18; 1:15). Brass, then, is a symbol of endurance and strength. (See also *Gold; Iron.*)

Brazen Serpent. See *Serpent.*

Bread. The manna which fed the Israelites in the desolate deserts of Sinai, the feeding of bread to the multitudes on the shores of Galilee, and the bread of the sacrament are but figures of the "true bread," which is the body of the Savior. "The bread that I will give is my flesh" (John 6:51), Jesus Christ said; and to the Nephites, he taught, "He that eateth this bread eateth of my body to his soul" (3 Ne. 20:8).

Bread, a common but important element of the diet during biblical times, played a crucial role in sustaining physical life. Perhaps it was for this reason that the Lord gave a sermon comparing himself to bread. In the testimony of John, Jesus declared that he was the "true bread" and the "living bread" who descended from heaven to give spiritual life to those who would partake. Jesus' own words were, "I am the bread of life: he that cometh to me shall never hunger; and he that believeth on me shall never thirst." (John 6:35; see also 6:32, 51.) Similar statements are found throughout the sixth chapter of John: "If any man eat of this bread, he shall live for ever"; "I will raise him up at the last day"; "He that believeth on me hath everlasting life" or "eternal life"; and "He that eateth me, even he shall live by me" (John 6:44, 47, 51, 54, 57). Thus, as physical bread sustains physical life, spiritual bread sustains the life of the spirit. (See also *Leaven; Manna; Shewbread;* part 2: *Bread.)*

Breastplate. The "breastplate of righteousness" (D&C 27:16; Eph. 6:14) and the "breastplate of faith and love" (1 Thes. 5:8) are worn by the Saints to protect their hearts and souls from the fiery darts of Satan and his host. (See also *Armor.)*

Breath of God. As the breath of man is essential for mortal existence, so the "breath of God" gives life and destroys life. Therefore, by his breath the foundations of the earth were laid (2 Sam. 22:16), and the Lord God "breathed" into both man and animals "the breath of life" (Moses 3:7, 19; Ps. 33:6; Job 33:4). Furthermore, with his breath, which is "like a stream of brimstone" (Isa. 30:33), the Lord performs divine acts, and with it he will give life unto those who sleep at the time of the resurrection (Job 37:10; Ezek. 37:5-10). Paradoxically, Isaiah records that "with the breath of [God's] lips shall he slay the wicked" (Isa. 11:4).

Bride. The "holy city, new Jerusalem" (Rev. 21:2, 9, 27), Zion (Isa. 54:1-6), and the Church (D&C 109:73-74) are spoken of as being the bride of the Lord. These are the faithful Saints, "they which are written in the Lamb's book of life" (Rev. 21:27), they who are as the wise virgins (Matt. 25:1-13), those who are "holy and without blemish" (Eph. 5:27; see also verses 23-32); they are the "Lamb's wife" (Rev. 21:9).

Apparently, the marriage between the bride and the Bridegroom will take place at the time of the Second Coming (Matt. 22:1-14; 25:1-13; Rev. 19:7-9; 21:2, 9; Zeph. 1:7-8). (See also *Bridegroom; Woman; Harlot.)*

Bridegroom. In a spiritual sense, Jesus Christ is the "Bridegroom" (Matt. 9:15; D&C 33:17-18; 65:3; 133:10) and is married to those who are faithful, pure, and just. "He that hath the bride is the bridegroom" (John 3:29), declared John the Baptist. (See also *Bride; Woman;* part 2: *Bridegroom.)*

Brimstone. 1) Brimstone, or sulfur, is a highly combustible mineral which, when ignited, can become very destructive.

The cities Sodom, Gomorrah, Admah, and Zeboim were obliterated when the Lord sent fire and brimstone upon them (Gen. 19:24-25; Deut. 29:22-23; Hosea 11:8). So great and absolute is the destruction by this substance that neither animal nor plant life can survive, nor is the land productive for generations thereafter. Moses described a land destroyed by brimstone: "The whole land thereof is brimstone, and salt, and burning, that it is not sown, nor beareth, nor any grass groweth therein" (Deut. 29:22-23). Brimstone, therefore, is a sign of the wrath and judgment of God upon the wicked (Ps. 11:6). In the last days, many of the wicked will be destroyed by brimstone (Rev. 9:18; D&C 29:21; Ezek. 38:22). (See also *Gomorrah.*)

2) So complete is the suffering and destruction of those plagued with burning sulfur that the prophets pictured hell as being "as a lake of fire and brimstone, whose flame ascendeth up forever and ever" (Alma 12:17).

Buckler. A buckler is a small shield generally held with the left hand to stop or parry the blows of an enemy. Speaking in a symbolic sense, the Lord is a buckler "to all them that trust in him" (2 Sam. 22:31; Ps. 18:2) and "to them that walk uprightly" (Prov. 2:7), meaning that he will shield and protect the righteous from the fiery darts and evil weaponry of the devil and his host.

Builder. God is the master builder. He is the builder of the celestial city (Heb. 11:10; Ps. 127:1), his Church (Matt. 16:18), and "all things" (Heb. 3:4; Jer. 24:6).

Building. 1) To the Saints of Corinth, the Apostle Paul wrote, "Ye are God's building" (1 Cor. 3:9). To the Saints of Ephesus he further explained that Jesus is the "chief corner stone," the Apostles are the foundation, and the Saints are the building, all "fitly framed together" to become one edifice (Eph. 2:12-22).

2) Lehi and Nephi told of a peculiar building which "stood as it were in the air, high above the earth" (1 Ne. 8:26). Called "the large and spacious building" (1 Ne. 12:18), this edifice represents the "vain imaginations and the pride of the children of men" (1 Ne. 12:18; 11:36).

Cain. Cain, who "loved Satan more than God" (Moses 5:18), whose philosophy it was to "murder and get gain" (Moses 5:31), and who made an oath with the devil himself (Moses 5:29), symbolizes any person whose main goal is wickedness and corruption (Moses 5:25; 1 John 3:12; Jude 1:11; D&C 124:75).

Candle / Candlestick. See *Lamp.*

Cankerworm. The cankerworm is a locust in an early stage in its development—probably at the nymph form. The word *canker* speaks of a spreading sore which quietly consumes and devours its victim. Prophetic imagery, therefore, portrays the cankerworm as being a destructive agent which corrupts and kills a people and their foodstuffs due to their wickedness (Joel 2:25; 1:4; Nahum 3:15-16). (See also *Locust.*)

Caterpillar. The biblical caterpillar, like the cankerworm, is a stage in the development of the locust. These creatures represented one of the great plagues of Egypt (Ps. 78:46; 105:34-35) as well as of other periods (2 Chr. 6:28). Figuratively, the caterpillar represents either horses (Jer. 51:27) or men (Jer. 51:14). (See also *Locust.*)

Cedar. During the biblical period, the cedar trees of Lebanon produced the finest and most valued lumber. So precious was cedar that it was used in the great sanctuary built under Solomon's direction (1 Kgs. 6:9-10). Fittingly, then, the magnificent cedar tree has come to represent the upright and stalwart of the Lord's people. "The righteous . . . shall grow like a cedar in Lebanon" (Ps. 92:12; Isa. 14:7-9)—that is, like the mighty men of the earth (2 Kgs. 14:9-10; Isa. 2:11-13; Ezek. 31:3). (See also *Tree.*)

Chaff. Anciently, threshers of grain understood well the art of separating the seed from the husks, or chaff. This simple matter was accomplished by tossing the grain into the air. By so doing, the valuable seed immediately returned to the threshing floor, and the slightest breeze would carry the worthless chaff away.

So it is with the wicked. They are "as the chaff that is driven with the whirlwind out of the floor" (Hosea 13:3; Ps. 1:4; 35:5), or are "led about by Satan, even as chaff is driven before the wind" (Morm. 5:18).

Chains. Chains of steel, employed during the biblical period for the purpose of binding captives and prisoners (Jer. 39:7; 40:1; Mark 5:3), are used with perfect prophetic imagery to portray those who are bound, either by the power of God or by the power of Satan.

1) Those who are held captive by Deity include the "angels which kept not their first estate" (Jude 1:6). Also, disembodied spirits who kept not their second estate are held in "chains of darkness" until the great Day of Judgment (2 Pet. 2:4; D&C 38:5; Moses 7:57).

2) The chains of the devil, on the other hand, are referred to as "awful chains" (2 Ne. 1:13), "everlasting chains" (2 Ne. 28:19), "chains of hell" (Alma 5:9), and "chains of death" (D&C 138:18). These diabolical fetters are utilized by Satan to encircle and bind those unrepentant souls who allow him to control their lives.

3) The scriptures liken the wicked traditions and customs of men to an "iron yoke" and a "strong band." They are as "handcuffs, and chains, and shackles, and fetters of hell" (D&C 123:8). These shackles of Satan hinder many from obtaining the truths of the gospel of Jesus Christ. (See also *Yoke.*)

Chariot. 1) During the days of old the chariot was a carriage employed principally during periods of war. For this reason the prophets made mention of the chariot in their descriptions of future battles and wars. This includes the great battle of Armageddon, a religious war which will be fought during an age when modern and sophisticated weaponry is known to man. In a figurative sense, then, the chariot is a vehicle of war (Ezek. 39:20; Dan. 11:40; Joel 2:5; Rev. 9:9).

2) In connection with the celestial chariots of God, it is written that "the chariots of God are twenty thousand" (Ps. 68:17) and that God "maketh the clouds his chariot" (Ps. 104:3). The prophet Zechariah told of four heavenly chariots (Zech. 6:1-7), and Ezekiel gave a description of the heavenly chariot (Ezek. 1, 10).

3) The elements wind and fire are often used in connection with the word *chariot.* Abraham declared that "the wind and the fire" are God's chariot (Abr. 2:7); Elijah was taken "up by a whirlwind into heaven" by a "chariot of fire" (2 Kgs. 2:11); the writer of 2 Kings mentions heavenly "chariots of fire" (2 Kgs. 6:17); and at the Second Coming, "the Lord will come with fire, and with his chariots like a whirlwind" (Isa. 66:15).

Cherubim. Cherubim are angels. In the Garden of Eden, cherubim were placed to guard the tree of life, so that fallen man would not partake of the fruit of the tree (Gen. 3:24; Alma 42:2-3). Huge cherubim of gold were placed on either side of the throne of Jehovah in the Holy of Holies (Ex. 25:18-22; 1 Sam. 4:4; 2 Sam. 6:2). Symbolic likenesses of cherubim were embroidered into the veil of the tabernacle (Ex. 26:31) and carved into the walls, doors, and panels of the temple (1 Kgs. 6:29-35; 7:29, 36). In the future temple of Ezekiel will also be found images of cherubim (Ezek. 41:18-25).

In angelic hierarchy, the role of cherubim is to guard the path which leads to Deity's presence. They are sentinels, so to speak, "The cherubim are obviously so stationed" in these various places, then, "to see that the holiness of God is not violated by those in transgression or those who have not complied with the proper rituals (see D&C 132:19)." (*Gospel Symbolism*, p. 256.) At times cherubim are depicted as animals (Ezek. 1, 10). This personifies their role as monitors and watchmen of the sacred things of God.

Chicken. Metaphorically, the people of God are young chicks whom the Lord desires to protect and nourish. Four times the Lord repeated to those slain of the Nephites, "O ye people . . . who are descendants of Jacob, yea, who are of the house of Israel, how oft have I gathered you as a hen gathereth her chickens under her wings, and have nourished you . . . and ye would not." (3 Ne. 10:4-6.) These words had been uttered to those of the Old World (Matt. 23:37); and in this dispensation the Lord said, "Listen to the voice of Jesus Christ . . . who will gather his people even as a hen gathereth her chickens under her wings, even as many as will hearken to my voice and humble themselves before me, and call upon me in mighty prayer" (D&C 29:1-2; 10:65). (See also *Eagle; Hen; Wings.*)

Child/Children. 1) Every person who humbles himself and repents of his sins becomes "as a child" (Mosiah 3:19). Jesus told the people of both hemispheres: "Except ye be converted, and become as little children, ye shall not enter into the kingdom of heaven" (Matt. 18:3), and, "Therefore, whoso repenteth and cometh unto me as a little child, him will I receive, for of such is the kingdom of God" (3 Ne. 9:22). It is in this sense that the elders of this dispensation are denominated "little children" by Deity (D&C 61:36). Similarly, righteous men and women are called "children of light" (D&C 106:5), each individual being referred to as a "child of Christ" (Moro. 7:19).

2) Diametrically opposed to those who are named "children of God" are those of mankind who are kin to the devil through their wickedness. Alma explained that "whosoever bringeth forth evil works, the same becometh a child of the devil" (Alma 5:41; see also Acts 13:10) or a "child of hell" (Alma 11:23). It is appropriate, therefore, that the "devil and his children" (1 Ne. 14:3) be given such disgraceful nomenclatures as "children of disobedience" (Eph. 2:2), "children of transgression" (Isa. 57:4), "children of this world" (Luke 16:8), and "children of them which killed the prophets" (Matt. 23:31).

3) The word *children* is employed with special significance in many scriptural idioms. For instance, the expression "children of Israel" (D&C 103:16) refers to those who are spiritually or physically of the blood of Israel. "Children of the prophets" (3 Ne. 20:25) are those who have hearkened unto the words of the Lord's messengers. Other phrases of particular note are the "children of Zion" (D&C 101:81), "children of Jacob" (D&C 109:61), "children of Ephraim" (D&C 133:30), "children of God" (Moses 6:8), "children of the covenant" (3 Ne. 20:26), and "children of Noah" (Moses 7:60).

4) Jesus is called the "Holy Child" (Moro. 8:3), a title which suggests his childlike qualities.

5) In several hundred instances, the scriptures use the idiomatic phrase "children of men" (Moro. 7:31-32). This expression simply refers to those who are the children of mortal men and women, or mankind.

Circumcision. The ceremonial act of circumcision was ordained by the Lord: "And I will establish a covenant of circumcision with thee . . . that thou mayest know for ever that children are not accountable before me until they are eight years old" (JST, Gen. 17:11-12). "This covenant, sealed in the flesh, typified the subjugation of passion and the consecration of the body to God, or a putting away of the sins of the flesh (Col. 2:11). The imagery is frequently drawn upon as those who would be acceptable to the Lord are told to circumcise their hearts, their ears, and their lips." (*Gospel Symbolism*, p. 256.)

Cities of Refuge. Six cities of ancient Palestine were set apart as cities of refuge for anyone committing accidental manslaughter, so that the avenger of blood would not slay the innocent (Num. 35:6-34; Deut. 19:1-13; Josh. 20). The ancient cities of refuge find symbolic fulfillment in two ways:

1) Zion is the quintessential city of refuge. It is "called the New Jerusalem, a land of peace, a city of refuge, a place of safety for the Saints of the Most High God" (D&C 45:66). Another scripture talks of "Zion, and . . . her stakes, and . . . Jerusalem, those places which I have appointed for refuge" (D&C 124:36).

2) Jesus Christ is a refuge unto those fleeing the storms and calamities of the world (Heb. 6:18). King David employed many metaphors to depict the refuge found only in Christ: "The Lord is my rock, and my fortress, and my deliverer; . . . he is my shield, . . . my high tower, and my refuge, my saviour; thou savest me from violence" (2 Sam. 22:2-3). (See also part 2: *Refuge.*)

Clap. 1) The clapping of hands as an expression of joy reaches to the most ancient of days (Mosiah 18:11; Ps. 47:1; 98:8; Isa. 55:12).

2) The striking of the hands together was also a sign of derision (Job 34:37; 27:23; Lam. 2:15).

Clay. 1) God is the Creator, we are his creations. He is the potter, we the clay. "But now, O Lord, thou art our father; we are the clay, and thou our potter; and we all are the work of thy hand" (Isa. 64:8; Job 10:9; 33:6; Jer. 18:6). Some of humanity are easily molded into valuable earthenware, others become hardened "vessels of wrath" (Rom. 9:20-24).

Jesus' body was called "a tabernacle of clay" (Mosiah 3:5), as are those of all men (Moro. 9:6).

2) The washing of clay from the eyes was used to dramatize the washing of the things of the earth (i.e., worldly things), that we might see the things of the Spirit. Thus Enoch anointed and washed his eyes prior to a great seeric vision (Moses 6:35). The man born blind washed from his eyes that which was earthly and saw not only the earth but the things of the Spirit (John 9:6-7, 17).

Cloud. 1) Clouds are called the garments of the earth (Job 38:9; Ps. 104:5-6; Prov. 30:4). It is recorded that "the earth . . . is clothed with the glory of her God" (D&C 84:101), which glory finds symbolic fulfillment in a cloud (D&C 84:5).

2) The glory of God is equated with the clouds of heaven. It was revealed to the Prophet Joseph Smith that after the temple in the New Jerusalem is built, "a cloud shall rest upon it, which cloud shall be even the glory of the Lord" (D&C 84:5; Ezek. 10:3-4). Many passages of scripture reveal that at the time of the Second Coming, Jesus Christ will come "in the clouds of heaven with power and great glory" (Matt. 24:30; Rev. 14:14; D&C 34:7; 45:16; 76:102). Interestingly, the same clouds which reveal the glory of the Lord often conceal his personal presence from onlookers (3 Ne. 18:38; Ether 2:4, 5).

3) The Lord symbolically causes the clouds to be his chariot; he "maketh the clouds his chariot" (Ps. 104:3). "Behold, the Lord rideth upon a swift cloud" (Isa. 19:1). (See also *Chariot.*)

4) Clouds represent the veil through which we must pass to stand in the divine presence (Ex. 19:9, 16; 24:15-18; Luke 9:34-35). (See also *Curtain; Veil.*)

Coal. The burning of hot coals of the goldsmith's fire simultaneously removes the dross—that is, sin or wickedness—and purifies the precious element—purity or cleanliness (Prov.

25:22; Ezek. 1:13; 10:2; 24:11). To Isaiah, the angel explained, "Lo, this [coal] hath touched thy lips; and thine iniquity is taken away, and thy sin purged" (Isa. 6:6–7). (See also *Gold; Dross*.)

Cockatrice. The cockatrice, a venomous reptile mentioned four times in the scriptures, symbolizes a dangerous or destructive circumstance (Isa. 14:29; 59:5; Jer. 8:17). To demonstrate the blissfulness and peacefulness that will prevail during the Millennium, Isaiah wrote that even this creature of destruction will not "hurt nor destroy" the babe found playing by his den (Isa. 11:8–9). (See also *Adder; Asp; Serpent*.)

Colors. Some colors "have symbolic meaning in the scriptures. Those most often used in this way are: white, black, purple, red, blue, gold, and silver. White signifies spotless purity, chastity, sanctification, righteousness, and sinlessness. God and heavenly beings are always clothed in white. It is also associated with transcendent perfection, simplicity, light, the sun, illumination, innocence, holiness, and sacredness. It is a statement of triumph of the spirit over the flesh, of good over evil. Black and darkness are often a symbol of evil or wickedness. Black is also associated with mourning. Purple (or scarlet) is the color of royalty, imperial and sacerdotal power. Red (or scarlet) naturally associates itself with blood and suffering and hence with the blood of atonement. Blue as the color of the heavens becomes associated with the idea of revelation and its source. Gold is the color of the sun; it represents divine power, the splendor of enlightenment; radiance, and glory. Because of its great value, and its radiance, gold is known to us as the possession of kings and great kingdoms. It is a symbol common to scriptural descriptions of God and the heavenly kingdom. Silver, like gold, is of great value and hence is associated with Christ. Traditionally, it is associated with the idea of a Reconciler, Savior, and Redeemer." (*Gospel Symbolism*, pp. 256–57). (See also *Green; Red*.)

Coney. The coney (Ps. 104:18), better known as the "rock-badger," is a small, weak, and unclean mammal (Lev. 11:5; Deut. 14:7). Solomon said of them that although they "are but a feeble folk" they are "exceeding wise" for they "make . . . their houses in the rocks" (Prov. 30:24, 26). The coney, then, is a symbol of those who are wise.

Cormorant. This unclean bird (Lev. 11:13–17) is described as being black in color, possessing a long, hooked beak, and having a peculiar, humanlike beard. Known to inhabit desolate places, it is used as a symbol of the utter destructions caused by

Deity against wicked cities and nations (Isa. 34:10-11; Zeph. 2:13-14).

Cornerstone. Jesus Christ is the "head of the corner" (Acts 4:11), or the "chief corner stone" of the Church (Eph. 2:20). (See also part 2: *Chief Cornerstone.*)

Crane. The crane possesses a distinctive voice which is heard from a great distance. Possibly for this reason, King Hezekiah, after recovering from a deathly illness, declared that "like a crane . . . did I chatter" (Isa. 38:14).

Also, the migrations of the crane are seasonal, and their movements can be predicted with great accuracy. Therefore we find Jeremiah contrasting the predictable migration of the crane to the uncertainty of the inhabitants of Jerusalem, who "know not the judgment of the Lord" (Jer. 8:7) or the time of his coming.

Cross. 1) As Jesus "endured the cross" (Heb. 12:2) of Calvary, in the literal sense of the word, all of his disciples must bear their own cross, meaning that all must "believe in Christ, and view his death, and suffer his cross and bear the shame of the world" (Jacob 1:8). As Jesus explained, "Now for a man to take up his cross, is to deny himself all ungodliness, and every worldly lust, and keep my commandments" (JST, Matt. 16:26). "Take up your cross" (3 Ne. 12:30), Jesus has commanded the Saints, for "he that will not take up his cross and follow me, and keep my commandments, the same shall not be saved" (D&C 56:2). Further, "If any man will come after me, let him deny himself, and take up his cross daily, and follow me" (Luke 9:23). There are many who refuse to carry their cross. These wicked ones are "the enemies of the cross of Christ" (Philip. 3:18).

2) Jesus introduced a second symbolic meaning of the word *cross.* In the Day of Judgment, both the wicked and the righteous will "be lifted up by the Father" in the same manner that Christ was lifted up on the cross, and they will be judged of God (3 Ne. 27:14-15). And then, after the Day of Judgment, those who are found to be righteous will be "lifted up at the last day" to dwell with God (3 Ne. 27:22).

Crown. Crowns and diadems, as worn by Deity, royalty, and the priesthood, are symbols of kingship and thus dominion, authority, and power. The crowns worn by the various biblical kings, the priests of the temple (Ex. 39:30), and elders of the Church (Rev. 4:4) are all types of the heavenly crown of God (Rev. 14:14; 6:2; 19:12), which crown is a "crown of eternal light" (Abr., facsimile 2:3). All faithful men of the priesthood who have become "kings and priests" (Rev. 1:6) are given crowns; nevertheless, they are yet subject unto the King of kings.

Speaking symbolically, their crown is as a "crown of eternal life" (D&C 20:14); a "crown of righteousness" (D&C 25:15); a "crown of immortality" (D&C 81:6); a "crown of glory" (D&C 104:7) or of "celestial glory" (D&C 101:65); and a "crown of life" (James 1:12). Furthermore, they are crowned "with blessings and great glory" (D&C 124:17) and "with sheaves" (D&C 79:3).

Cup. 1) Every man chooses whether to drink from the "cup of the Lord" or from the "cup of devils." Those who "have fellowship with devils . . . cannot drink of the cup of the Lord" but only of "the cup of devils," and this wicked communion occurs at "the table of devils" (1 Cor. 10:20–21). Perhaps these are they who are made to drink of the cup of "the great persecutor of the church, the apostate, the whore, even Babylon" (D&C 86:3). They "drink the dregs of a bitter cup" (Alma 40:26).

However, "when the cup of their iniquity is full" (D&C 101:11) with their transgressions (D&C 103:3), then the Lord will share of his cup, which is the cup of "fury" (2 Ne. 8:17, 22), "wrath" (Mosiah 3:26), and divine "indignation" (D&C 29:17; Rev. 14:10). These are they who have "drunk damnation to their own souls" (Mosiah 3:25), and "the portion of their cup" will be "snares, fire and brimstone, and an horrible tempest," and the sword (Ps. 11:6; Jer. 25:15–28).

2) Not only bitter drink flows from God's cup. Sweet refreshment is also found there. "For in the hand of the Lord there is a cup, and the wine is red; it is full of mixture; and he poureth out of the same: but the dregs thereof, all the wicked of the earth shall wring them out, and drink them" (Ps. 75:8). The wicked partake of the sediment and scum, but the righteous sip of the red wine. It is in this context that the guest says to the Lord, his divine Host, "Thou preparest a table before me . . . ; my cup runneth over" (Ps. 23:5). He partakes of the "cup of salvation" (Ps. 116:13).

3) The Only Begotten, who "descended below all things," partook of a bitter cup. He told his disciples at Bountiful, "Behold, I am the light and the life of the world; and I have drunk out of that bitter cup which the Father hath given me" (3 Ne. 11:11; D&C 19:18).

Curtain. 1) The heavenly temple, not unlike the Mosaic Tabernacle and the Temple of Solomon, has a veil or curtain which conceals the holy things of Deity from the profane eyes of the world. The Lord, who dwells in the celestial spheres, "stretcheth out the heavens as a curtain, and spreadeth them out as a tent to dwell in" (Isa. 40:22; Ps. 104:2). Only in special circumstances are mortals allowed to peer through the curtain to view God sitting on this throne.

However, the day is fast approaching when "the curtain of heaven [shall] be unfolded, as a scroll is unfolded after it is rolled up, and the face of the Lord shall be unveiled" (D&C 88:95). This is called "the veil of the covering of my temple, in my tabernacle, which hideth the earth," and it "shall be taken off, and all flesh shall see me" (D&C 101:23), declared the Lord.

2) As curtains are employed for concealing things from the outside, they are also used as door coverings to protect those who dwell within from the destructive elements of nature. Many ancient tent dwellers, such as the Patriarchs, knew the importance of the tent curtain, or door covering. Perhaps it is for this purpose that a metaphor is used describing the stakes of Zion as "the curtains or the strength of Zion" (D&C 101:21; 3 Ne. 22:2). Those who dwell within the spiritual boundaries of the stake are protected from the evil elements of the world. However, when the curtains are lost or destroyed, then comes destruction (Hab. 3:7; Jer. 49:29; 4:20). (See also *Veil.*)

Cyrus. As the Lord's anointed (the Hebrew word for "anointed" is *Messiah*), and as deliverer of the tribes of Israel from Babylon. Cyrus (Isa. 45:1-5) is a type of Jesus the Anointed, who delivers his people from spiritual Babylon, or the world. (See also part 2: *Christ; Messiah.*)

Dance. Dances of the biblical period, when performed with modesty and righteous intentions, symbolized joy and gladness (1 Sam. 18:6; Ps. 30:11; Jer. 31:4, 13; Lam. 5:15; Luke 15:23-25; Mosiah 20:1). Through dancing, the Saints were able to visibly and physically "praise . . . the Lord" (D&C 136:28; Ps. 149:3; 150:4).

Darkness. Darkness pertains to Satan, his kingdom, his disciples, and their works. The devil is the perpetuator of dark and evil things (2 Ne. 9:9; Hel. 6:28-29). "Everlasting darkness" is equated with "destruction" and is opposed to "everlasting light" and "everlasting salvation" (Alma 26:15; Col. 1:12-13; 1 Thes. 5:5). Darkness does not comprehend the light (John 1:5; D&C 88:49), and those who are wicked are "walking in darkness at noon-day" (D&C 95:6). To his son Helaman, Alma said that "the works of darkness" are "wickedness and abominations" (Alma 37:21). (See also *Light; Night.*)

Darkness, Mists of. "The mists of darkness are the temptations of the devil, which blindeth the eyes, and hardeneth the hearts of the children of men, and leadeth them away into broad roads, that they perish and are lost" (1 Ne. 12:17; 2 Pet. 2:17). Followers of Christ avoid the mists of darkness by holding fast to the rod of iron (1 Ne. 8:23-24).

When actual "mists of darkness" are found upon the earth, there is "not any light seen, neither fire, nor glimmer, neither the sun, nor the moon, nor the stars" (3 Ne. 8:22; see also Ex. 10:21-23).

Darkness, Outer. Outer darkness is the habitation of "the spirits of the wicked, yea, who are evil—for behold, they have no part nor portion of the Spirit of the Lord; . . . and these shall be cast out into outer darkness; there shall be weeping, and wailing, and gnashing of teeth. . . . Now this is the state of the souls of the wicked, yea, in darkness, and a state of awful, fearful looking for the fiery indignation of the wrath of God upon them; thus they remain in this state . . . until the time of their resurrection." (Alma 40:13-14.) It was revealed to Joseph Smith that the Lord "in his hot displeasure, and in his fierce anger, in his time, will cut off those wicked, unfaithful, and unjust stewards, and appoint them their portion among hypocrites, and unbelievers; even in outer darkness" (D&C 101:90-91).

Darts, Fiery. "Fiery darts" are the temptations of Satan which are continually hurled at the righteous by Lucifer and his hosts (1 Ne. 15:24; Eph. 6:16). It is only by the "shield of faith" that one can be protected from these instruments of destruction (D&C 27:17). (See also *Shield.*)

Daughter / Son. Those who take upon themselves the name of Jesus Christ and receive his gospel are "spiritually begotten" of Christ. They are then spiritually "born of him" and become his sons and his daughters (Mosiah 5:7; D&C 25:1; Mosiah 27:25; Ether 3:14; 2 Cor. 6:17-18). In this sense, therefore, a daughter or a son is one who has become part of the eternal family of God.

Daughter of Zion. "Daughter of Zion" is the prophetic appellation given to the city of Jerusalem and its inhabitants (Lam. 1:6-8; 2:8-11; Zech. 9:9; 2 Ne. 8:25). Other lands and cities are also designated by the title "daughter," such as Egypt (Jer. 46:24), Babylon (Ps. 137:8), Gallim (Isa. 10:30), Moab (Isa. 16:2), Chaldea (Isa. 47:5), and Edom (Lam. 4:22).

David. Many events in the life of King David prefigure the life and ministry of Jesus, making David an important archetype of Christ. 1) He, like the Son of God, was born under humble circumstances in the village of Bethlehem (1 Sam. 16:1). 2) During his early years, he was despised by his brothers (1 Sam. 17:28). 3) He was a good shepherd. 4) Christ's ancestry came through the lineage of David (Matt. 9:27; 12:23). 5) The name of David is a prophetic name for Christ (Ezek. 34:23–24). 6) David slew Goliath, the great enemy of Israel, and Jesus slew the last enemy of Israel, which is death. 6) David was anointed with holy oil (1 Sam. 16:12–13) and became king (2 Sam. 5:4–5), uniting the kingdom of Israel under one head. David's reign thus symbolizes the glorious reign of the Lord during the millennial period. 7) David's name means "beloved," and Jesus is called the "beloved Son" (Matt. 3:17). (See also part 2: *David.*)

Day. 1) A day, in prophetic terms, signifies a period of a year (Ezek. 4:6; Num. 14:34; Isa. 34:8; 63:4).

2) A day can represent an unspecified period of time (Isa. 34:8; 22:5; Joel 2:2).

3) Peter admonished, "Be not ignorant of this one thing, that one day is with the Lord as a thousand years" (2 Pet. 3:8), thus explaining a truth that was revealed centuries before to Abraham (Abr. 3:4; 5:13). In connection with this, the Lord has stated that "now it is called today until the coming of the Son of Man. . . . For after today cometh the burning—this is speaking after the manner of the Lord—for verily I say, tomorrow . . . I will burn them [the wicked] up." (D&C 64:23–24.)

Day of Atonement. Many symbols were evident in the events of this most sacred day of the Israelite calendar (Lev. 16), when atonement was made for the sins and transgressions of the children of Israel. The high priest, the sacrificial offering, and the scapegoat, each playing their role on the Day of Atonement, are symbols of Jesus Christ. Incense typified the prayers of the Saints. The linen garments of the temple officiants symbolized the righteousness of the Saints, and the Holy of Holies was built in similitude of the celestial kingdom (see Lev. 16; Heb. 7–9). (See also *Feast of Tabernacles; Feast of Weeks; Passover; Sabbatical Year.*)

Day of the Lord. In the great majority of instances, when the prophets used the expression "the day of the Lord," they were referring to the day of the Lord's second coming, when he will come to the earth in power and great glory (see Isa. 13:6; Mal. 4:5; Acts 2:20; 2 Pet. 3:10; D&C 45:42).

Deaf. People who are deaf to hearing the words of God are those who "have ears to hear, and hear not" (Ezek. 12:2; Matt. 13:15; Isa. 42:18-20; Ps. 38:13-14). These will perish (2 Ne. 9:31). However, due to the restoration of the gospel and through the bringing forth of the Book of Mormon, many of the deaf will hear and understand the things of God (Isa. 29:18; 2 Ne. 27:29). (See also *Ear.*)

Death, Spiritual. A soul who suffers spiritual death is one who is dead to the things of the Spirit. These are they who are living, mortal souls, but are "dead in trespasses and sins" (Eph. 2:1; Col. 2:13; Luke 9:60; Jude 1:11-12). As Timothy explained, "She that liveth in pleasure is dead while she liveth" (1 Tim. 5:6). However, those who repent and obtain the baptism or "burial" (JST, Gen. 17:5) are then "raised up from the dead . . . in newness of life" (Rom. 6:1-10; 8:10-11).

Deep, Great. The great seas and mighty oceans are often termed "the deep" or "the great deep" by the prophets (D&C 133:20; 2 Ne. 4:20).

Deer. The deer is found variously in the King James Version as "hart," "hind," "roe," "roebuck," and "fallow deer." Because of its qualities of speed and fleetness of foot, the deer is often compared to athletic and warriorlike men who possess similar qualities. Hence certain men are described as being "light of foot as a wild roe" (2 Sam. 2:18) and "as swift as the roes upon the mountains" (1 Chr. 12:8; Prov. 6:5; Isa. 35:6; 2 Sam. 22:34). According to the Mosaic code, the deer were pronounced ritually clean for food (Deut. 14:5; 12:15).

Desert. See *Wilderness.*

Dew. In ancient Palestine, dew was considered vital to the agricultural base (1 Kgs. 17:1; Micah 5:7), often of value equal to rain (Deut. 32:2). On one hand, dew was considered a blessing from God (Hosea 14:5), and on the other, the lack of this moisture may have been the result of a prophetic curse (Hag. 1:10; 1 Kgs. 17:1; 2 Sam. 1:21). For these reasons it was natural for the prophets to symbolically equate dew with prosperity and abundance (Gen. 27:28; Deut. 33:13, 28; Zech. 8:12). The doctrines and teachings of the Lord are also "as the dews from heaven" (D&C 121:45; Deut. 32:2). (See also *Rain*; part 2: *Dew.*)

Disease. 1) Those of the Aaronic order possessing certain physical defects and diseases were disallowed from participating in specific temple ordinances and sacrifices, because they were considered ritually impure (Lev. 21). Such sicknesses symbolized spiritual diseases (i.e., sins and transgressions), which caused defects in the soul of man. Of course, the great Physician (Luke 4:23), Jesus Christ, has the power to heal all spiritual afflictions. It is he who is spoken of in a synonymous parallelism as the one "who forgiveth all thine iniquities; who healeth all thy diseases" (Ps. 103:3). (See also *Leprosy*.)

2) Physical diseases are often the result of a judgment from God. "I will put none of these diseases upon thee, which I have brought upon the Egyptians" (Ex. 15:26; Deut. 7:15; 28:60), the Lord told Israel. Concerning diseases in the last days, it is written that "an overflowing scourge" or "a desolating sickness shall cover the land," yet the wicked will still "curse God and die" (D&C 45:31–32). Because many partake of the sacrament unworthily, "many are weak and sickly . . . and many sleep" (1 Cor. 11:27–30).

However, there are notable exceptions — not all diseases can be considered divine judgments. For instance, Job, a "perfect and upright" man (Job 1:1), was smitten with "sore boils from the sole of his foot unto his crown" (Job 2:7).

Ditch. One of the lowest conditions or states that a human can find himself in, speaking symbolically, is a ditch (Job 9:31). Ironically, the enemies of God dig a ditch for others to fall into, and afterwards tumble into it themselves (Ps. 7:15). Elsewhere, a prostitute is called a "deep ditch" (Prov. 23:27).

Dogs. People whose lives are unworthy and reprobate are often referred to as dogs. For instance, unrighteous watchmen and shepherds are "all dumb dogs, they cannot bark; sleeping, lying down, loving to slumber. Yea, they are greedy dogs" (Isa. 56:10–11; Philip. 3:2). Those who turn from righteousness are "like the dog" who returns "to his vomit" (3 Ne. 7:8). While righteous souls hereafter will live in the celestial city, "dogs, and sorcerers, and whoremongers, and murderers, and idolaters" (Rev. 22:14–15) will cower and grovel outside the city's gates. Furthermore, those who crucified Jesus (Ps. 22:16), male prostitutes (Deut. 23:17–18), and the Gentiles (Matt. 15:23–28) are referred to as "dogs."

To the Nephites, Jesus instructed, "Give not that which is holy unto the dogs" (3 Ne. 14:6). Similarly, to the Church of this dispensation it is written, "It is not meet that the things which belong to the children of the kingdom should be given to them that are not worthy, or to dogs" (D&C 41:6). (See also *Fox; Wolf*.)

Door. 1) In a principal sense, a door is a passageway leading from one place to another. Through one door awaits death (Job

38:17). Through the "door of faith" one accepts and receives the gospel (Acts 14:27). Through the doors of the Lord's inner sanctuary, one symbolically enters heaven (1 Kgs. 6:31–35).

2) Christ is the door, or the way, to salvation. He explained to his disciples, "I am the door of the sheep. . . . I am the door: by me if any man enter in, he shall be saved" (John 10:7, 9). Symbolically, the Lord's presence is found at the door of the righteous (Ex. 12:22; Rev. 3:20). (See also *Gate; Key of David;* part 2: *Door.*)

3) Several scriptural idioms and expressions employ the word *door.* Some of these express the nearness of an event or thing, such as "Sin lieth at the door" (Moses 5:23); "The great and dreadful day of the Lord is near, even at the doors" (D&C 110:16); "He is near, even at the doors" (JS–M 1:39). The expression "An effectual door shall be opened" suggests that an opportunity will come (D&C 112:19; 100:3; 1 Cor. 16:9). (See also *Gate.*)

Dove. "The sign of the dove," taught the Prophet Joseph Smith, "was instituted before the creation of the world, a witness for the Holy Ghost, and the devil cannot come in the sign of a dove. The Holy Ghost is a personage, and is in the form of a personage. It does not confine itself to the *form* of the dove, but in [the] *sign* of the dove. The Holy Ghost cannot be transformed into a dove; but the sign of a dove was given to John to signify the truth of the deed, as the dove is an emblem or token of truth and innocence." (*Teachings,* p. 276.) (See also 1 Ne. 11:27; 2 Ne. 31:8; D&C 93:15; Matt. 3:16; Abr., facsimile 2:7.)

Dragon. 1) The dragon represents Satan. John wrote, "And the great dragon was cast out, that old serpent, called the Devil, and Satan" (Rev. 12:9; 20:2). One of Satan's chief mortal representatives, "Pharaoh king of Egypt" (Ezek. 29:3), was also known as a dragon.

2) Mighty warriors who fight and battle with fierceness almost beyond human comprehension are compared to dragons. Thus the scriptures say, "They exerted themselves and like dragons did they fight" (Mosiah 20:11; Alma 43:44). (See also *Jackal.*)

Dregs. The righteous are privileged to drink of the pure sacramental wine when they partake of the cup of the Lord, but the wicked "drink the dregs of a bitter cup" (Alma 40:26); indeed, "all the wicked of the earth shall . . . drink them" (Ps. 75:8; Isa. 51:17, 22). (See also *Cup; Wine.*)

Dross. Dross is waste matter on the surface of molten metal. For the blacksmith, dross altogether lacks value and is therefore cast away. For this reason dross symbolizes the wicked. According to the scriptures, "The wicked of the earth [are] like dross" (Ps. 119:119; Prov. 26:23), even "as dross, which the refiners do cast out, (it being of no worth) and is trodden under foot of men" (Alma 34:29). After the destruction of the first temple, while Israel was in exile, they were compared to the dross of silver (Ezek. 22:18–19). But in the last days they will be purged of their dross, and will become valuable to the Lord (Isa. 1:22–25). (See also *Furnace; Gold;* part 2: *Purifier; Refiner.*)

Dung. Dung, or the excrement of animals, is so vile and loathsome that even the creatures and beasts have no use for it. Therefore, this substance has become the symbol of the lowly and worthless state of depraved souls who have experienced the terrible judgments and punishments of God. This was the case with Jezebel, under whose bidding many of the prophets of Jehovah were murdered. Subsequent to the death of Jezebel, and after dogs had devoured her flesh, it is recorded that "the carcase of Jezebel" became "as dung upon the face of the field in the portion of Jezreel" (2 Kgs. 9:37). The prophet Job was very descriptive in his language when he said that the wicked man "shall perish for ever like his own dung" (Job 20:7). Others of similar dispositions of wickedness have received like judgments (Morm. 2:15; Ezra 6:11; Jer. 8:2; 16:4).

Dust. 1) To demonstrate the nothingness of man, the prophets often compare humanity to dust (Mosiah 2:25–26; Zeph. 1:17). This is due partly to the fact that the majority of mankind disregards the word of God, but every particle of dust obeys his commands: "O how great is the nothingness of the children of men; yea, even they are less than the dust of the earth. For behold, the dust of the earth moveth hither and thither, to the dividing asunder, at the command of our great and everlasting God" (Hel. 12:7–8). Even the great patriarch Abraham, while in the presence of the Lord, exclaimed, "I . . . am but dust and ashes" (Gen. 18:27).

2) The word *dust* is used to express the commonness and abundance of a given thing. For example, Isaac was promised that his seed would be "as the dust of the earth" (Gen. 28:14; see also 13:16; Num. 23:10); and so plentiful was the silver of Tyrus that it was "as the dust" (Zech. 9:3).

3) Deliberately sitting in the dust (Isa. 47:1; Micah 1:10) or sprinkling it upon the head (Josh. 7:6; 2 Sam. 1:2; Job 2:12) is a

sign of humility. Dust was also employed in other ways to express the humility of a person or people (Job 16:15; 1 Sam. 2:8; Isa. 2:9–11; Lam. 3:29; 1 Sam. 4:12). An expression in the Book of Mormon best equates dust with humility. The people of Limhi, after suffering great losses in battle against the Lamanites, "did humble themselves even to the dust. . . . And they did humble themselves even in the depths of humility." (Mosiah 21:13–14; Alma 34:38.)

4) Great significance is attached to the act of shaking dust from the feet of the elders. "And in whatsoever place ye shall enter, and they receive you not in my name, ye shall leave a cursing instead of a blessing, by casting off the dust of your feet against them as a testimony, and cleansing your feet by the wayside" (D&C 24:15; 75:20; Matt. 10:14; Acts 13:51).

Eagle. This most majestic of birds is swift (Jer. 4:13; Lam. 4:19; Job 9:26; Deut. 28:49), soars high in the heavens (Obad. 1:4), possesses excellent eyesight (Job 39:27–29), and has stamina (Ps. 103:5; Isa. 40:31). Three different things are symbolized by this creature.

1) Kingdoms or nations are likened to the eagle, such as Bozrah (Jer. 49:16), Chaldea (Hab. 1:6–8), Rome (Deut. 28:49–50), and others (Jer. 48:40; Ezek. 17:3–7; Dan. 7:4).

2) The Lord led Israel through the desert "as an eagle stirreth up her nest, fluttereth over her young, spreadeth abroad her wings, taketh them, beareth them on her wings: so the Lord alone did lead" them (Deut. 32:9–12; Ex. 19:4; Jer. 49:22; D&C 124:18). (See also *Dove; Hen; Wings;* part 2: *Eagle.*)

3) Certain individuals, possessing great swiftness and stamina, are likened to the eagle (2 Sam. 1:23; Isa. 40:30–31).

Ear. An audience or individual which is spiritually responsive to the things of God is said to have an "opened" ear (Isa. 50:4–5), whether the message is transmitted by God, the Holy Spirit, an angelic being, or a prophet; and whether the word is written, spoken, or simply felt. Thus the followers of Deity are instructed to "give ear" (Deut. 32:1; Isa. 1:10) and "incline [their] ear" (Ps. 45:10; Prov. 4:20) unto the word of God. In relation to this, King Benjamin instructs, "Hearken unto me, and open your ears that ye may hear, and your hearts that ye may understand, and your minds that the mysteries of God may be unfolded to your view" (Mosiah 2:9).

On the other hand, the wicked possess an ear that is "not opened" (Isa. 48:8). They are not responsive unto the things of

God. Of them it is written: "Their hearts have waxed hard, and their ears are dull of hearing, and their eyes cannot see afar off" (Moses 6:27). Furthermore, "their ear is uncircumcised, and they cannot hearken: behold, the word of the Lord is unto them a reproach" (Jer. 6:10). Also, it was said of the wicked that they "hearkened not, nor inclined their ear" (Jer. 7:24). The wicked man is "he that turneth away his ear from hearing the law" of God (Prov. 28:9). (See also *Deaf; Eyes.*)

Earth. The word *earth* often means "earth's inhabitants." For instance, a synonymous parallelism (Ps. 33:8) says:

>Let all the earth fear the Lord:
>let all the inhabitants of the world stand in awe of him.

Another (Gen. 6:11) uses *earth* similarly:

>The earth also was corrupt before God,
>and the earth was filled with violence.

Other passages of scripture demonstrate that the word *earth* can be substituted for "inhabitants." "And the whole earth was of one language, and of one speech" (Gen. 11:1). "And all the earth sought to Solomon, to hear his wisdom, which God had put in his heart" (1 Kgs. 10:24).

Earthquake. Earthquakes are one of the "great and terrible judgments of the Lord" (1 Ne. 12:4–5) reserved principally for "they that kill the prophets, and the saints" (2 Ne. 26:5–6), and "they that believe not" in God (2 Ne. 6:15). These frightening upheavals of the earth are designed to be a warning voice and a testimony (D&C 43:24–25; 88:89) so that the unrepentant will "feel the wrath, and indignation, and chastening hand of an Almighty God" (D&C 87:6).

East. East is the sacred direction. Holy temples are oriented eastward, and the east wind (the "wind of God") originates from this direction. Jesus Christ enters his temples from the east (Ezek. 43:1–2; see also Ezek. 10:19); and at the time of the Second Coming, the Lord will come from the east (JS-M 1:26; Matt. 24:27; *Teachings*, p. 287).

As dawn breaks forth in the east, and the light of the sun sheds light on the inhabitants of the earth, east (from the Hebrew verb *zerach*, which means "to rise, to come forth") symbolizes light, truth, and Christ (Isa. 60:1–3; Deut. 33:2; Ps. 112:4).

East Wind. The east wind is a destructive wind which originates in the east, the symbolic direction of Deity's presence.
Also called "the wind of the Lord" (Hosea 13:15), it is "prepared" by God (Jonah 4:8) for the purpose of destroying the ungodly and unrighteous. The Lord has stated, "If my people shall
sow filthiness they shall reap the east wind, which bringeth immediate destruction" (Mosiah 7:31). Hence they are "smitten
with the east wind" (Mosiah 12:6; see also Job 27:21).

Eden, Garden of. 1) Notwithstanding the fact that the
Garden of Eden was not enclosed within a building structure or
found within walls, this sacred space represented the first sanctuary known to mankind. Sacred oaths, eternal marriage, ceremonial clothing, sacrifices, revelation, and other temple rites
and ordinances were found within the Garden of Eden. (Moses
3-4.)

2) During Old Testament times, the Garden of Eden was a
byword for prosperity and abundance (Isa. 51:3; Ezek. 36:35;
Joel 2:3). (See also *Garden.*)

Edom / Idumea. During the biblical era Edom was the region
situated southeast of the Dead Sea and directly south of the area
known as Moab. It was not included as part of ancient Israel.
From the period of the Hasmonean kingdom and onward, Edom
was called Idumea.

Perhaps due to the fact that from earliest times Edom was
unfriendly towards the covenant people (Num. 20:14-21; 1
Sam. 14:47), and due to their gross wickedness, Edom, or
Idumea, has become a symbol for the wicked nations of the
earth, or "the world." The Prophet Joseph Smith wrote that the
Lord will "come down in judgment upon Idumea, or the world"
(D&C 1:36). It is the *world* that the Lord will destroy because of
wickedness, not the earth (Ezek. 35:15; Jer. 49:7-22; Isa.
34:5-6). (See also *Babylon; Egypt.*)

Egypt. Once called "the basest of the kingdoms" (Ezek.
29:15), Egypt symbolizes worldliness and "that which is forbidden." Abraham wrote about "the land of Egypt," which was
"first discovered by a woman, who was the daughter of Ham,
and the daughter of Egyptus, which in the Chaldean signifies
Egypt, which signifies that which is forbidden" (Abr. 1:23).
John the Revelator referred to Jerusalem as that "great city,
which spiritually is called Sodom and Egypt, where also our
Lord was crucified" (Rev. 11:8), equating Egypt with Sodom
and thus with gross wickedness. (See also *Assyria; Babylon;
Edom; Promised Land.*)

Eight. Church doctrine dictates that children should enter the waters of baptism at the age of eight years (D&C 68:25; JST, Gen. 17:11). Peter compared the eight souls found on Noah's ark to this age of baptism by saying: "In the days of Noah, . . . the ark was a preparing, wherein few, that is, eight souls were saved by water. The like figure whereunto even baptism doth also now save us." (1 Pet. 3:20-21.) In other words, temporal salvation came to eight souls because of water in the same way that eternal life comes to those who are baptized at the age of eight. (See also *Seven.*)

Elijah. Many of the prophetic actions of Elijah, whose name means "my God is Jehovah," prefigured the divine ministry of Jesus Christ. Elijah and Jesus Christ both uttered prophecy (1 Kgs. 17:1; Matt. 24:3-51), fearlessly denounced sin (1 Kgs. 21:17-24; Matt. 11:22-23), miraculously multiplied food (1 Kgs. 17:14-16; Luke 9:13-17), raised the dead (1 Kgs. 17:17-23; Matt. 9:18-25), demonstrated power over the elements (1 Kgs. 18:41-45; 2 Kgs. 2:8; Luke 8:23-24), fasted forty days and forty nights (1 Kgs. 19:8; Matt. 4:2), and were taken up into heaven (2 Kgs. 2:11; Acts 1:9-11). (See also *Prophet.*)

Elisha. The miracles of Elisha typified many of the wonders and marvels which were performed by the Lord during his earthly ministry. Both Elisha and Jesus healed lepers (2 Kgs. 5:9-14; Matt. 8:2-3) and both raised the dead (2 Kgs. 4:20-37; Mark 5:21-43). Miracles employing the use of food or bread (2 Kgs. 4:38-44; Mark 6:30-44) and water (2 Kgs. 6:1-7; Mark 6:45-52) were executed by both. And Elisha, the leading prophet of the northern kingdom for more than fifty years, and Jesus, who was reared in the northern portion of Palestine, both provided food for the hungry (2 Kgs. 6:24-7:20; Mark 8:1-9). (See also *Prophet.*)

Ensign. 1) Zion and its inhabitants are "as a beacon upon the top of a mountain" and "as an ensign on an hill" (Isa. 30:17; Zech. 9:16; D&C 64:41-42).

2) In the last days the gospel banner will be lifted "on the mountains" so that "a people scattered" may be brought to "mount Zion" (Isa. 18:3, 7; D&C 45:9). "And he [God] will lift up an ensign to the nations from far, and will hiss unto them from the end of the earth" (Isa. 5:26) and gather them into the land of Zion. (See also part 2: *Ensign.*)

Ephod. The ephod or "shoulder dress" was a sacred vestment worn by the high priest (Ex. 28:6-14). Attached to the ephod was the linen "breastplate of judgment" (Ex. 28:15-30), which bore twelve precious stones and the Urim and Thummim. Furthermore, two onyx stones were fastened to the shoulders of the vestment. Written upon the twelve precious stones, and again upon the two onyx stones, were the names of the twelve tribes of Israel, so that the high priest would "bear their names before the Lord upon his two shoulders" (Ex. 28:12).

In two principal ways the ephod was a symbol of Christ. First, the Urim and Thummim (Hebrew for "lights and perfections") represented the perfect Jesus, who, as the "light of the world," reveals his truths to the prophets. Second, the high priest (also a symbol of Christ) donned the ephod and entered the Holy of Holies to make atonement for the children of Israel. By having the names of the children of Israel twice attached to the ephod, the high priest (representing Christ) symbolically carried the twelve tribes into the Holy of Holies and there made atonement for them.

Eve. The name *Eve* signifies life and speaks of a great posterity and offspring. "And Adam called his wife's name Eve, because she was the mother of all living; for thus have I, the Lord God, called the first of all women, which are many" (Moses 4:26).

Eye. 1) Through the physical eyes one gains much knowledge of temporal things, and through the spiritual eyes one "sees" or understands the things of God. Prophets of all ages have referred to the eyes as the means by which spiritual illumination and truth are gained. For instance, the Psalmist pleaded with God, "Open thou mine eyes, that I may behold wondrous things out of thy law" (Ps. 119:18; Ps. 123:1). Using similar imagery the Apostle Paul wrote to the Ephesians about "the eyes of your understanding being enlightened" (Eph. 1:18) concerning the things of God.

Concerning the eyes of the beasts mentioned in the fourth chapter of the book of Revelation, Joseph Smith asked, "What are we to understand by the eyes . . . which the beasts had?" The revealed answer was that "their eyes are a representation of light and knowledge, that is, they are full of knowledge" (D&C 77:4; see also Matt. 6:22–23).

God, of course, has all knowledge and is full of light. Thus it is said of him that his eye is an "all-searching eye" (2 Ne. 9:44) and a "piercing eye" (Jacob 2:10), meaning there is no place that his eye cannot penetrate and nothing that he does not know. He is omniscient. (See also *Blind; Ears.*)

2) The "lust of the eyes" (1 John 2:16) pertains to those that have "eyes full of adultery, and that cannot cease from sin" (2 Pet. 2:14; Matt. 5:28).

Ezekiel. Instructed by God, Ezekiel performed certain peculiar actions which made him "a sign unto the house of Israel" (Ezek. 12:6) that they would be taken from Jerusalem and scattered among all nations (Ezek. 12:1-16). (See also *Prophet.*)

Famine. 1) Famines signify a scarcity of spiritual bread, a lack of divine knowledge. Amos wrote of such a figurative famine: "Behold, the days come, saith the Lord God, that I will send a famine in the land, not a famine of bread, nor a thirst for water, but of hearing the words of the Lord: and they shall wander from sea to sea, and from the north even to the east, they shall run to and fro to seek the word of the Lord, and shall not find it" (Amos 8:11).

2) Ezekiel listed famines as being one of God's "four sore judgments" (Ezek. 14:21). Famines frequently originate from and are controlled by heaven (Jer. 14:12; Ps. 105:16; Ezek. 5:16-17), often at the word of the prophets (Hel. 10:6; 11:4-15; Abr. 2:17). During various ages they have been referred to as "great desolations" and "grievous judgments" (JS-H 1:45), and as "sore afflictions" (Mosiah 12:4). They are sent "according to the wickedness of [the] people" (Hel. 10:6), due to unfaithfulness (Mosiah 1:17). They are sent to those who are "slow to remember the Lord" (Mosiah 9:3) and to those who do not repent (Alma 10:23). Further, they are sent to "chasten [God's] people" so that they will "remember him" (Hel. 12:3; Mosiah 1:17). By famine and other judgments will "the inhabitants of the earth be made to feel the wrath, and indignation, and chastening hand of an Almighty God" (D&C 87:6).

Fat. 1) A "fat land" is a land "full of all goods, wells digged, vineyards, and oliveyards, and fruit trees in abundance." Anciently, those that dwelt in such a place "did eat, and were filled, and became fat, and delighted themselves in [the Lord's] great goodness" (Neh. 9:25; see also Deut. 31:20; 32:13-14). Thus, fat things represent an abundance of earthly blessings (Gen. 45:18; Prov. 13:4). These things are reserved for the righteous: "He that putteth his trust in the Lord shall be made fat" (Prov. 28:25; see also Isa. 30:23).

2) Under the law of Moses the fat of sacrifices belonged to the Lord (Lev. 3:16). This regulation may have been a type of the "feast of fat things" which will be enjoyed at the wedding feast during "the marriage of the Lamb" (D&C 58:8, 11).

Feast of Tabernacles. The Feast of Tabernacles or the Feast of Booths is celebrated in the fall, at the completion of the harvest (Lev. 23:42–44). Its symbolical significance was explained by Elder Bruce R. McConkie: "The fact that [the Feast of Tabernacles] celebrated the completion of the full harvest symbolizes the gospel reality that it is the mission of the house of Israel to gather all nations to Jehovah, a process that is now going forward, but will not be completed until [the] millennial day." (*Promised Messiah*, p. 433.) (See also *Day of Atonement; Feast of Weeks; Passover; Sabbatical Year*.)

Feast of Weeks. Called Pentecost by the Christians, the symbolism attached to this festival has been explained as follows: "All the fires on all the altars of the past, as they burned the flesh of animals, were signifying that spiritual purification would come by the Holy Ghost, whom the Father would send because of the Son. On that first Pentecost of the so-called Christian Era such fires would have performed their purifying symbolism if the old order had still prevailed. How fitting it was instead for the Lord to choose that very day to send living fire from heaven, as it were, fire that would dwell in the hearts of men and replace forever all the fires on all the altars of the past." (*Promised Messiah*, p. 432.) And so it was that on the day of Pentecost, there were "cloven tongues like as of fire. . . . And they were all filled with the Holy Ghost." (Acts 2:1–4.) (See also *Day of Atonement; Feast of Tabernacles; Passover; Sabbatical Year*.)

Field. When used figuratively, the word *field* represents the wicked inhabitants of the world. The word of the Lord as revealed in the Doctrine and Covenants states, "Concerning the parable of the wheat and of the tares: Behold, verily I say, the field was the world" (D&C 86:1–2). Similarly, Lehi beheld in a dream "a large and spacious field, as if it had been a world" (1 Ne. 8:20). (See also *World*.)

Fig Tree. A fig tree is represented in Judges 9:10–11 as being a noble and fruitful man. (See also *Tree*.)

Fire. Fire is connected with the presence of Deity and holy men, God's judgments, his power to cleanse repentant souls, and various other divine occurrences.

1) The scriptures declare that "God is a consuming fire" (Heb. 12:29; Deut. 4:24) and "a wall of fire" (Zech. 2:5). Concerning this, Joseph Smith taught, "God Almighty Himself dwells in eternal fire; flesh and blood cannot go there, for all corruption is devoured by the fire" (*Teachings*, p. 367). To the Lawgiver, Moses, he appeared "in a flame of fire" (Ex. 3:2; 19:18). At his second coming the Lord will descend from heaven

"in flaming fire" (2 Thes. 1:8; see also Isa. 66:15) or "in a pillar of fire" (D&C 29:12) or "as the melting fire that burneth, and as the fire which causeth the waters to boil" (D&C 133:41).

2) On certain occasions and in special circumstances, holy men of God are accompanied with fire or are as fire (Ps. 104:4; Isa. 33:14–15; Judg. 13:20; Hel. 5:23–24, 43–45; D&C 7:6).

3) Fire is known for its cleansing powers. A simile portrays God as being "like a refiner's fire" and tells us that "he shall purify . . . and purge" various people (D&C 128:24; see also Isa. 6:6–7; Mal. 3:2; 1 Pet. 1:7; Rev. 3:18). Likewise, the Holy Ghost cleanses souls with fire (2 Ne. 31:13–14; Matt. 3:11). It is written that after one is baptized by water, "then cometh a remission of your sins by fire and by the Holy Ghost" (2 Ne. 31:17).

4) Fire has been sent as a judgment upon Syria, the Philistines, Tyre, Edom, Ammon, and Moab (Amos 1:4–14; 2:2). It was "brimstone and fire" that cursed Sodom and Gomorrah with destruction (Gen. 19:24). In a future day, fire will be sent to destroy the forces of Gog and Magog (Rev. 20:9; see also Isa. 47:14; Deut. 32:22; Jer. 23:29).

Interestingly, the same divine fire that cleanses the righteous also destroys the wicked. The unrighteous will burn in the "lake which burneth with fire and brimstone" (Rev. 21:8) or in "everlasting fire" (Matt. 25:41). They "shall burn as stubble" (JS-H 1:37), but the righteous will "dwell with the devouring fire" and "with everlasting burnings" (Isa. 33:14). "If the fire can scathe a green tree for the glory of God, how easy it will burn up the dry trees to purify the vineyard of corruption," wrote John Taylor (D&C 135:6). Thus, in sum, heavenly fire purifies the righteous (Isa. 43:1–2) but destroys the wicked (2 Ne. 30:10).

Firstborn. Before the law of Moses was introduced, the entire nation of Israel was God's firstborn (Ex. 4:22). At that time the rights and powers of the priesthood were available to all worthy males. During the Old Testament period when the Israelites were obliged to heed to the Mosaic law, however, the tribe of Levi became the firstborn (Num. 3:12, 40–45; 8:18). Firstborn creatures, both man and beast, were to be dedicated to God and made holy; Jehovah commanded, "Sanctify unto me all the firstborn, . . . both of man and of beast: it is mine" (Ex. 13:2, 12; 22:29). They belonged to the Lord (Num. 3:12–13), and were therefore called "holy to the Lord" (Luke 2:22–23).

The symbolical significance of the firstborn, both of man and of beast, has been explained as follows: "The consecration of the firstborn to the Lord as priest or as a sacrificial offering was a type for Christ, who as the firstborn in the spirit of all the Father's children was chosen in the heavenly council to be our priest or mediator and 'the Lamb slain from the foundation of the world' (Rev. 13:8)." (*Gospel Symbolism*, p. 260.) (See also part 2: *Firstborn*.)

Firstfruit. The law of Moses dictated that the firstfruits of the harvest be offered unto the Lord (Deut. 26:2; Prov. 3:9; Num. 18:12-13). These, considered "holy unto the Lord" (Ezek. 48:14), represent the righteous Saints of the first resurrection. These are they who were first plucked from the grave, those who are first gathered to rise from the dead. After their resurrection, they will be "presented as the first-fruits of Christ unto God" (Jacob 4:11). Christ is "the firstfruits of them that slept" (1 Cor. 15:20, 23; 2 Ne. 2:9), and those who arise at the first resurrection "are Christ's, the first fruits" (D&C 88:97-98). (See also *Fruit;* part 2: *Firstfruits*.)

Fish. Fish are symbols of men (Hab. 1:14; Eccl. 9:12). The law of Moses declared some fish clean and others unclean (Lev. 11:9-12; Deut. 14:9-10). So also are the children of men; some are pure and holy, while others are filthy. Likening men unto the fish of the sea, Jesus stated: "Again, the kingdom of heaven is like unto a net, that was cast into the sea, and gathered of every kind: which, when it was full, they drew to shore, and sat down, and gathered the good into vessels, but cast the bad away" (Matt. 13:47-48). (See also *Fishermen; Net.*)

Fishermen. Consistent with the typology that fish represent individuals, fishermen are those who catch and gather people into the gospel net. Thus Jeremiah wrote, "Behold, I will send for many fishers, saith the Lord, and they shall fish them" (Jer. 16:16), referring to those who would accept the gospel. Six centuries later Jesus told "Simon called Peter, and Andrew his brother, . . . Follow me, and I will make you fishers of men" (Matt. 4:18-19; Mark 1:17). (See also *Fish; Net.*)

Flea. The idiomatic saying "The king of Israel is come out to seek a flea" is found twice in the Old Testament (1 Sam. 26:20; 24:14). In this context, the tiny flea signifies a creature or thing of comparable insignificance.

Flesh. When used in a figurative sense, the word *flesh* pertains to the things of carnality (Ps. 56:4; John 3:6). In a scriptural parallelism, flesh is equated with iniquities (2 Ne. 4:17), many of which are listed by the Apostle Paul. He wrote, "Now the works of the flesh are manifest, which are these; Adultery, fornication, uncleanness, lasciviousness, idolatry, witchcraft, hatred, variance, emulations, wrath, strife, seditions, heresies, envyings, murders, drunkenness, revellings, and such like" (Gal. 5:19-21).

Accordingly, Jacob contrasted "the will of God" to "the will of the devil and the flesh" (2 Ne. 10:24). Man should not "trust in the arm of flesh" (D&C 1:19) but in the arm of the Lord. It is the flesh which serves sin (JST, Rom. 7:5, 26; 2 Ne. 4:27, 34) and finally dies the spiritual death (Rom. 8:12-13).

Other parallels and comparisons are made in the scriptures. Unlike the flesh of Christ (John 6:51-58), the flesh of mankind is made of corruptible substance (2 Ne. 9:4, 7). For this reason "no man has seen God at any time in the flesh, except quickened by the Spirit of God" (D&C 67:11), lest his corruptible flesh become destroyed. And Nephi wrote that "there is no flesh that can dwell in the presence of God" (2 Ne. 2:8).

Flock. Christ is the Shepherd, and those who hearken to his call are the sheep of his flock (Alma 5:38; Matt. 26:31; Jer. 13:17; Ezek. 34:31) or his "little flock" (Luke 12:32; D&C 6:34; 35:27). Often the flock is led by the servants of the Shepherd, or the prophets (Ps. 77:20; Acts 20:28). Isaiah wrote that the Lord "shall feed his flock like a shepherd: he shall gather the lambs with his arm, and carry them in his bosom, and shall gently lead those that are with young" (Isa. 40:11). (See also *Shepherd*; part 2: *Shepherd*.)

Flood. 1) During the days of Noah the destructive waters from heaven covered the entire earth, and all those found outside of the ark were drowned (Gen. 6:5-17). This deluge served as a prototype and symbol for other subsequent destructions, which also would cover the earth like a flood and destroy the children of men.

For instance, many of the great and terrible armies of the earth were said to be as the floods that "cover the earth" and "destroy . . . the inhabitants thereof." In this manner various nations were destroyed by their enemies (Jer. 46:7-8; 47:2; Amos 8:8), as was Jerusalem, for example, by the Romans (Dan. 9:26). Jesus compared the flood of Noah to the destructions of the Second Coming (Matt. 24:38-39). These figurative floods may originate from God (Isa. 28:2; Nahum 1:8; Matt. 7:27; 3 Ne. 18:13), Satan (Rev. 12:15), or man. (See also *River*.)

2) The deluge at the time of Noah represented the baptism of the planet earth. Similar to mortal beings who receive the

covenant of baptism, the earth was totally immersed under the waters of the Flood (Gen. 7:19; Ether 13:2).

Flower. Man in his temporary state has been compared to the flower of the field, whose beauty lasts for but a moment. After this fleeting glory, man, like the "fading flower" (Isa. 28:1–4; 40:6–8), dies and returns to the earth. Job taught that "man that is born of a woman is of few days. . . . He cometh forth like a flower, and is cut down." (Job 14:1–2; see also Ps. 103:15–16.) Both man and flower, like all corruptible things, cannot bear the heat of the day, "for the sun is no sooner risen with a burning heat, but . . . the flower . . . falleth" to the ground, and "perisheth" (James 1:10–11; 1 Pet. 1:24).

Even the great ones of the earth, the "high-minded governors" and the "kings and authorities" and "as the flowers thereof which soon falleth" (D&C 124:3–7); and, like the flower of the field, "it is gone; and the place thereof shall know it no more" (Ps. 103:15–16).

Footstool. The word *footstool* has three figurative usages.

1) Heaven is the "throne" of the Lord, and the earth is his "footstool" (1 Ne. 17:39; Matt. 5:34–35; D&C 38:17).

2) The enemies of the Lord are his "footstool" (Ps. 110:1; Matt. 22:44; Heb. 1:13).

3) The temple of Jerusalem is referred to as God's "footstool" (1 Chr. 28:2). The Psalmist wrote, "Exalt ye the Lord our God, and worship at his footstool" (Ps. 99:5), and affirmed that "we will go into his tabernacles: we will worship at his footstool" (Ps. 132:7).

Forehead. Perhaps due to the high visibility of the forehead, many persons in antiquity have placed identifying marks upon their foreheads. This was done both to distinguish themselves from others and to identify a peculiar social stance or position. Such was the case of prostitutes of the late Old Testament period who distinguished themselves with a mark on their foreheads (Jer. 3:3; Ezek. 16:12). In the Book of Mormon "the Amlicites were distinguished from the Nephites, for they had marked themselves with red in their foreheads after the manner of the Lamanites" (Alma 3:4, 13, 18). Aaron, the high priest, wore "a plate of pure gold" on his forehead. This emblem had written upon it the words "HOLINESS TO THE LORD" (Ex. 28:36–38).

Both righteous and unrighteous causes have employed marks in the forehead to identify their followers. At times of righteousness the Saints of God will reign in the celestial kingdom, with the name of their God written upon their foreheads (Rev. 22:4); the 144,000 chosen high priests will stand on Mount Zion, having the "Father's name written in their foreheads" (Rev. 14:1; D&C 133:18). And the four angels of Revelation chapter 7 were told, "Hurt not the earth, neither the sea, nor the trees, till we have sealed the servants of our God in their foreheads" (Rev. 7:3; 9:4; D&C 77:9).

Perhaps attempting to counterfeit the true religion, Satan's crowd of followers bear upon their foreheads distinguishing signs and words. John the Revelator explained that these individuals are identified as being followers of the devil, because they bear "a mark . . . in their foreheads" (Rev. 13:16; 14:9). Babylon the great has written upon her forehead "MYSTERY, BABYLON THE GREAT, THE MOTHER OF HARLOTS AND ABOMINATIONS OF THE EARTH" (Rev. 17:5).

Forest. Since a tree is often made to represent a man, it follows that the word *forest* symbolizes many men (Jer. 22:7; 21:14; Zech. 11:1-2; Isa. 10:17-18). Ezekiel spoke a parable of the "forest of the south," referring to the men of the south. "The word of the Lord came unto me, saying, Son of man, . . . prophesy against the forest of the south field; and say to the forest of the south, Hear the word of the Lord; Thus saith the Lord God; Behold, I will kindle a fire in thee, and it shall devour every green tree in thee, and every dry tree" (Ezek. 20:45-47; for an explanation of the parable, see Ezek. 21:1-5). (See also *Tree.*)

Foundation. Speaking symbolically, *foundation* has been used to represent Jesus Christ, the Apostles, the Saints of God, and followers of the devil.

1) Paul identifies Jesus Christ as the "chief corner stone" (Eph. 2:19-20). Not only is the chief cornerstone an integral part of the foundation—it is the most prominent and signal component. For this reason it is written of Christ that he is the "stone" which "shall become the great, and the last, and the only sure foundation" upon which all may build (Jacob 4:16). All true followers of God are to "remember that it is upon the rock of our Redeemer, who is Christ, the Son of God," that we must build, " . . . which is a sure foundation, a foundation whereon if men build they cannot fall" (Hel. 5:12).

2) The scriptures establish that the true Saints of God represent a building (1 Cor. 3:9-12), that the Apostles and prophets are the "foundation" (Eph. 2:19-20), and that Christ is the "chief corner stone" (Eph. 2:19-20; Isa. 28:16; Ps. 118:22; 1 Pet. 2:6). (See also *Building.*)

3) All who choose to follow the example of the Savior and who are obedient to the counsel of the prophets are considered "an everlasting foundation" (Prov. 10:25; Luke 6:47-48; 1 Tim. 6:19). They then become like their exemplars, Jesus and the Apostles.

4) The wicked "are laying the foundations of the devil" (Alma 10:17), meaning that through their impure activities, they attend to Satan's diabolical schemes and become part of his organization.

Fountain. In addition to possessing aesthetic beauty, a fountain of water provides all living creatures with life, and the water is used for cleansing purposes. So it is with Jesus. He is "the fountain of living waters" (Jer. 17:13; see also Rev. 21:6; Ps. 36:8-9), giving life to those who drink of the waters of salvation. He also is "the fountain of all righteousness" (Ether 12:28; 8:26; 1 Ne. 2:9), cleansing those who wash themselves to rid themselves of the stains of the world.

However, many have rejected Jehovah, the "living waters." Jeremiah recorded these words: "For my people have committed two evils; they have forsaken me the fountain of living waters, and hewed them out cisterns, broken cisterns, that can hold no water" (Jer. 2:13). (See also *Water; part 2: Fountain.*)

Fox. Unrighteous persons, with their evil cunning and deceitful actions, are said to be like the wily fox. Thus false prophets of Ezekiel's day were considered to be "like foxes in the deserts" (Ezek. 13:4; see also Lam. 5:18). The infamous King Herod was called a fox by Jesus Christ, who created the entire animal kingdom (Luke 13:31-32). (See also *Dog; Wolf.*)

Frankincense. See *Incense.*

Friend. The friends of God are those who are obedient to his commands. "Ye are my friends, if ye do whatsoever I command you" (John 15:14) was the divine word of Jesus to his disciples. And to those who are called friends in this dispensation, the Lord adds the promise, "And ye shall have an inheritance with me" (D&C 93:45; D&C 84:63). In other words, those who are God's friends will enjoy an everlasting "sociality" with their Father in Heaven, "coupled with eternal glory" (D&C 130:2).

In contrast to the friends of God are those who will receive an inferior station in the hereafter. These are called "servants" (D&C 76:112; John 15:14-15). (See also *Servants*; part 2: *Friend of Sinners.*)

Fringes. The law of Moses demanded that the children of Israel make "fringes in the borders of their garments" (Num. 15:38; Deut. 22:12). Religious Jews of today still comply with this ritual. Its significance was that whenever a person would look upon the fringes, he would "remember all the commandments of the Lord, and do them" (Num. 15:39).

Frog. The great plagues of Egypt, sent from God to humble the community of Pharaoh (Ps. 78:45; 105:30; Ex. 8), were types and figures of things to come. These plagues included frogs, lice, flies, locusts, hail, and fire. According to John, frogs represent "unclean spirits" or "the spirits of devils" (Rev. 16:13–14).

Fruit. 1) In the scriptures, trees often represent men, and their fruits represent their qualities and their works. Therefore, the righteous man, like the fruitful tree, will be fruitful "in his season" (Ps. 1:3). He will perform good works even in "old age" (Ps. 92:12–14), and he will never "cease from yielding fruit" (Jer. 17:7–8). These "fruits of righteousness" originate when one accepts and follows Jesus (Philip. 1:11).

The scriptures list many of these "peaceable fruit[s] of righteousness" (Heb. 12:11; 2 Cor. 9:10). Paul wrote that the "fruit of the Spirit is love, joy, peace, longsuffering, gentleness, goodness, faith, meekness, temperance" (Gal. 5:22–23). He further explained, "For the fruit of the Spirit is in all goodness and righteousness and truth. . . . Have no fellowship with the unfruitful works of darkness." (Eph. 5:9, 11.)

Not every tree, however, produces "fruits of righteousness." Matthew explained that "every good tree bringeth forth good fruit; but a corrupt tree bringeth forth evil fruit. A good tree cannot bring forth evil fruit, neither can a corrupt tree bring forth good fruit." (Matt. 7:17–18; 12:33.) Corrupt trees are "trees whose fruit withereth, without fruit, twice dead" (Jude 1:12; Hosea 9:16). Their fruits are "unfruitful works of darkness" (Eph. 5:9, 11); as Paul wrote to the Romans, "the motions of sins . . . did work in our members to bring forth fruit unto death" (JST, Rom. 7:5).

2) The seed and offspring of a person is often called his fruit. Hence, such idioms as the "fruit of my loins" (2 Ne. 3:4; Acts 2:30) and the "fruit of the womb" (Gen. 30:2; Deut. 7:13; Ps. 21:10) are commonly used to indicate posterity. In a similar manner, Moses called an unborn child "fruit" (Ex. 21:22); and to Adam and Eve the Lord commanded, "Be fruitful, and multiply, and replenish the earth" (Moses 2:28).

3) The fruit of the tree of life signifies "the bread and the waters of life" (Alma 5:34), or the body and blood of Jesus Christ. In other words, those who partake of this fruit are those who have been baptized into the Lord's true Church (Alma

5:62) and are making Jesus' atoning sacrifice effective in their lives. This fruit is "most precious and most desirable above all other fruits; yea, and it is the greatest of all the gifts of God" (1 Ne. 15:36; Alma 12:21). (See also *Tree of Life*.)

Furnace. 1) To set forth the extreme terror, horror, and anguish awaiting those who will inherit hell, the prophets have described this place of torment as a "furnace of fire" where one finds "wailing and gnashing of teeth" (Matt. 13:42, 50).

2) Through the "furnace of affliction," the Lord's people are refined, purified, and sanctified before the Lord (Isa. 48:10; 1 Pet. 1:7; Deut. 4:20). The Lord instructed Ezekiel, "Son of man, the house of Israel is to me become dross: all they are brass, and tin, and iron, and lead, in the midst of the furnace; they are even the dross of silver. . . . I will gather you, and blow upon you in the fire of my wrath, and ye shall be melted in the midst thereof. As silver is melted in the midst of the furnace, so shall ye be melted in the midst thereof." (Ezek. 22:18-22.) The same concept was taught to Zechariah: "And I will bring the third part through the fire, and will refine them as silver is refined, and will try them as gold is tried: they shall call on my name, and I will hear them: I will say, It is my people: and they shall say, The Lord is my God" (Zech. 13:9). (See also *Gold; Dross*.)

Gall. Gall, a poisonous plant, denotes an extremely bitter thing. The "gall of bitterness" speaks of hell, or the "darkest abyss" (Mosiah 27:29; Morm. 8:31; Moro. 8:14).

Garden. 1) "Three sacred gardens are central to the whole plan of salvation: the Garden of Eden, the place of the Fall; the Garden of Gethsemane, with Golgotha the place of the Atonement; and the Garden of the Empty Tomb, the place of the Resurrection" (*Gospel Symbolism*, p. 260). (See also *Eden; Gethsemane*.)

2) The tents and tabernacles of Israel were compared to the "gardens by the river's side" (Num. 24:5-6; see also Lam. 2:6).

3) The righteous are "like a watered garden" (Isa. 58:11), but the wicked are "as a garden that hath no water" (Isa. 1:30).

Garment. 1) To Moroni and the Nephite armies, "rending their garments" was a "token," or a "covenant, that they would not forsake the Lord . . . ; or, in other words, if they should transgress the commandments of God, . . . the Lord should rend them even as they had rent their garments" (Alma 46:21).

2) During ancient times, rending the garments was a sign of mourning (Isa. 37:1; Job 1:20; Gen. 37:34).

3) Joseph's garment (coat of many colors) represented

priesthood authority and the blessings of the birthright. Jacob, possessing a remnant of this garment, declared: "Even as this remnant of garment of my son hath been preserved, so shall a remnant of the seed of my son be preserved by the hand of God, and be taken unto himself, while the remainder of the seed of Joseph shall perish, even as the remnant of his garment" (Alma 46:24; see also 1 Kgs. 11:29–32).

4) Garments are often put for the whole man (Morm. 9:35; Ether 13:10). The expression "that our garments may be pure" speaks of the purity of the whole person (D&C 109:76). Similarly, the phrase "those who have washed their garments in my blood" refers to those souls who have become clean through "their faith, and the repentance of all their sins" (3 Ne. 27:19).

Gates. When the prophetic writer used the word *gates,* he used the word to signify an entrance or an exit into another area or realm. Also, judgment and law were given at this locale.

1) The place by ancient city gates was a place of judgment (Deut. 16:18–19; 2 Sam. 15:2; Amos 5:15; Josh. 20:4; Ruth 4:1–2; Zech. 8:16), and the thrones of kings and princes often were set at this locale (1 Kgs. 22:10; 2 Chr. 18:9; Jer. 38:7; 39:3). It is also written that the law was read at the gates of Jerusalem (Neh. 8:1–3).

2) The "gates of death" (Job 38:17; Ps. 9:13) are those portals through which dying souls pass at the time that their spirit exits the physical body and enters into the world of spirits. When the time was at hand for King Hezekiah to leave this sphere of existence, he mournfully said, "I shall go to the gates of the grave" (Isa. 38:10).

3) The scriptures inform us that the gates to spiritual death are "broad" and "wide" (D&C 132:25; Matt. 7:13). For this reason many will locate these gates of Satan and enter therein.

4) The expression "gates of hell" is a common scriptural expression (D&C 10:69; 17:8; Matt. 16:18). "The gates of hell are ready open to receive" the wicked (3 Ne. 18:13).

5) The gate of heaven, in contrast to the gates of hell, is "strait" and "narrow" (Matt. 7:14). It should be noted that there is only one gate to heaven, but there are many gates which open unto hell. Clearly, only the righteous are able to walk over the threshold of heaven's doorway (Isa. 26:2; 60:10–12; 62:9–10). The Psalmist referred to "this gate of the Lord, into which the righteous shall enter" (Ps. 118:20), and Helaman wrote that "the gate of heaven is open unto all . . . who will believe on the

name of Jesus Christ" (Hel. 3:28). One enters these divine portals by repentance and baptism (D&C 22:1-2; 2 Ne. 31:17-18). Incidentally, Jacob, the great patriarch, was shown the gate of heaven in a vision (Gen. 28:12-17).

Significantly, Christ is the "door" of the gate (John 10:7, 9) and "the keeper of the gate" (2 Ne. 9:41; Moses 7:53). All who enter into the celestial realm must pass by the Lord, and become approved by him. (See also part 2: *Keeper of the Gate*.)

Gethsemane. The Garden of Gethsemane (a Hebrew word meaning "oil press") signifies the place of the Atonement, where Jesus Christ, the Anointed One, was crushed, squeezed, and pressed, where the symbolical purgation took place. (See also *Olive Leaf; Olive Oil; Olive Tree*.)

Girdle. Anciently, men of war prepared for battle by girding their swords or weapons around their loins (1 Sam. 25:13; 1 Ne. 4:19). From this practice have come the idioms "to gird up your loins" and "to gird yourself with a girdle." Such phraseology speaks of the Lord's soldiers who prepare for spiritual warfare (D&C 27:15-16; 2 Ne. 30:11). Among the Lord's warriors are his Apostles (D&C 112:7, 14) and the faithful of the Church (D&C 105:16, 26), who, having prepared themselves spiritually, have made war or will make war against Satan and his evil hosts (Rev. 12:7-9; D&C 76:29).

Gnashing of Teeth. While "gnashing their teeth," the captors and persecutors of Alma and Amulek asked the two prophets, "How shall we look when we are damned?" (Alma 14:21.) The expression "gnashing of teeth" describes the horrible condition of the "wicked, unfaithful, and unjust stewards, . . . hypocrites, and unbelievers" (D&C 101:90-91). These, in their final state, will be "cast out into outer darkness" (Alma 40:13) and "into a furnace of fire" (Matt. 13:42; 8:12), placed at the "left hand" of God (D&C 19:5), and "cut asunder" (D&C 85:9), where they will continually "howl, and weep, and wail, and gnash their teeth" (Mosiah 16:2; Matt. 13:42).

Gnat. To avoid swallowing a gnat, an insect declared unclean by the law of Moses (Lev. 11:23), the Jews of Jesus' day were accustomed to straining out their wine through a cloth. In this manner, the wine would filter through the cloth and become acceptable for drinking, but the gnat would be caught up in the cloth. Understanding this Jewish practice sheds light on the declaration of Jesus to the scribes and Pharisees: "Ye blind guides, which strain at a gnat [should read 'strain out a gnat'], and swallow a camel" (Matt. 23:24). In this context, therefore, the gnat signifies something which is small and insignificant, as compared to the camel, a large animal which, according to the Mosaic law, is also unclean (Lev. 11:4).

Goat. Two goats have significant roles in the sacred ceremony of the Day of Atonement: the goat of Jehovah and the scapegoat. Both are types of the Lord Jesus, prefiguring his great atoning sacrifice. The goat of Jehovah was sacrificed as a sin offering and its blood was sprinkled on the mercy seat and on the horns of the altar, making atonement for the sins of Israel (Lev. 16:8-19).

Upon the head of the scapegoat, the high priest laid his hands and pronounced "all the iniquities of the children of Israel, and all their transgressions in all their sins, putting them upon the head of the goat" (Lev. 16:21). Afterward the scapegoat was sent into the wilderness. (See also *Scapegoat; Sacrifice.*)

2) At the great Day of Judgment, the Great Shepherd will separate the goats and the sheep. The sheep will gain a place of honor, distinction, and glory at the right side of the Lord, but the goats will be set at the left hand, where weeping, wailing, and darkness are found (Matt. 25:33). (See also *Lamb; Shepherd; Sheep; Right; Left.*)

Gog and Magog. Gog and Magog are the prophetic names given to the evil and warring nations which will fight two great battles of the future. The first battle, known as Armageddon, will be in progress when the Lord returns at the time of the Second Coming (see Ezek. 38; 39; Zech. 11; 12; 13; Rev. 16:14-21). The second will take place at the end of the Millennium (Rev. 20:7-9; D&C 88:111-116).

Gold. 1) Gold, which belongs to God (Hag. 2:8; Joel 3:5) and is given to whom he pleases (Ezek. 16:17), represents that which is pure, incorruptible, and precious. For this reason, gold is connected with divine and sacred things, such as the ancient sanctuary (Ex. 36:34, 38; 1 Kgs. 6:21-22; 1 Chr. 22:14, 16; 29:2-7), its candlesticks (Ex. 25:31-38; 37:17-24), vessels (Ex. 25:26, 29, 38-39; 37:16), cherubim (2 Chr. 3:10), the ark of the covenant (Ex. 25:11-13), the altar (1 Kgs. 7:48), and other articles and utensils (1 Kgs. 7:48-51; 2 Kgs. 25:15; Jer. 52:19). Furthermore, gold is associated with the celestial city of Jerusalem and its inhabitants. Its streets will be as "pure gold" (Rev. 21:18, 21), and Christ and the exalted elders will wear "crowns of gold" (Rev. 14:14; 4:4). After having seen Jesus in a vision, Joseph Smith noted that he had been standing upon "a paved work of pure gold" (D&C 110:2).

Babylon, the city of wickedness, attempting to imitate the heavenly city, has gold as one of its chief desires (1 Ne. 13:7-8; Rev. 17:4; 18:16).

2) Both the sons of Levi and the Saints of God are tried and purged as gold in the great furnace of Jehovah (D&C 128:24; Mal. 3:3; 1 Pet. 1:7), meaning that through their trials and afflictions, they become pure and precious before God. (See also *Brass; Dross; Furnace; Iron;* part 2: *Purifier; Refiner.*)

Gomer. See *Hosea.*

Gomorrah/Sodom. During the days of Abraham, the sister cities Sodom and Gomorrah were destroyed by a rain of fire and brimstone (Gen. 19:24-28; Deut. 29:23; 32:32). This heavenly judgment was the result of sins and gross wickedness found among their inhabitants, sins which are enumerated within the Bible (Ezek. 16:49-50; Jude 1:7).

The very definition of the Hebrew names of these cities describes their final desolate condition—i.e., Sodom is defined as being a "volcanic" or "bituminous" area, and Gomorrah, "a ruined heap." So thorough was the destruction of these cities that they became "the breeding of nettles, and saltpits, and a perpetual desolation" (Zeph. 2:9), and it is written that "no man shall abide there, neither shall a son of man dwell in it" (Jer. 49:18; 50:40).

The names *Sodom* and *Gomorrah*, therefore, have become a byword for evil (Isa. 13:19; 3:9; Jer. 23:14) and symbols of the divine wrath and judgment of God (Matt. 10:15; Rom. 9:29) upon the abominable practices of mankind. Further, these two cities "are set forth for an example" (Jude 1:7) of the type of heavenly judgment awaiting "those that after [Sodom and Gomorrah] should live ungodly" lives (2 Pet. 2:6). (See also *Babylon; Edom; Egypt.*)

Grass. The temporal and fragile nature of man's existence has been compared to "the grass of the field" (Isa. 37:27). Man, therefore, is like the grass, because "in the morning it flourisheth, and groweth up; in the evening it is cut down, and withereth" (Ps. 90:5-6). Using metaphoric language, Isaiah taught, "All flesh is grass. . . . The grass withereth . . . : surely the people is grass." (Isa. 40:6-8; 1 Pet. 1:24.) Even those who claim to be mighty, the "kings and authorities" and "high-minded governors" are "as grass, and all their glory [is] as the flower thereof which soon falleth" (D&C 124:3-7; James 1:10-11; Ps. 72:16).

Grasshopper. Metaphors, similes, and other figures of speech are employed by the prophets to compare the grasshopper to mankind. In four principal ways, human beings are like the grasshopper—in their smallness, in their great number, in their insignificance when considered in the light of God's mighty works, and in their ability to devastate and spoil the land.

1) The spies which Moses commissioned to "search the land of Canaan" (Num. 13:2) returned with this report: "And there we saw the giants, the sons of Anak, which come of the giants: and we were in our own sight as grasshoppers, and so we were in their sight" (Num. 13:33).

2) In order to describe a great multitude of people, the hyperbolic expression "They are more than the grasshoppers, and are innumerable" (Jer. 46:23; Judg. 7:12; 6:5) is often employed by the writers of the scriptures.

3) In comparison to the marvelous works and creations of Deity, the children of men are but grasshoppers, or lowly creatures (Isa. 40:22).

4) Warriors and fighting men, like the locust family, are agents of destruction. These armies of creatures ravage, destroy, and make bare the land. Thus the Lord described the men that "hath laid my vine waste, and barked my fig tree: [they] hath made it clean bare, and cast it away; the branches thereof are made white" (Joel 1:1-7; Isa. 33:4; Nahum 3:15-17). (See also *Locusts.*)

Green. The color green pertains to fruitful and living things, speaking of both spiritual things and physical things (Job 15:32; Jer. 11:16-17; Hosea 14:8; Ps. 37:2; D&C 135:6). (See also *Colors.*)

Hagar. In an epistle to the Galatians, Paul employed an allegory comparing the old law with the new. In his analogy, Hagar represented the law of Moses and Sarah the fullness of the gospel (Gal. 4:22-31). (See also *Sarah.*)

Hail. Hail is one of many "judgments" sent forth from God to encourage mortals toward repentance and righteousness (D&C 109:30; D&C 43:25; Hag. 2:17). Through this destructive device, crops are destroyed (D&C 29:16), and the tribes of the earth are smitten and slain (Josh. 10:11; Ezek. 38:22; Mosiah 12:6).

Hair. Cutting and shaving off the hair symbolizes mourning and grief (Jer. 7:29; Job 1:20; Ezra 9:3). (See also *Baldness.*)

Hand. 1) The Hebrew *yad* means "hand" or "power." In priesthood ordinations, blessings, and conferrals, when the laying on of hands is performed, the power of the Lord is manifest through the hands of the administrator or priesthood participant (D&C 36:1-2). In scores of scriptural instances, the hand represents power (1 Ne. 5:14; Alma 37:4). (See also *Arm; Left; Right.*)

2) *Hand* is often put for the whole man (2 Ne. 25:16; Mosiah 11:21).

Harlot. Speaking of Jerusalem and its inhabitants, the prophet Isaiah exclaimed, "How is the faithful city become an harlot!" (Isa. 1:21.) Ezekiel added this charge: "Thou . . . playedst the harlot . . . and pouredst out thy fornications on every one that passed by" (Ezek. 16:15; see also verses 16ff.). Other cities have been accused of acting as a harlot by their treacherous actions and deeds, such as Tyre (Isa. 23:15-16), Samaria (Ezek. 23:5, 44), Ninevah (Nahum 3:4), and Babylon (Rev. 17:5). Therefore, the wicked of these cities practiced spiritual harlotry, by selling their souls for cheap sins and base transgressions.

Those who symbolically represented the bride of Jehovah, the children of Israel, "played the harlot with many lovers" (Jer. 3:1). The Lord said, "And I saw, when for all the causes whereby backsliding Israel committed adultery I had put her away, and given her a bill of divorce; yet her treacherous sister Judah feared not, but went and played the harlot also" (Jer. 3:8). (See also *Adultery.*)

Harvest. The word *harvest* pertains to members of the Church, the preaching of the gospel, and the acceptance or rejection of the gospel by the inhabitants of the world. Commenting on the parable of the wheat and tares, Joseph Smith explained, "The harvest and the end of the world have an allusion directly to the human family in the last days" (*Teachings*, p. 101). Associated with harvest imagery are many symbols — harvest, sowing, reapers, field, wheat, and tares (D&C 86; Matt. 13; *Teachings*, pp. 98-101). Joseph Smith added to the biblical interpretation of these symbols.

1) "The good seed [the wheat] are the children of the kingdom" or the righteous (Matt. 13:38).

2) "The tares are the children of the wicked one" (Matt. 13:38).

3) The field is the world, upon which the seeds (mankind) are planted (D&C 86:2).

4) The sowers of the good (wheat) seed are the Apostles (D&C 86:2).

5) The tares are "sown by the enemy" (*Teachings*, p. 98), or the devil.

6) The harvest represents the "end of the world" or "the destruction of the wicked" (*Teachings*, p. 98).

7) The angels of God are the reapers who "shall first gather out the wheat from among the tares, and after the gathering of the wheat, behold and lo, the tares are bound in bundles, and the field remaineth to be burned" (D&C 86:5, 7; Rev. 14:15; *Teachings*, p. 101). (See also *Field; Sheaves; Tares*.)

Hear. Often the verb *to hear* should be interpreted as meaning "to believe" or "to obey," as in the case of 1 Nephi 22:20, which says, "And it shall come to pass that all those who will not hear that prophet shall be cut off from among the people" (see also Jacob 6:6; Alma 10:6; 21:11). (See also *Ears; Eyes*.)

Heart. The word *heart* is used throughout the scriptures in scores of idiomatic expressions. Some of its usages are:

1) *Heart* is put for the entire soul, the whole person: "And now [I desire] that my soul might have joy in you, and that my heart might leave this world with gladness because of you" (2 Ne. 1:21; 2 Ne. 4:16).

2) The heart is thought to be the seat of emotions, the center of feelings—for example, Lehi spoke "according to the feelings of his heart" (2 Ne. 4:12). The heart sorrows, groans, weeps, and rejoices (see 2 Ne. 4:17, 19, 26, 28).

3) The word *heart* pertains to the evil disposition of a man—as shown by the phrases "harden his heart" (Alma 12:35) and "lifted up in the pride of his heart" (Alma 1:6)—or to his spiritual disposition, which may be "pure in heart" (Jacob 3:2) or "poor in heart" (Alma 32:3).

4) The heart is associated with the intellect and is the seat of thought, as in the phrases "I said in my heart" (1 Ne. 4:10) and "my heart pondereth" (2 Ne. 4:15).

5) Since the heart is located in the central part of the body, it represents the geographical center of a particular place: "The Lamanites durst not come into the heart of their lands" (Hel. 1:18).

Helmet. The "helmet of salvation" (Isa. 59:17; Eph. 6:17; 1 Thes. 5:8; D&C 27:18) is part of the divine armor worn by the warriors and soldiers of God as a protection from the fiery darts of Satan and his hordes. (See also *Armor.*)

Hen. Jesus, "as a hen" to the "descendants of Jacob" (3 Ne. 10:4), offers them nourishment and protection from predators. To the Nephites the Lord recited the same lamentation which he had spoken to the Jews (Matt. 23:37): "How oft have I gathered you as a hen gathereth her chickens under her wings, and have nourished you. . . . and ye would not." (3 Ne. 10:4, 6.) The Psalmist invoked the Lord to "hide me under the shadow of thy wings" (Ps. 17:8). Also, the Lord "shall cover thee with his feathers, and under his wings shalt thou trust" (Ps. 91:4). (See also *Chicken; Dove; Eagle; Wings.*)

High Priest. Faithful high priests of all ages and of every dispensation are similitudes of the "great high priest, that is passed into the heavens, Jesus the Son of God" (Heb. 4:14; 3:1). High priests who served Jehovah during the dispensation of Moses were to have no physical "blemish" (Lev. 21), in similitude of the Savior, who was spiritually "without blemish" (1 Pet. 1:19). The high priest was anointed with holy oil, as was the Messiah, or the Christ. They wore temple crowns (Zech. 6:11), as did Jesus (Rev. 19:12). The high priest is ordained "to administer in spiritual things" (D&C 107:12) so that "he may offer both gifts and sacrifices for sins" (Heb. 5:1). Such is the divine calling of Jesus. Also, a high priest is "rightful heir . . . holding the right belonging to the fathers" (Abr. 1:2), as is Jesus (Heb. 1:2). (See also *Apostle; Bishop; Priest;* part 2: *High Priest.*)

Highway. A highway represents the way of the just and the path of the righteous. It is the road that holy Saints travel as they journey toward their heavenly home. "The highway of the upright is to depart from evil" (Prov. 16:17; Jer. 31:21). Concerning the returning ten tribes, they will travel the strait and narrow highway of righteousness. "And an highway shall be there, and a way, and it shall be called The way of holiness; the unclean shall not pass over it" (Isa. 35:8; 62:10; see also 2 Ne. 31:18, 21; D&C 133:26–29). (See part 2: *Way.*)

Holy of Holies. The Holy of Holies of the temple is but a figure "of a true" Holy of Holies, which is "heaven itself" (Heb. 9:1–10, 12, 24–25). Housed within this sacred edifice in ancient days were many items symbolically associated with Jesus Christ, such as the ark of the covenant, the mercy seat, the cherubim, the jar of manna, Aaron's rod, and the tablets of the law. (See also *Temple.*)

Honey / Honeycomb. 1) The common expression that a place is a "land flowing with milk and honey" (Ex. 33:3) occurs twenty-one times in the scriptures. This and other idiomatic expressions employing the word *honey* (Job 20:17; Isa. 7:22; Deut. 32:13) describe its symbolic usage. Honey, during the biblical days, was a byword for abundance and divine blessing.

2) Honey also signified the heavenly boon of wisdom and knowledge. The eating of honey was said to enlighten the mind of the partaker (1 Sam. 14:27, 29). It was equated with wisdom (Prov. 24:13–14), divine books (Ezek. 3:3; Rev. 10:9–10), and knowledge (Isa. 7:15). The words of the Lord were "sweeter than honey" to those who feasted upon them (Ps. 119:103).

Horn. 1) Horns are representative of power and strength (1 Sam. 2:10; Jer. 48:25; Ps. 75:10). (See also part 2: *Horn of Salvation.*)

2) A great key to understanding Daniel's usage of the word *horns* (see Dan. 7; 8) is given in the same account. Speaking metaphorically, Daniel explains that "the ten horns out of this kingdom are ten kings" (Dan. 7:24), and that "the ram which thou sawest having two horns are the kings of Media and Persia" (Dan. 8:20; see also 8:21). John the Revelator employs similar imagery in his writings (Rev. 12:3; 13:1; 17:3, 7, 12).

Horse. Before the warring machines of the modern era, the principal vehicle of ancient warfare was the horse and chariot. Such instruments of combat often struck fear into the hearts of the people (Isa. 31:3; Jer. 4:13; 8:16). Job's description of the warhorse (Job 39:19–24) demonstrates the terribleness of this warring creature:

> Hast thou given the horse strength?
> hast thou clothed his neck with thunder?
> . . . .
> the glory of his nostrils is terrible.
> He paweth in the valley,
> and rejoiceth in his strength:
> he goeth on to meet the armed men.
> He mocketh at fear, and is not affrighted;
> neither turneth he back from the sword.
> The quiver rattleth against him,
> the glittering spear and the shield.
> He swalloweth the ground with fierceness and rage.

Prophetically speaking, therefore, the horse is connected with warfare; in other words, prophecies which associate the

horse with combat and war always associate the horse with ve-
hicles of war, warriors, battles, and conquest (Jer. 46:4; Ezek.
38:4; Hosea 1:7).

Notwithstanding this, disciples of Jehovah are taught not to
fear the horse nor seek protection from the chariot in times of
war, but to trust the Lord. "The horse is prepared against the
day of battle: but safety is of the Lord" (Prov. 21:31; Ps. 20:7;
33:17; Isa. 31:1; Hosea 1:7). (See also *Ass.*)

Hosea. Each of the family of Hosea was a sign unto the
children of Israel. Hosea, as the husband and bridegroom, symbolized Jehovah. Gomer, Hosea's "wife of whoredoms," represented unfaithful Israel who had "committed great whore-
dom" by "departing from the Lord."

The names of the children of Hosea and Gomer also held special significance. All three were named by Jehovah. Jezreel was
so named because, as the Lord stated, "I will break the bow of
Israel in the valley of Jezreel." Lo-ruhamah (Hebrew) for "not
having obtained mercy") received her name because Jehovah
promised that he would "no more have mercy upon the house
of Israel." After the third child of Hosea and Gomer was named
Lo-ammi (Hebrew for "not my people"), the Lord declared, "Ye
are not my people, and I will not be your God" (Hosea 1:2–9).

Hot Drinks. The Word of Wisdom instructs, "And again, hot
drinks are not for the body or belly" (D&C 89:9). Hyrum Smith,
the brother of the Prophet, defined *hot drinks* by saying, "There
are many who wonder what this can mean; whether it refers to
tea, or coffee, or not. I say it does refer to tea, and coffee."
(*Times and Seasons*, 1 June 1842, p. 800.)

Hour. An *hour* can represent an unspecified period of time.
For example, such expressions as "The hour of his judgment is
come" (Rev. 14:7), "The hour is close at hand" (Alma 5:29), "It
is the eleventh hour" (D&C 33:3), and "The hour cometh" (D&C
27:5) cannot refer to a time period of sixty minutes.

House. The word *house* often indicates the house's inhabitants (Alma 10:11; Ether 9:12, 16).

Hunters. 1) The Lord's missionaries are called hunters, signifying the way in which they seek for converts "from every
mountain, and from every hill, and out of the holes of the rocks"
(Jer. 16:16). (See also *Fishermen.*)

2) The wicked employ devious methods to trap and ensnare
their fellow humans. They "hunt every man his brother with a
net" (Micah 7:2). Also, "the proud have hid a snare . . . and
cords; they have spread a net by the wayside; they have set gins
[traps]" (Ps. 140:5).

Husband. In the scriptures, God acts as the husband (Hebrew word *ba'al* means "husband," "lord," or "owner"), and the house of Israel, or the Church, is his wife. God is the bridegroom and the Church is the bride. As the scriptures explain, "For thy Maker is thine husband" (Isa. 54:5); "I was an husband unto them, saith the Lord" (Jer. 31:32); "For the husband is the head of the wife, even as Christ is the head of the church" (Eph. 5:23). (See also *Bride; Bridegroom*; part 2: *Husband.*)

Husbandman. The role of a husbandman is to care for the vineyard. It is quite a natural thing, then, to see the husbandmen of Jesus' parables as ecclesiastical overseers, whose duty it is to cultivate the spiritual growth of those for whom they are responsible. Thus, a parable recorded by the Apostle Matthew describes the chief priests and Pharisees of Christ's day as being husbandmen, albeit wicked overseers (JST, Matt. 21:33-56).

Another parable sets forth God the Father as the husbandman, with Jesus as the vine, and his followers as the branches. In these inspired words the Father is shown to be the chief overseer, who directs the affairs of the vineyard, or kingdom of God upon the earth (John 15:1-6). Paul wrote to the Corinthians, saying, "Ye are God's husbandry" (1 Cor. 3:9). This phrase could also be written "Ye are God's cultivated field."

Hyssop. An herb with cleansing and purifying qualities, hyssop was employed during specific ceremonies and rites under the Mosaic law. For instance, hyssop was used to cleanse the leper and his household (Lev. 14:4-6, 49, 52), and it was employed to ritually purify persons who had had contact with "one slain, or one dead, or a grave" (Num. 19:18). Conclusively, the symbolic purpose of hyssop is expressed by the Psalmist: "Purge me with hyssop, and I shall be clean: wash me, and I shall be whiter than snow" (Ps. 51:7).

Incense. Incense, which performed an integral role in the sacrificial process of the Mosaic system (Ex. 30:7-8, 34-36), signifies the prayers of the righteous. Twice daily the smoke of the burning incense ascended heavenward, filtering through the atmosphere of the temple precinct. In a like manner the prayers uttered by the faithful also rose upward through the heavens to the ears of Deity. It was more than a coincidence that the moment of prayer coincided with the time of the burning of incense upon the altar. "And the whole multitude of the people were praying without at the time of incense" (Luke 1:10), explained Luke. The Psalmist added this truth: "Let my prayer be set forth before thee as incense" (Ps. 141:2).

The Apostle John fully understood the signification of incense. In his Revelation he wrote of a certain angel found in the temple of heaven who was given "much incense, that he should offer it with the prayers of all saints upon the golden altar which was before the throne. And the smoke of the incense, which came with the prayers of the saints, ascended up before God." (Rev. 8:3-4.) John also wrote, "Four and twenty elders fell down before the Lamb, having . . . golden vials full of odours [incense], which are the prayers of saints" (Rev. 5:8).

Iron. 1) Iron symbolizes great strength and permanence (Deut. 28:48; Judg. 1:19; Micah 4:13). So strong is this substance that it "subdueth all things" (Dan. 2:40-41). Iron is precious unto the Lord (Josh. 6:19; D&C 124:27), but on a scale of value, iron is more valuable than clay but worth less than gold or silver (Dan. 2:31-42).

2) The children of Israel were as iron which Jehovah tried, tempered, and hardened in the furnace (Ezek. 22:20; Deut. 4:20). It was Jehovah who brought them "forth out of Egypt, from the midst of the furnace of iron" (1 Kgs. 8:51; Jer. 11:4). (See also *Gold; Brass.*)

Isaac. The story of the binding of Isaac, recorded in Genesis 22, contains important symbology. In this account, Abraham symbolized the Father, and Isaac was a type for Christ who was to become a sacrifice. The Book of Mormon prophet Jacob explained that "Abraham . . . in offering up his son Isaac . . . is a similitude of God and his Only Begotten Son" (Jacob 4:5). Paul called Isaac the "only begotten son" of Abraham (Heb. 11:17), obviously creating a symbolic link between Isaac and Jesus, who also is the "Only Begotten Son" (John 1:18). (See also *Abraham; Prophet.*)

Isles. All lands, both islands and continents, to which the Lord has led families and peoples, are called the "isles of the sea" (1 Ne. 22:4; 21:1). Jacob, writing from the American continent, said concerning the Nephites, "We are upon an isle of the sea" (2 Ne. 10:20-22). (See also *Field.*)

Jackal. The jackal (translated "dragon" in the King James Version) is known to inhabit desolate areas (Isa. 13:22; 34:13), and is distinguished by a long, mournful, piercing howl. It may be due to these facts that these doglike beasts symbolize all creatures that mourn and grieve (Job 30:28–29; Micah 1:8; Jer. 9:10–11).

Jeremiah. The prophetic ministry of Jeremiah (Hebrew for "he shall exalt Jehovah") prefigured the divine ministry of Jesus. Most notable, the foreordination of Jeremiah (Jer. 1:4–5), the numerous persecutions which he was called upon to endure (Jer. 11:18–20; 12:6; 20:1–2; 26; 37; 38:13–28), and the prophetic powers which he possessed were types and shadows of the greater Prophet who would minister unto the people of the land. (See also *Prophet.*)

Jerusalem. Jerusalem is the holy city. It was made sacred in bygone days by the presence of God's sanctuary, sanctified by righteous prophets and Apostles who walked her streets, and hallowed by the life, ministry, and infinite atonement of Jesus Christ. The city's many names and titles describe her sacred calling and divine mission. This "princess among the provinces" (Lam. 1:1) was called "the throne of the Lord" (Jer. 3:17), "the holy city" (Isa. 52:1), "the Lord our righteousness" (Jer. 33:16), the "city of truth" (Zech. 8:3), "the city of God" (Ps. 46:4), "the city of the great King" (Ps. 48:2), the "joy of the whole earth" (Ps. 48:2), "the city of righteousness" (Isa. 1:26), "the faithful city" (Isa. 1:26), "the city of the Lord" (Isa. 60:14), "the perfection of beauty" (Lam. 2:15), and "the Lord is there" (Ezek. 48:35). It was in Jerusalem where the name of God was found (2 Chr. 6:6).

Jewels. The expression "in that day when I make up my jewels" is used four times in holy writ (Mal. 3:17; 3 Ne. 24:17; D&C 60:4; 101:3). Here jewels represent the Saints of God. As jewels are of great value to their owner, faithful disciples are precious unto the Lord.

Job. Job epitomizes the man of grief who is tried in all things. He is the quintessential example of all "the prophets, who have spoken in the name of the Lord," and have become "an example of suffering affliction, and of patience" (James 5:10–11). The trials and tribulations of the Prophet Joseph Smith were compared to those of Job (D&C 121:10). (See also *Prophet.*)

Jonah. The "sign of the prophet Jonas [Jonah]" (Matt. 12:39) refers to the three days and three nights that Jonah remained in the belly of the fish. This momentous act prefigured the death, burial, and resurrection of the Lord. Thus Jesus explained concerning the sign of the prophet Jonah: "For as

[Jonah] was three days and three nights" in the belly of the great fish, "so shall the Son of man be three days and three nights in the heart of the earth" (Matt. 12:39–40). (See also *Prophet*.)

Jordan River. "Crossing over the Jordan is a metaphor for entering heaven, because the children of Israel were miraculously enabled to go over it dryshod on their way to the Promised Land (Josh. 3)" (*Gospel Symbolism*, p. 263).

Joseph of Egypt. Joseph of Egypt was a type for Christ, Joseph Smith, and the Latter-day tribe of Joseph (i.e., Ephraim and Manasseh).

Joseph served as a type for Christ in the following ways: 1) Both were granted a new name: Joseph was denominated Zaphnath-paaneah by Pharaoh (Gen. 41:45); Jesus' divine name was Christ. 2) Both were good shepherds. 3) Both were known as the most loved of their father. 4) Both were clothed in authority and power of their father. Joseph, for instance, was given the "coat of many colours" (Gen. 37:3), a symbol of priesthood authority. 5) Both were revelators, and revealed things pertaining to the future (JST, Gen. 50:24–38; Matt. 24). 6) Both were fully obedient to the will and wishes of their fathers and responded to their calls to serve, saying, "Here am I" (Gen. 37:13; Abr. 3:27). 7) Both were promised a future sovereignty, speaking equally of a temporal and an eternal rule. 8) Both were betrayed by their brothers, at which time they were stripped of their garments. 9) Both were cast into a pit—Christ to the world of spirits, Joseph into an empty cistern. 10) Both were betrayed with the utmost hypocrisy (Gen. 37:27; John 18:31). 11) Both were sold. It was Judah that sold Joseph for twenty pieces of silver (Gen. 37:26–28), as it was Judas (Greek for Judah) who sold Jesus for thirty pieces of silver (Matt. 26:15). 12) The blood-sprinkled coat of each was presented to his father. Joseph's coat of many colors was dipped in the blood of the goat (Gen. 37:31–32); the blood of Jesus Christ as the blood of the scape-goat, a sin offering, was symbolically presented to the Father. 13) Both blessed those with whom they labored in prison (Gen. 39:21–23; D&C 138). 14) Both were servants, and as such all that they touched were blessed. 15) Both were tempted with great sin and both refused its enticements (Gen. 39; Matt. 4:1–11). 16) Both were falsely accused: Joseph by Potiphar's wife, Christ by false witnesses. 17) Both stood as the source of divine knowledge to their day and generation. 18) Both were triumphant, overcoming all. 19) Both were granted rule over all

(Gen. 41:40; 1 Pet. 3:22). 20) Both were thirty years old when they began their life's work (Gen. 41:46; Luke 3:23). 21) Both were saviors to their people, giving them the bread of life. Joseph saved his family with a temporal salvation; Christ as the Bread of Life saves the family of mankind with a spiritual salvation. 22) The rejection of both brought bondage upon the people. 23) Both were unrecognized by their people (Gen. 45:3-5; D&C 45:51-53). 24) Both would be recognized and accepted by their brothers only at the "second time" (Acts 7:13; D&C 45:51-53). 25) As Joseph's brothers bowed to him in fulfillment of prophecy, so all will yet bow the knee to Christ (Gen. 43:26-28; D&C 76:110). 26) Through both, mercy is granted to a repentant people. As Joseph's brothers sought forgiveness of him, so Christ's brothers will eventually seek forgiveness of him. 27) After the reconciliation, Israel is gathered. Having manifest himself to his brothers, Joseph charged them to return and bring their father and families to Egypt. So it shall be in the last days. After Israel have returned to their God, they, like Joseph's brothers, shall be sent to bring all the family of Israel into the kingdom ruled by Christ. (Adapted from *Gospel Symbolism*, pp. 30-36.)

Joseph of Egypt also served as a type for Joseph Smith in several ways, including the following: 1) Both were familiar with the spirit of revelation. 2) Both shared the same name. 3) Both were hated by their "Christian" brothers—Joseph by his actual brothers, and Joseph Smith by the ministers of religion and others of his day. 4) It is of interest that the promise of future destiny was given to Joseph of Egypt when he was seventeen years of age (Gen. 37:2). Similarly, it was when Joseph Smith was seventeen that Moroni appeared to him and unfolded the great destiny that was his (JS-H 1:33-41). 5) Both were betrayed by those who held positions of trust. 6) Both were cast into prison, being guilty of nothing. 7) Both were given the authority over the "prisoners that were in prison" (Gen. 39:22). The latter-day Joseph stands at the head of this dispensation of the gospel on earth, and so stands at its head in the spirit prison. 8) As Joseph of Egypt interpreted the dreams of those in prison anciently, so Joseph Smith by the power of that same Spirit has been able to interpret revelations given to others (the Bible, the papyrus of Abraham, and so on) in our day. 9) As Joseph of Egypt was lifted up and sustained by a foreign power, thus enabling him to restore his family, so Joseph of the last days has been lifted up by a great Gentile nation and granted the power to again restore Israel. (Adapted from *Gospel Symbolism*, pp. 38–42.)

Joseph served as a type for the latter-day tribe of Joseph (Ephraim and Manasseh) as follows: 1) Both the ancient prophet and the modern tribe of Joseph have been clothed in the same coat or robes of authority. These are the "robes of righteousness" (D&C 109:76). 2) As Joseph was sold into Egypt, so Joseph (the Church in the last days) was forced into the bondage of a desert. As this happened to Joseph when he was seventeen, so it happened to the Church in 1847, or in its seventeenth year. 3) Joseph's brothers, the ten tribes, will yet come to him (the Church) seeking the bread of everlasting life (D&C 133:26–32). 4) As the whole nation of Egypt was blessed anciently because of Joseph, so the United States and all nations of the earth will be blessed because of the labors of the latter-day Joseph. (Adapted from *Gospel Symbolism*, pp. 38–42.) (See also *Prophet*.)

Joseph Smith. As a seer, Apostle, prophet, lawgiver, restorer, elder, teacher, and revelator, Joseph Smith is a type of Jesus Christ. He "has done more, save Jesus only, for the salvation of men in this world, than any other man that ever lived" (D&C 135:3; see also 2 Ne. 3:15). (See also *Prophet*.)

Joshua. 1) Joshua was a type for Jesus. The name Joshua means "he shall save" or "salvation of Jehovah." The Greek form of Joshua is Jesus (see Acts 7:45, note *a*; Heb. 4:8, note *a*, indicating that the name Jesus should be written "Joshua"). Through his name, and by leading Israel through the waters of the Jordan into the promised land (Joshua 3), Joshua prefigured the baptism of Jesus in the Jordan River. Christ, through baptism, leads his followers into the better promised land, which is heaven. (See also *Jordan River; Promised Land*.)

2) A second Joshua also was a type for Christ. Joshua, the son of Josedech, as a high priest, prefigured the priesthood ministry of the Lord. Further, Joshua was given a crown, a motif which demonstrated his kingship and priesthood powers (Zech. 6:11–13). Jesus was portrayed by John as wearing crowns at the Second Coming (Rev. 19:12). (See also *Prophet; High Priest*.)

Jubilee Year. Certain aspects of the Jubilee Year remind us of the atonement of Jesus Christ. Fittingly, it was proclaimed on the "tenth day of the seventh month" (Lev. 25:9), or on the Day of Atonement.

1) During the Jubilee Year, every fiftieth year, the Israelites

were required to allow the land to rest. They were not to sow nor reap for the entire year. Thus the children of Israel were required to demonstrate faith that Jehovah would provide for the period of the Jubilee.

2) As slaves and servants were freed during the Jubilee Year, and debts were forgiven, so Jesus frees us from sin and forgives our debts.

3) During the Jubilee Year, liberty is proclaimed "throughout all the land unto all the inhabitants thereof" (Lev. 25:10). The Atonement brings liberty unto all the inhabitants of the spirit prison, and allows for the resurrection of all men. (See *Day of Atonement; Sabbatical Year.*)

Judah. Zephaniah prophesied concerning the destruction of the people of Judah and the "inhabitants of Jerusalem," which prophecy was fulfilled during the days of Lehi and Jeremiah (Zeph. 1). This ruin and downfall of Judah was in similitude of those who will suffer similar desolations at the time of the Second Coming.

Judges. The book of Judges tells of thirteen protagonists of Israel, who were "deliverers," "judges," and "saviours" unto the tribes of Israel. When these judges acted with righteous intent under the direction of the Holy Spirit, they were archetypes for Jesus. Nehemiah called the judges "saviours." "According to thy manifold mercies thou gavest them saviours, who saved them out of the hand of their enemies" (Neh. 9:27). Christ, as the Savior, saves mankind from the enemies of death and hell. (See also part 2: *Judge.*)

Key of David. "In ancient Israel, David was a man of blood and battle whose word was law and whose very name was also a symbol of power and authority. Accordingly, when Isaiah sought to convey a realization of the supreme, directive control and power resident in our Lord, the Son of David, he spoke these words in the Lord's name: 'And *the key of the house of David* will I lay upon his shoulder; so he shall open, and none shall shut; and he shall shut, and none shall open.' (Isa. 22:22.) . . . Thus, the *key of David* is the absolute power resident in Christ whereby his will is expressed in all things both temporal and spiritual." (*Mormon Doctrine*, p. 409.) (See also *Door.*)

Keys. Many passages of scripture equate power and authority with keys. For instance, D&C 107:18 informs us that "the power and authority of the higher, or Melchizedek Priesthood, is to hold the keys of all the spiritual blessings of the church" (see also D&C 68:17; 107:15; 132:45). Therefore, in the gospel sense, keys represent the power and authority to open the doors which lead mankind to eternal life.

King. 1) All righteous kings, such as Melchizedek (Alma 13:17), Moses (Deut. 33:4-5), Benjamin (Mosiah 1:1), and other worthy "kings and priests unto God" (Rev. 1:6; 5:10), are but shadows of the "King of kings" (see Rev. 19:16), who is Jesus Christ. He is "the King of all the earth" (Ps. 47:6, 7; 44:4) and rules and reigns in the kingdom of God.

2) For the time being, Satan rules with power and darkness over his host. Called Abaddon and Apollyon, the devil is the "king . . . of the bottomless pit" (Rev. 9:11). (See also part 2: *King of Kings.*)

Kiss. The kiss is generally a token of affection and tenderness which one shares with a loved one (Gen. 33:4; Ruth 1:9; Moses 7:63). However, when Judas betrayed the Son of God, he did so as "a sign, saying, Whomsoever I shall kiss, that same is he: hold him fast" (Matt. 26:48). This act represented an extreme insult, for he betrayed God with the symbol which generally demonstrates love and trust. At times, the kiss is even employed by worshippers who are in the presence of the Lord (Luke 7:37-38; 3 Ne. 11:19; 17:10). Little wonder that Jesus inquired of the fallen Apostle, "Judas, betrayest thou the Son of man with a kiss?" (Luke 22:48.)

Knee, Kneeling. 1) Kneeling, as a posture of prayer, was known and practiced during the biblical days (2 Chr. 6:13; Luke 22:41; Acts 7:60; Eph. 3:14). For example, three times a day the prophet Daniel "kneeled upon his knees . . . and prayed, and gave thanks before his God" (Dan. 6:10). The Psalmist also made a connection between kneeling and divine worship when he wrote, "O come, let us worship and bow down: let us kneel before the Lord our maker" (Ps. 95:6). "Kneeling the knees," therefore, signifies an attitude of reverence and worship belonging to the communicant.

2) Often the knees of a person are a symbol of the whole person. For instance, the common expression "Strengthen the feeble knees" (D&C 81:5; Job 4:4; Isa. 35:3) is an idiom meaning "Strengthen those who are feeble."

Ladder. The ladder seen in vision by Jacob represents progression from the telestial kingdom (or this earthly existence) upward into the celestial kingdom. Standing at the head of the ladder is God, who waits for those who have successfully endured the rigors of their journey (Gen. 28:12–19; *Teachings*, pp. 304–5).

Lake. To identify the woeful anguish and racking torment which must be suffered by the wicked, the prophets define hell as being like a "lake of fire and brimstone, whose flame ascendeth up forever and ever" (2 Ne. 9:16; Rev. 20:10; Jacob 3:11). Although such a lake is figurative, the phraseology employed sets forth the terribleness of hell.

Lamb. 1) Jesus Christ is the "Lamb of God, which taketh away the sin of the world" (John 1:29). (See also part 2: *Lamb.*)

2) Proclaiming his innocence shortly before his martyrdom, the Prophet Joseph Smith said, "I am going like a lamb to the slaughter. . . . I SHALL DIE INNOCENT, AND IT SHALL YET BE SAID OF ME—HE WAS MURDERED IN COLD BLOOD." (D&C 135:4.) (See also *Sheep.*)

Lamp. Lamps produce light and dispel darkness. They are therefore identified with righteous people, divine revelation, and the Church of God. (It should be noted that wherever the King James Version has *candlestick*, it should be written *lamp* or *lampstand.*)

1) Those who allow the Holy Ghost to guide them are like a living, glowing lamp. In connection with this, the scriptures explain that "the spirit of man is the candle of the Lord" (Prov. 20:27) and that "the light of the righteous rejoiceth: but the lamp of the wicked shall be put out" (Prov. 13:9; Job 18:5–6).

John the Revelator understood well this imagery and employed it often. He explained that the "seven lamps of fire burning before the throne" of God in heaven are "the seven servants of God" (JST, Rev. 4:5). Also, the two prophets spoken of in Revelation 11 are "the two candlesticks standing before the God of the earth" (Rev. 11:4; Zech. 4:2–14). Further, John the Baptist was depicted as being "a burning and a shining light" (John 5:35).

2) The word of God directs mankind toward their heavenly home, thus becoming "a lamp unto [the] feet, and a light unto [the] path" (Ps. 119:105; Prov. 6:23).

3) The "seven golden candlesticks" which John saw in vision represent "the seven churches" of Asia. They are called Ephesus, Smyrna, Pergamos, Thyatira, Sardis, Philadelphia, and Laodicea (Rev. 1:11, 12, 20). (See also *Light.*)

Law of Moses. Paul wrote that the law of Moses "was our schoolmaster to bring us unto Christ" (Gal. 3:24). Similarly,

Jacob explained, "For this intent we keep the law of Moses, it pointing our souls to [Jesus Christ]" (Jacob 4:5). That is to say, all ablutions, performances, rituals, covenants, sacrifices, observances, functions, solemnities, ministrations, devotionals, rites, vows, propitiations, offerings, ordinances, and commandments which were connected with the law of Moses—"all these things were types of things to come" (Mosiah 13:31). Nephi summed up the whole purpose of the law of Moses by saying, "Behold, my soul delighteth in proving unto my people the truth of the coming of Christ; for, for this end hath the law of Moses been given; and all things which have been given of God from the beginning of the world, unto man, are the typifying of him" (2 Ne. 11:4). (See also part 2: *Lawgiver*.)

Leaven. 1) "As an agent which causes fermentation, [leaven] symbolically represents any corrupting influence" (*Gospel Symbolism*, p. 265). Thus the false doctrines taught by the Pharisees and the Sadducees (Matt. 16:11–12), as well as their "hypocrisy" (Luke 12:1), is called the "leaven of the Pharisees and of the Sadducees."

2) Leaven is also an agent which causes a thing to spread slowly and to expand. Matthew recorded a parable in which Jesus likened the "kingdom of heaven" unto "leaven, which a woman took, and hid in three measures of meal, till the whole was leavened" (Matt. 13:33). Joseph Smith gave an inspired application of this parable, explaining "that the Church of the Latter-day Saints has taken its rise from a little leaven that was put into three witnesses" of the Book of Mormon (*Teachings*, p. 100).

3) Unleavened bread, or "the bread of affliction" (Deut. 16:3), was eaten during Passover week to remind the ancient Israelites of the day when they went "forth out of the land of Egypt in haste" (Deut. 16:3) at the time that "they were thrust out of Egypt, and could not tarry" (Ex. 12:39). So strict was this law concerning unleavened bread that during this memorial festival, no leaven was to be found in their homes, nor could anyone be seen with leaven. Whosoever transgressed this law would be cut off from Israel (Ex. 12:19; 13:7). (See also *Bread*.)

Left. The primary sense of the Old English *lyft* (now spelled "left") is "weak" or "worthless." So it was during the biblical days, in which the word *left* represented those who were emotionally infirm (Eccl. 10:2), or those who were spiritually debilitated. Several passages describe the condition of those accursed souls who are found to be on the "left hand of God." These will burn in the fires of hell with great "weeping, wailing and gnashing of teeth" (D&C 19:5), forever in the presence of the devil and his host (Matt. 25:33–41; Mosiah 5:10, 12; D&C 29:27). In contrast to the wicked, the righteous will "be gathered on [God's] right hand unto eternal life" (D&C 29:27). (See also *Arm; Hand; Right.*)

Leprosy. A leper was excluded from holding the priesthood (Lev. 22:2–4), declared ceremonially unclean (Lev. 13:8, 11, 22, 44), and commanded to "dwell alone" outside the camp of Israel (Lev. 13:46; Num. 5:2). Additionally, the leper was directed to rend his clothes, bare his head, cover his upper lip, and cry aloud, "Unclean, unclean" (Lev. 13:45). A leper, therefore, represents the spiritually unclean, who, through their sins, are excluded from the priesthood and are not allowed to enter into the camp of God. (See also *Disease.*)

Liahona. The "Liahona, which is, being interpreted, a compass" (Alma 37:38), is likened to the words of Christ. The words of the Lord are as a compass to the followers of Christ, and "will point to [them] a straight course to eternal bliss" (Alma 37:44). As the Liahona worked by faith and pointed the Nephites to the promised land, so will the "words of Christ" lead the disciples of God to "a far better land of promise" (Alma 37:45), referring to heaven.

Light. All things associated with light are of the Lord, his Church, his revelations, and his disciples. "That which is of God is light" (D&C 50:24).

1) Jesus Christ is "Alpha and Omega, the beginning and the end, the light and the life of the world—a light that shineth in darkness and the darkness comprehendeth it not" (D&C 45:7). (See also part 2: *Light.*)

2) Light is a symbol of the gospel, which produces things pertaining to Deity, and truths which lead men toward eternal life (D&C 45:9, 28–29).

3) Truth, understanding, wisdom, knowledge, and revelation are associated with light (D&C 84:45; 93:28–29; Alma 19:6; 39:6).

4) Disciples of Jesus Christ are lights unto the world (D&C 103:9; 88:67). Jesus has admonished his followers: "Hold up your light that it may shine unto the world. Behold I am the light which ye shall hold up—that which ye have seen me do." (3 Ne. 18:24.)

Lightning. 1) The awe-inspiring shafts of lightning which pierce the heavens represent the arrows of Deity. Such effulgent arrows proceed forth from God's throne, which rests in the temple of heaven (Rev. 4:5; 11:19), and they bring discomfort to the wicked (2 Sam. 22:15; Ps. 18:14; Zech. 9:14). This "shaft of death" brings destruction upon the unrepentant (2 Ne. 26:6; D&C 85:8; Ps. 144:6), causing them to "feel the wrath, and indignation, and chastening hand of an Almighty God" (D&C 87:6). It is the shafts of lightning which "utter forth their voices . . . , saying these words—Repent ye, for the great day of the Lord is come" (D&C 43:22; 43:25; 88:90).

2) Due to the extreme brilliance and whiteness of this celestial light, heavenly personages are often described as having a countenance like lightning (Dan. 10:6; Matt. 28:3; D&C 20:6; JS–H 1:32).

Linen. During the biblical period, linen was associated with the holy tabernacle and its appurtenances, the sacred vestments of the priesthood, heavenly beings, and God. For instance, the curtains (Ex. 26:1), veil (Ex. 26:31), and outer door hangings (Ex. 28:42) of the tabernacle were all composed of linen. Similarly, the ephod, coats, mitre, bonnets, and breeches belonging to the temple officiants were made of fine linen (Ex. 39:2, 27-28). These items were called the "holy garments" (Lev. 16:4, 32).

Also, the "seven angels" that came forth from the heavenly temple, the armies of heaven, and the Saints of God all are "arrayed in fine linen, clean and white" (Rev. 19:7-8; 15:6; 19:14). Interestingly, the crucified body of Jesus was wrapped and buried in linen cloth (Matt. 27:59-60). What does linen represent? John explained that linen symbolizes "the righteousness of saints" (Rev. 19:8). (See also *Garment; Robe.*)

Lion. Individuals or groups of persons having lionlike qualities are often metaphorically represented as being lions. They are described as being courageous, mighty, or having "the faces of lions" (1 Chr. 12:8). They demonstrate ferocity, dignity, or majesty.

1) The majestic lion is thought to be the "king of beasts" or the "king of the jungle." Thus many prophets referred to kings and rulers as being like a lion. "Pharaoh king of Egypt" was "like a young lion of the nations" (Ezek. 32:2); and "a wicked ruler" is "as a roaring lion" (Prov. 28:15; see also 19:12; 20:2).

2) On many occasions God is referred to as a lion (Isa. 31:4; Hosea 5:14; 11:10; 13:7-8; Num. 24:8-9). As the "Lion of the tribe of Juda" (Rev. 5:5), the Lord represents the Prince, Ruler, and King of the Jews. (See also part 2: *Lion.*)

3) Satan, as the ruler of this earth, is "as a roaring lion, [who] walketh about, seeking whom he may devour" (1 Pet. 5:8).

4) The tribes of Judah (Gen. 49:9), Gad (Deut. 33:20), Dan (Deut. 33:22), the entire house of Israel (Micah 5:8; 3 Ne. 20:16), and other individuals or groups (Num. 23:24; 2 Sam. 1:23; 23:20; Alma 14:29; Morm. 5:24) are as the lion.

Lips. The word *lips* often represents the attitude of the whole person. Thus one who has "lying lips" (Prov. 12:22; 10:18; Ps. 120:2) is a dishonest person; one who has "righteous lips" (Prov. 16:13) is an upright and just soul. The expression "A fool's lips enter into contention" (Prov. 18:6) relays the meaning that the entire individual is involved, not just his lips.

Locust. Four principal stages in the life of the locust are named in the scriptures. Metaphorically, all stages of the locust speak of invading armies and their accompanying consumption and devastation of the land and its people.

1) Cankerworm (in Hebrew, *yeleg,* meaning "licker"). An early stage in the development of the locust, most likely at the nymph form. The word *canker* speaks of a spreading sore or ulcer which slowly consumes and corrupts (Joel 2:25; 1:4; Nahum 3:15–16). (See also *Cankerworm.*)

2) Palmerworm (in Hebrew, *gazam,* meaning "gnawer"). As the Hebrew demonstrates, the palmerworm gnaws away at a substance until nothing is left (Joel 1:4; 2:25; Amos 4:9).

3) Caterpillar (in Hebrew, *chasil,* meaning "consumer"). Listed as one of the plagues of Egypt (Ps. 78:46), the caterpillar consumes and eats away the foliage by degrees (2 Chr. 6:28; Ps. 105:34; Joel 1:4; 2:25; see also Jer. 51:14, 27). (See also *Caterpillar.*)

4) Locust (in Hebrew, *arbeth,* meaning "many"). At times, so plentiful are the locusts that the sky becomes darkened. Moses described the manner in which the locusts ravaged and devoured the land of Egypt. "For they covered the face of the whole earth, so that the land was darkened; and they did eat every herb of the land, and all the fruit of the trees which the hail had left: and there remained not any green thing in the trees, or in the herbs of the field, through all the land of Egypt" (Ex. 10:15). The full-grown locust, then, like the cankerworm, the palmerworm, and the caterpillar, refers to the warring hosts and multitudes that swarm upon and devour their enemies (Joel 1:4; Rev. 9:3, 7). (See also *Grasshopper.*)

Loins. The loins are the hips and lower abdomen, or the region of the body where the procreative powers are found. The expression "fruit of the loins" speaks of one's posterity or descendants (2 Ne. 3:19, 21; Jacob 2:25). The phrase "gird up your loins" (D&C 61:38) signifies a person's preparation to do something difficult. (See also *Girdle.*)

Lot's Wife. Those who desire to "flee unto Zion" by forsaking the world and its carnal ways are instructed: "Let him not look back lest sudden destruction shall come upon him" (D&C 133:12, 14–15; Luke 9:62). Those who look back will be destroyed, as was the case with the wife of Lot (Gen. 19:17, 26).

Mammon. An Aramaic word for riches, *mammon* refers to any type of worldly wealth. "Ye cannot serve God and mammon," warns the Lord unto those who desire to become his disciples (D&C 82:22; Luke 16:13).

Man. In the scriptures, the word *man* is often used in place of all of humanity (1 Ne. 10:20; Mosiah 4:18, 30). (See also *Adam.*)

Manna. Manna has been described as being "like coriander seed, white; and the taste of it was like wafers made with honey" (Ex. 16:31). It was called "bread" (Ex. 16:15), "the corn of heaven," and "angels' food" (Ps. 78:24). As a memorial to the miraculous manner in which manna came down from heaven, a jar of manna was kept within the ark of the covenant (Heb. 9:4).

Manna, which saved the children of Israel temporally, represents Jesus Christ, the "living bread," who saves his people everlastingly. Jesus said, "I am [the] bread of life. Your fathers did eat manna in the wilderness, and are dead. This is the bread which cometh down from heaven, that a man may eat thereof, and not die. I am the living bread which came down from heaven: if any man eat of this bread, he shall live for ever." (John 6:48–51.) Concerning those who overcome the world, they will be given "to eat of the hidden manna" (Rev. 2:17). (See also *Bread; Leaven.*)

Mantle. The mantle of Elijah was called an *adderet,* a Hebrew word which signifies "glory" or "magnificence." This garment of glory symbolized authority and spiritual power (1 Kgs. 19:19; 2 Kgs. 2:8–14). A parallel is found in the modern revelations in which Latter-day Saints are instructed to "clothe [themselves] with the bond of charity, as with a mantle, which is the bond of perfectness and peace" (D&C 88:125). (See also *Garment.*)

Marriage. Speaking metaphorically, Jehovah told ancient Israel, "For I am married unto you" (Jer. 3:14). The Lord is the bridegroom and husband, Israel the bride and wife.

In this dispensation, the faithful of the Church are the Lamb's bride. Concerning the great wedding feast which will take place, John prophesied: "The marriage of the Lamb is come, and his wife hath made herself ready. And to her was granted that she should be arrayed in fine linen, clean and white. . . . Blessed are they which are called unto the marriage supper of the Lamb." (Rev. 19:7-9; D&C 58:6-11; Matt. 25:1-13.) (See also *Husband; Bridegroom; Bride.*)

Marrow. Figuratively, a soul who has "marrow and fatness" (Ps. 63:5; Isa. 25:6) or "marrow to [his] bones" (D&C 89:18; Prov. 3:8) is one who has received an abundance of temporal blessings from God. (See also *Bone.*)

Meat. 1) A generic scriptural term for edible seeds, herbs, and other comestibles is *meat* (Gen. 1:29-30; Ezek. 16:19).

2) Meat, meaning the mysteries of the gospel, is for those who have a mature knowledge of the doctrines of the gospel and are able to digest "the greater portion of the word" of God (Alma 12:10). "Babes," however, must be nurtured with milk (Heb. 5:14; 1 Cor. 3:1-3; D&C 19:22). (See also *Milk.*)

Melchizedek. Melchizedek, the "king . . . of Salem" (Alma 13:17), was a prototype of Jesus Christ. *Salem* is a Hebrew word signifying "peace." As "Prince of peace" (JST, Gen. 14:33) and "King of peace" (JST, Gen. 14:36), Melchizedek typified the "King of kings" (Rev. 19:16), or the Lord. Fittingly, the name Melchizedek means "my king is righteous," meaning "my king (Jesus) is righteous."

The priesthood ministry of Melchizedek also prefigured that of Jesus. Paul explained that "after the similitude of Melchisedec there ariseth another priest," who is Christ (Heb. 7:15). As the "priest of the most high God," Melchizedek "brought forth bread and wine: and he brake bread and blest it; and he blest the wine" (JST, Gen. 14:17), a clear reference to the sacramental emblems. Out of respect for the sacred name of Deity, and to honor the great high priest Melchizedek, the priesthood was called the Melchizedek Priesthood, rather than "*the Holy Priesthood, after the Order of the Son of God*" (D&C 107:2-4; italics in original). (See also *Prophet.*)

Mercy Seat. The mercy seat, or the throne of Jehovah, was located in the Holy of Holies of the temple (Ex. 26:34). Made of pure gold, the throne acted as the covering or lid of the ark of the covenant and was situated between two gold cherubim (Ex. 25:17-19; 1 Sam. 4:4; Ps. 99:1; Heb. 4:16).

It is incorrectly termed the "mercy seat"; the expression originates from the Hebrew word *kapporeth,* which means "propitiatory," "covering," or "seat of atonement." The *kapporeth* was the place where atonement and expiation was made. Once a year on the Day of Atonement the blood of the sacrificial bullock and goat was sprinkled seven times by the high priest upon the throne. This ritualistic act was performed to "make an atonement . . . because of the uncleanness of the children of Israel, and because of their transgressions in all their sins" (Lev. 16:14–16). Further, it was upon the throne that Jehovah sat when he communed with his prophets (Ex. 25:22; 30:6; Isa. 6:1). Thus the throne represented Jesus Christ, his divine presence, and his atoning sacrifice. (See also *Ark of the Covenant.*)

Michael. Michael, who is Adam, is a type of the Lord. Jesus is God; Michael, as his Hebrew name signifies, is one "who is like God." Jesus is first in authority; Michael stands second in authority (*Teachings*, p. 157). Jesus is the Firstborn of all spirits; Michael, the firstborn of all flesh. Jesus is the Father of those who believe in his gospel; Michael is the father of all flesh. Christ is the "Resurrection" (John 11:25); Michael, by blowing his trump, announces the resurrection (D&C 29:26). (See also *Adam; Prophet.*)

Milk. 1) Milk signifies abundance, plenty, and blessing (Deut. 32:14; Job 21:24; 2 Ne. 26:25). The expression "a land flowing with milk and honey" denotes a land containing a great harvest of produce and goods (Ex. 3:8; D&C 38:18).

2) "Whom shall he teach knowledge? and whom shall he make to understand doctrine?" asked Isaiah. He answered, "Them that are weaned from the milk, and drawn from the breasts" (Isa. 28:9). Milk is for the babes of the gospel, those who are "unskilful in the word of righteousness," while the greater knowledge, the "strong meat," is reserved for those who are "of full age" (Heb. 5:13–14; 1 Cor. 3:2; 1 Pet. 2:2; D&C 19:22). (See also *Meat.*)

Mire. Men who are sunk in the mire, either figuratively or literally, are those who experience extreme humility and lowliness (Job 30:19; Ps. 69:2, 14; Jer. 38:22).

Monster. Satan, death, and hell, each of which produce fear and horror in the hearts of men, are described as being an "awful monster." It is only in and through the atoning sacrifice of Jesus Christ that these most awful monsters are overcome. (2 Ne. 9:10, 19, 26.)

Moon. 1) In a dream, Joseph saw his father Jacob represented by the sun, his mother by the moon, and his brothers by eleven stars (Gen. 37:9–10).

2) The light of the moon is compared to the glory which will exist in the terrestrial kingdom (1 Cor. 15:41; D&C 76:78, 81). This is in contrast with the light of the sun (the celestial kingdom) and the light of the stars (the telestial kingdom). (See also *Sun; Stars.*)

Moriah. As early as the patriarchs Abraham and Isaac, Mount Moriah symbolized a sanctuary of the Lord (Gen. 22:2). However, unlike many mountain sanctuaries, an actual temple building once stood upon Mount Moriah (2 Chr. 3:1). (See also *Mountain.*)

Moses. Moses was a quintessential archetype for the Son of God. As God explained to him, "Thou art in the similitude of mine Only Begotten" (Moses 1:6). Like the Lord, he was a mediator (Ex. 20:19-22; 1 Tim. 2:5), deliverer (Ex. 3:1-12), king (Deut. 33:5; Matt. 21:5), teacher (Deut. 4:5; Matt. 5:2), prophet (Deut. 18:15-19; 1 Ne. 22:21), and lawgiver (John 1:17; Isa. 33:22). Both Jesus and Moses were called "faithful" (Heb. 3:1-6), were "mighty in words and deeds" (Acts 7:22; John 1:1), performed signs and miracles (Ex. 4:28-31; John 20:30), fasted forty days (Ex. 34:28; Matt. 4:2), controlled the sea (Ex. 14:21; Matt. 8:26), and were sent from God (Ex. 3:1-12; John 6:57). Both called "seventy" (Num. 11:16-17; Luke 10:1), and both came forth out of Egypt (JST, Gen. 50:29; Matt. 2:15). Finally, miraculous circumstances attended the birth of both Moses and Jesus (Ex. 2:1-6; Luke 1:27-38). (See also *Prophet.*)

Mountain. Mountains are sanctuaries designed and fashioned by Jehovah (Ex. 15:17). They are the temples of nature, where the prophets receive theophanic experiences, where God descends from heaven to reveal his will unto his people. Mount Sinai, Mount Moriah, the Mount of Transfiguration; the mountains associated with Nephi, the brother of Jared, Ezekiel, and others; and, in these days, Ensign Peak—all in their own time represented the Lord's temple. Each could rightly be called a "holy mountain" or the "mount of God" (Ex. 4:27; 18:5).

The Psalmist wrote, "Worship at his holy hill [the Hebrew word is *mountain*]" (Ps. 99:9), meaning "Worship at God's temple." "The Lord will dwell" in his holy hill (Hebrew, *mountain*) (Ps. 68:16), exclaims the writer of this Psalm. Two scriptural parallelisms connect *mountain* to the *temple.*

> Come ye, and let us go up to the mountain of the Lord,
> to the house of the God of Jacob (Isa. 2:3).

Even them will I bring to my holy mountain,
and make them joyful in my house of prayer (Isa. 56:7).

(See also *Mount of Transfiguration; Moriah; Sinai; Temple.*)

Mount of Transfiguration. This "high mountain" (Mark 9:2) was one of nature's temples. Sacred ordinances and events transpired here (Matt. 17:1–13; 2 Pet. 1:16–18), and it was in this location that Peter, James, and John "received their endowments" (*Doctrines of Salvation,* 2:165). (See also *Mountain; Moriah; Sinai; Temple.*)

Mouth. The word *mouth* is often used to indicate the whole person. The expression "that which had been spoken by the mouth of Jared" (Ether 1:39; see also 3 Ne. 1:13) simply means "that which had been spoken by Jared." Similarly, the "mouth of God" (Moro. 7:25; 10:28) and the "mouth of the Lord" (D&C 88:84–85) signifies Deity himself, his will, mind, word, and voice (see D&C 68:4).

Whenever men of God "speak as they are moved upon by the Holy Ghost" (D&C 68:3–4), it is as if the mouth of the Lord has spoken it (D&C 1:38; 21:5).

Murder. Figuratively, those who lead the children of men "away unto destruction" (Alma 36:14; Matt. 10:28), speaking of spiritual destruction, are guilty of murder.

Mustard Seed. In the parable of the mustard seed, Jesus stated, "The kingdom of heaven is like to a grain of mustard seed" (Matt. 13:31). Making an inspired application of this parable, Joseph Smith taught, "The Kingdom of Heaven is like unto a mustard seed. Behold, then is not this the Kingdom of Heaven that is raising its head in the last days in the majesty of its God, even the Church of the Latter-day Saints . . . ?" (*Teachings,* pp. 98–99.)

Nakedness. 1) Nakedness is used to denote shame. "Thy nakedness shall be uncovered, yea, thy shame shall be seen" (Isa. 47:3; Rev. 3:18; 2 Ne. 9:14).

2) The impoverished, the needy, the destitute, those who lack the very necessities of life, are said to be "naked" (James 2:15; Mosiah 18:28; Alma 4:12).

3) Nakedness is a synonymous term for bare, revealed, and exposed. In other words, persons and institutions that are naked are those which are open and displayed for all to see (Job 26:6; Ezek. 16:37; Heb. 4:13).

Navel. The navel, as the umbilical cord, from which everyone once received nourishment and life from his or her mother, represents the life force of the entire body (Job 40:16; Prov. 3:8; D&C 89:18).

Neck. The neck typifies the spirit and attitude of nations and men, usually denoting callousness and hardness (2 Ne. 6:10; Prov. 29:1). Men having necks of "iron sinew" (1 Ne. 20:4) or having "stiffness of necks" (2 Ne. 25:12; 1 Ne. 2:11) are those who are unable to glance sidewards at the concerns of their neighbor or to look upward toward their Creator.

Neighbor. 1) In a general sense, a neighbor is anyone of the human race, one's fellowman (D&C 45:68; 59:6; 88:81).

2) When a certain lawyer inquired of the Lord, "Who is my neighbor?" Jesus presented the parable of the good Samaritan (Luke 10:29-37). As the parable demonstrates, a neighbor is anyone who shows compassion and mercy to others.

Nest. Figuratively, a nest is the dwelling place of a person or people (Job 29:18; Prov. 27:8; Jer. 48:28). Concerning Jesus, however, it is written that "the foxes have holes, and the birds of the air have nests; but the Son of man hath not where to lay his head" (Matt. 8:20). (See *Dove; Eagle; Hen*.)

Net. 1) One who is trapped and ensnared by a net is one who is experiencing hardship and affliction. God tries his people by casting them into a net (Ps. 66:11; Job 19:6), but afterwards "plucks" them "out of the net" (Ps. 25:15; 31:4). At times, people unknowingly tumble into the net of the wicked, or, ironically, evil persons often become entangled in their own nets (Ps. 9:15; Eccl. 9:12; Prov. 29:5).

2) Matthew recorded the words of Jesus, "Again, the kingdom of heaven is like unto a net, that was cast into the sea, and gathered of every kind" (Matt. 13:47). Concerning this parable Joseph Smith explained, "Behold the seed of Joseph, spreading forth the Gospel net upon the face of the earth, gathering of every kind, that the good may be saved in vessels prepared for that purpose, and the angels will take care of the bad. So shall it be at the end of the world—the angels shall come forth and sever the wicked from among the just, and cast them into the furnace of fire, and there shall be wailing and gnashing of teeth." (*Teachings*, p. 102.) (See also *Fish; Fisherman*.)

Night. 1) As the darkness is called *night* (see Gen. 1:5), so also those whose minds are spiritually dark are of the night and wickedness (John 11:10; 1 Thes. 5:5; Alma 41:7; Micah 3:6). (See also *Darkness*.)

2) In contrast to the above, and despite the fact that darkness and nighttime symbolically are associated with evil, spiritual giants of all ages have envisioned the things of God and of eternity during the hours of the night. Israel (Gen. 46:2), Samuel (1 Sam. 3:3ff.), Daniel (Dan. 2:19), Paul (Acts 16:9), Nephi (2 Ne. 4:23), Joseph Smith (JS–H 1:29–30), and others have enjoyed the secrets of Deity while reposing upon their beds. (See also *Bed.*)

Nineveh. Nineveh, a mighty city of commerce and trade and the great capital of Assyria, was destroyed in 600 B.C. The destruction of Nineveh is in similitude of the destructions which will accompany the Lord's second coming (Nahum 2).

Noah. 1) Noah, whose name means "rest," was a type of Jesus Christ. He was "a just man, and perfect in his generation" (Moses 8:27), officiated in the Melchizedek Priesthood (D&C 107:52), offered sacrifices unto the Most High God (Gen. 8:20), and preached the gospel and declared repentance unto those of his generation (JST, Gen. 8:7–8). In similitude to the spiritual salvation which Jesus brings, Noah, through building the ark, saved his posterity "with a temporal salvation" (Moses 7:42). (See also *Prophet.*)

2) The deluge of Noah has been likened to national destructions and regional catastrophes. For instance, in the last days, "the coming of the Son of man" will be "as the days of Noe [Noah]" (Matt. 24:37), meaning that in the last days the wicked will be found "eating and drinking, marrying and giving in marriage" (Matt. 24:38), as were the unrighteous of Noah's day. Perhaps the principal difference between the two periods will be the method of destruction—God first destroyed the world with water, but at the time of the Second Coming he will destroy the world with fire. (See also *Flood.*)

Nose. See *Nostrils.*

Nostrils. 1) Through man's nostrils oxygen is inhaled, thus sustaining physical life. Symbolically, into the nostrils of man God breathes "the breath of life" so that man can become "a living soul" (Abr. 5:7; Moses 3:7; Job 27:3).

2) In the symbolic scriptural language, the anger of the Lord is vented through his nostrils (2 Sam. 22:9; Ps. 18:8). On many occasions the King James translators put the word *anger* in place of *nose* (Judg. 10:7; 1 Chr. 13:10; Jer. 49:37). Also, by the nostrils of Deity evil man is destroyed (Job 4:9). (See also *Breath of God.*)

Numberless. *Numberless* and *innumerable* are hyperbolic figures employed to express immense numbers (1 Ne. 1:8; Moses 1:28; Alma 58:8).

Oak. This term represents men who are "proud and lofty" or "high and lifted up" (Isa. 2:12–13; Amos 2:9; Zech. 11:2). But in the day of the Lord, these will be hewn down and cast into the fire. (See also *Tree.*)

Olive Leaf. Doctrine and Covenants section 88 was named the Olive Leaf by the Prophet Joseph Smith. Referring to this revelation, he explained it as "the 'olive leaf' which we have plucked from the Tree of Paradise, the Lord's message of peace to us" (*History of the Church* 1:316).

Olive Oil. This signifies the Holy Ghost. In the parable of the ten virgins, the five virgins who are prepared to meet the bridegroom are those whose lamps are full of oil, or whose lives are full of the Holy Ghost. These are they who are "wise and have received the truth, and have taken the Holy Spirit for their guide" (D&C 45:56–57; Matt. 25:1–14). John associates the anointing of oil with the Holy Ghost, or with receiving divine truth and being taught from on high (JST, 1 John 2:20–27). Other prophets mention the sanctifying and consecrating powers of olive oil (Lev. 8:10–12; Ex. 28:41) and the physical and spiritual healing which comes when one is anointed by the elders of the Church (James 5:14–15), all which point to the mission and calling of the Holy Ghost.

Luke identified olive oil as being representative of the Holy Ghost when he wrote, "God anointed Jesus of Nazareth with the Holy Ghost and with power" (Acts 10:38). Isaiah and others used the same imagery (Isa. 61:1; 1 Sam. 16:3; 10:1, 6). (See also *Anointing*; part 2: *Christ; Messiah.*)

Olive Tree. 1) The prophets have compared goodly men unto the olive tree (Judg. 9:8–9; Ps. 128:3). A righteous man is "like a green olive tree in the house of God" (Ps. 52:8). The two olive trees spoken of by Zechariah (Zech. 4:3, 11–14) have a dual fulfillment. They represent first Joshua and Zerubbabel; and second, the two prophets of the latter days who will be slain in Jerusalem (Rev. 11:1–4).

2) Paul (Rom. 11:17–24), Nephi (1 Ne. 10:12–14; 15:7–16), and Jacob (Jacob 5) have compared the house of Israel to an olive tree. Jacob recorded in a lengthy allegory, "Thus saith the Lord, I will liken thee, O house of Israel, like unto a tame olive-tree" (Jacob 5:3). Further, the tribe of Judah (Jer. 11:16) and

the tribe of Ephraim (Hosea 14:6) are symbolical representations of the olive tree. (See also *Tree*.)

Oven. Telestial souls that will experience the conflagration and holocaust accompanying the Second Coming are to be destroyed as by a "fiery oven" (Ps. 21:9; Mal. 4:1; D&C 133:64). (See also *Furnace*.)

Owl. Owls are among the "doleful creatures"—the owl, satyr, cormorant, bittern, raven, and dragon—which inhabit the wilderness and areas made desolate by the hand of God (Isa. 13:21-22; 34:14; Jer. 50:39).

Palmerworm. See *Locust*.

Palm Leaf. The palm leaf is an emblem of victory and triumph of Christ (John 12:13) and of the Saints (Rev. 7:9; Ps. 92:12).

Passover. The ordinances and events connected with the feast of the Passover point to the atoning sacrifice of Jesus Christ. The sacrificial lamb, the eating of its flesh, the partaking of the wine, the blood upon the doorposts, the unleavened bread, the hyssop, the bitter herbs—all of the hallowed ceremonials associated with the Passover meal—typified the great sacrifice of the Lamb of God (Ex. 12). (See part 2: *Lamb; Passover*.)

Path. A path is the route or way which a person chooses to travel. His choice may be to journey on the "path of the wicked" (Prov. 4:14), which is the way of darkness; or he may choose to walk the "path of the just," which is "as the shining light" (Prov. 4:18-19).

The "path of the just" is a "strait and narrow path" (2 Ne. 31:18) which leads the initiate first through the gate of baptism, then through the portal of eternal marriage. The candidate continues to "walk in the strait path which leads to life, and continue . . . until the end of the day of probation" (2 Ne. 33:9). The path is treacherous; many loose their way. However, the footing of the probationer is assured by his gripping tight unto the word of God (1 Ne. 15:23-24), by clinging to "the path of . . . duty," and by "walk[ing] circumspectly before God" (Hel. 15:5). Finally, the man of God reaches his final destination—the tree of life, or Jesus Christ. (See also *Highway*.)

Pavilion. Symbolizes the heavenly tabernacle or temple where the Most High dwells. The "thick clouds" which surround this holy residence signify the glory of God. God's pavilion is hidden from the eyes of mortal man (Ps. 18:11; 27:5; D&C 121:1, 4).

Pearl. Gospel knowledge and heavenly wisdom are of greater value than are gold and crystal, rubies and pearls (Job 28:18; Matt. 13:45). So precious are the things of the gospel that Jesus warned, "Give not that which is holy unto the dogs, neither cast ye your pearls before swine, lest they trample them under their feet" (Matt. 7:6; D&C 41:6). The Pearl of Great Price, chronologically the fourth volume of the standard works, is so called to establish its value to the Latter-day Saints.

Peniel. Peniel (Hebrew, "face of God") signifies the place that Jehovah appeared to Jacob. As it is written, "Jacob called the name of the place Peniel: for I have seen God face to face" (Gen. 32:30).

Perdition. The name / title Perdition means "utter loss" or "destruction" (John 17:12; 1 Tim. 6:9; D&C 76:25-27). Those who attach themselves to Satan and his plan of damnation receive this name. Their eternal position then becomes a state devoid of light, glory, and salvation.

Physician. Any true minister of the Lord that administers relief to the host of spiritual diseases which accompany fallen man is a "physician" (Matt. 9:12; Jer. 8:22; Moro. 8:8). Of all physicians, Jesus Christ, of course, is the greatest (Matt. 9:12). (See also part 2: *Physician.*)

Pillar. A pillar is the mainstay and strength of a building. In this sense Peter, James, and John, the chief Apostles of the New Testament era, were called "pillars"—they were the principal supports of the Church (Gal. 2:9). In connection with this, the Lord said of the righteous, "Him that overcometh will I make a pillar in the temple of my God" (Rev. 3:12).

To demonstrate the great strength which Jeremiah would have as the spokesman of the Lord, he was called "an iron pillar" (Jer. 1:18). This contrasts with Lot's wife, who became a "pillar of salt" (Gen. 19:26), a monument of God's judgment against the disobedient.

Pit. Known as the "horrible pit" (Ps. 40:2), the "pit of destruction" (Ps. 55:23), the "deeps" (Ps. 88:6), and "prison" (Isa. 24:22), the pit is hell, the realm where the spirits of the unrighteous dwell while awaiting the judgment (2 Ne. 24:15; Ezek. 32:21-23).

Plant. The scriptures compare men to plants. The "men of Judah" are known as God's "pleasant plant" (Isa. 5:7), and faithful priesthood holders are called "plants of renown" (D&C 124:61; see also Isa. 60:21). Saints are planted by God's own hand (Matt. 15:13; D&C 57:14; Jer. 42:10) in the sanctuary of the Lord (Ex. 15:17). (See also *Root; Stem of Jesse; Tree.*)

Priest. The ministerial duties and responsibilities of the priest of the Mosaic system appertain to the atoning sacrifice of Jesus (see Lev. 9, 16, 17). By acting on behalf of the people and making atonement for their sins (Lev. 4:20), the priest became a type and a shadow of Jesus Christ, the great High Priest.

Similarly, in the dispensation of the fulness of times, the priest that faithfully functions in the Aaronic Priesthood becomes a model of the Lord. His duties are not unlike those performed by Jesus while he lived upon the earth—that is, his "duty is to preach, teach, expound, exhort, and baptize, and administer the sacrament" (D&C 20:46). (See also *Apostle; Bishop; High Priest;* part 2: *Priest.*)

Promised Land. The concept of a "promised" land is that of a tangible symbol of the covenant between the Lord and his people. When a people are worthy of the divine presence they are granted a land of promise. The land is a symbol of the everlasting inheritance that will be theirs if they are true and faithful. If they break their covenants and reject their God, those lands will be taken from them, and they will be scattered.

The continent of America, for example, is called "the promised land" (1 Ne. 18:23). It is "a land which is choice above all the lands of the earth" (Ether 1:42). Notwithstanding its promise and choiceness, the land of America is but a shadow of a "far better land of promise," which is heaven (Alma 37:45). (See also *Babylon; Assyria; Edom; Egypt; Liahona.*)

Prophet. Every prophet is a type of Jesus Christ. It is the privilege of every prophet to prophesy, denounce sin, teach, preach, warn, and perform priesthood ordinances and functions —all of which point to the ministerial duties of Jesus. The very life of every prophet should reflect the perfect life of Jesus. (See also specific prophets, i.e., *Adam; Joseph; Moses;* and so on; part 2: *Prophet.*)

Race. With admonishment, Paul wrote, "Let us run with patience the race that is set before us, looking unto Jesus" (Heb. 12:1; see also 1 Cor. 9:23-25). Elder Bruce R. McConkie explained, "Life, [Paul] says, is a race. The Saints are in the stadium running toward the goal of salvation. . . . Those who look to Christ and run as he ran shall gain the victory as he did." (*Doctrinal New Testament Commentary*, 3:222.)

Rain. 1) Since it provides essential moisture to all forms of life—man, beast, and vegetation—rain signifies temporal blessings. When nations and peoples are righteous, the rains bring a harvest of plenty; but when they forget God, then the heavens are shut, and the lack of rain causes drought and famine (Deut. 11:14, 17; 1 Kgs. 8:35–36; Amos 4:7).

2) "Doctrine" and "righteousness" are said to "drop as the rain" upon the Saints of God (Deut. 32:2; Hosea 10:12). Upon the wicked, however, God rains "snares, fire and brimstone, and an horrible tempest: this shall be the portion of their cup" (Ps. 11:6). (See also *Dew*.)

Rainbow. The significance of the rainbow was explained to Noah. "And the bow shall be in the cloud; and I will look upon it, that I may remember the everlasting covenant, which I made unto thy father Enoch; that, when men should keep all my commandments, Zion should again come on the earth, the city of Enoch which I have caught up unto myself. And this is mine everlasting covenant, that when thy posterity shall embrace the truth, and look upward, then shall Zion look downward." (JST, Gen. 9:21–22.)

The Prophet Joseph Smith has added this application: "I have asked of the Lord concerning His coming; and while asking the Lord, He gave a sign and said, 'In the days of Noah I set a bow in the heavens as a sign and token that in any year that the bow should be seen the Lord would not come; but there should be seed time and harvest during that year: but whenever you see the bow withdrawn, it shall be a token that there shall be famine, pestilence, and great distress among the nations, and that the coming of the Messiah is not far distant.' " (*Teachings*, pp. 340–41; see also *Teachings*, p. 305.)

Reap. An eternal law dictates that "whatsoever a man soweth, that shall he also reap" (Gal. 6:7). Alma explained this principle in an understandable manner: "The time is at hand that all men shall reap a reward of their works, according to that which they have been—if they have been righteous they shall reap the salvation of their souls . . . and if they have been evil they shall reap the damnation of their souls" (Alma 9:28; 3:26; Mosiah 7:30–31). (See also *Harvest*.)

Reapers. See *Reap; Harvest*.

Red. In many instances, the color red symbolizes the blood spilt by the Savior during his atoning sacrifice (Rev. 19:13; D&C 133:48; Isa. 63:2; Num. 19:2). (See also *Colors; Green*.)

Reed. The reed is an emblem of frailty or weakness. Egypt was called a reed (Isa. 36:6; Ezek. 29:6–7), as were persons possessing physical weaknesses or bodily afflictions (Matt. 12:20; 1 Ne. 17:48).

Reins. The *reins,* an archaic word for "kidneys," represent the seat of emotions and the core of one's inner self (Ps. 7:9; 73:21; Prov. 23:16). (See also *Heart.*)

Rend or Rent. See *Garment.*

Right Hand. The right hand is used in covenant making, in performing sacred ordinances, and in sustaining various officers and authorities in the Church. Joseph Fielding Smith has explained, "The right hand is called the *dexter,* and the left, the *sinister;* dexter means *right* and sinister means *left.* Dexter, or right, means *favorable* or *propitious.* Sinister is associated with evil, rather than good. Sinister means *perverse.*" (*Doctrines of Salvation,* 3:108; italics in original.)

Thus, the right hand of God is associated with righteousness (Ps. 48:10; Isa. 41:10), power (Ex. 15:6, 12; Ps. 89:13), and covenant making (Isa. 62:8). With his right hand, the Lord executes justice (3 Ne. 29:4, 9), dispenses the law (Deut. 33:2), and saves his people (Ps. 17:7; 20:6); with his right hand he created the heavens and the earth (Isa. 48:13). After the divine judgment, the righteous will dwell eternally at the right hand of God (Mosiah 26:23-24; D&C 29:27). A simple but beautiful passage in Psalm 118:15-16 sums up the importance of the right hand:

> The right hand of the Lord doeth valiantly.
> The right hand of the Lord is exalted:
> The right hand of the Lord doeth valiantly.

(See also *Arm; Hand; Left.*)

Ring. 1) A ring is an emblem of eternity. Joseph Smith taught, "That which has a beginning will surely have an end; take a ring, it is without beginning or end — cut it for a beginning place and at the same time you have an ending place" (*Teachings,* p. 181).

2) During the biblical period, a ring symbolized prerogative and authority (Gen. 41:42; Luke 15:22).

River. 1) Unto the inhabitants of the city of Zion, the Lord will be like "a place of broad rivers and streams" (Isa. 33:21), meaning righteous souls will find spiritual refreshment and invigoration from God. (See also *Fountain; Water.*)

2) The word *river* is a metaphor for a mighty conquering army that flows into enemy nations, floods the land, and sweeps away its occupants (Isa. 8:7-8; Jer. 46:7-8; 47:2). (See also *Flood.*)

3) Lehi encouraged his son, Laman, toward a righteous life by saying, "O that thou mightest be like unto this river, continually running into the fountain of all righteousness!" (1 Ne. 2:9.)

4) The river beheld by Lehi and Nephi in the vision of the tree of life symbolizes "filthiness," and its depths are the "depths of hell" (1 Ne. 15:26–27; 12:16).

Robe. Those who clothe themselves in purity, virtue, and goodness wear the robes of righteousness. It is written concerning the great day of judgment that the wicked will be as if they are naked, but the righteous shall be "clothed with purity, yea, even with a robe of righteousness" (2 Ne. 9:14; D&C 29:12; Rev. 19:8). (See also *Garments; Linen; Nakedness.*)

Rock. 1) Jesus is called the Rock, the Rock of Heaven, and the Rock of Israel. (See also part 2: *Rock.*)

2) Jesus, the Rock of Heaven, dispenses the gospel unto mankind. The gospel, also a rock, brings permanence, stability, and strength into the life of the disciple of Christ. The Lord said, "Build upon my rock, which is my gospel" (D&C 11:24; 18:4–5; 33:12–13).

3) Joseph Smith explained the significance of Matthew 16:18: "Jesus in His teaching says, 'Upon this rock I will build my Church, and the gates of hell shall not prevail against it.' What rock? Revelation." (*Teachings*, p. 274.)

Rod. 1) The rod of Aaron is a symbol of Jesus—his chosenness, his regal power, his priesthood authority, and his ability to give life (Ex. 4:2–4; 7:9–20; Num. 17:2–10; Ps. 23:4).

2) The rod spoken of in Isaiah 11:1 is "a servant in the hands of Christ, who is partly a descendant of Jesse as well as of Ephraim, or of the house of Joseph, on whom there is laid much power" (D&C 113:3–4). The figurative reference is to Joseph Smith. (See also *Root.*)

Rod of Iron. The rod of iron is a representation of the "word of God" (1 Ne. 15:23–24). During the millennial era, Jesus will rule the nations with an iron rod, or with the word of God (Rev. 19:15). (See also *Iron; Rod.*)

Root. 1) The expressions "Root of David" (Rev. 5:5) and the "root out of dry ground" (Mosiah 14:2) refer to Christ. (See also part 2: *Root of David.*)

2) The "root of Jesse" mentioned in Isaiah 11:10 and Doctrine and Covenants 113:5–6 represents the Prophet Joseph Smith.

3) Scriptural metaphors portray men as being trees and as possessing roots, leaves, and fruit—the roots being the most

crucial extension of the tree. Water and nourishment enter the tree by way of the roots, and by the same is the tree held upright.

So it is with men. Concerning the righteous, spiritual nourishment and living waters enter in and are stored at their roots (Alma 32:37–42). In contrast, the roots of the wicked are "rottenness" (2 Ne. 15:24), or worse, they are "trees whose fruit withereth, without fruit, twice dead, plucked up by the roots" (Jude 1:12; see also Alma 5:52; 3 Ne. 25:1). (See also *Tree.*)

4) The house of Israel has been likened unto a tame olive tree, whose roots are sunk deep in the soil of her homeland (Jacob 5:8, 18). However, due to wickedness, the Lord of Israel often uproots and removes the olive tree and transplants it from one part of the earth to another (1 Kgs. 14:15; 2 Kgs. 19:30). (See also *Olive Tree; Branch.*)

Sabbath. Three events of signal importance are associated with the Sabbath. 1) The Creation: "For in six days the Lord made heaven and earth, . . . and rested the seventh day: wherefore the Lord blessed the sabbath day, and hallowed it" (Ex. 20:11). 2) The Exodus: Jehovah led the tribes of Israel out of the bondage of Egypt with a "mighty hand and by a stretched out arm," and "commanded [Israel] to keep the sabbath day" (Deut. 5:14–15). 3) The Resurrection: Jesus arose from the dead on the first day of the week, bringing forth the promise of immortality unto all mankind.

The Lord explained the significance of the Sabbath to the children of Israel: "Verily my sabbaths ye shall keep: for it is a sign between me and you throughout your generations; that ye may know that I am the Lord that doth sanctify you" (Ex. 31:13). (See also part 2: *Sabbath.*)

Sabbatical Year. In ancient times, the sabbatical year signified a period of rest for the earth. According to the law of Moses, the sabbatical year occurred every "seventh year." This was to be a "sabbath of rest unto the land, a sabbath for the Lord," when the Israelites were commanded by the Lord, "Thou shalt neither sow thy field, nor prune thy vineyard . . . for it is a year of rest unto the land." (Lev. 25:4–5.)

Sackcloth. A course, rough cloth usually made of goat's hair, sackcloth was worn anciently by those who wished to display an attitude of mourning (Gen. 37:34; 2 Sam. 3:31), extreme humility (Ps. 35:13), or repentance (Hel. 11:9; Matt. 11:21). The custom of donning sackcloth was often accompanied by the rending of garments, sitting in ashes, weeping, fasting, and prayer (Mosiah 11:25; Jonah 3:6–8; Dan. 9:3). (See also *Ashes; Garment.*)

Sacrifices. During the first four thousand years of the earth's temporal existence, thousands and tens of thousands of sacrifices were made unto the God of Israel. Each and every sacrifice, from the first to the last, was but a miniature model, a prototype of the last and great sacrifice offered up by Jesus. In each rite, consecration, and ordinance; in every solemnity, ritual, and ceremony; in all observances, duties, and ministrations; indeed, in the entire system of sacrifices and offerings given of God in all ages, the spiritually alert can identify aspects of Jesus' atonement. In short, all sacrifices were designed to be "a similitude of the sacrifice of the Only Begotten of the Father" (Moses 5:7).

One enlightened biblical scholar, Andrew Jukes, has written that in every sacrificial "offering there are at least three distinct objects presented. . . . There is the offering, the priest, the offerer." By *offering* is meant the sacrificial victim, such as the lamb, the pigeon, the fowl, the bull, the ram, and so on. By *priest* is meant the temple officiant who performs the sacrifice. By *offerer* is meant the man or family of Israel who presents the offering to the priest.

Juke explains, "What, then, is the offering? what the priest? what the offerer? Christ is the offering, Christ is the priest, Christ is the offerer. . . . As offerer, we see Him man under the law, standing our substitute, for us to fulfil all righteousness. As priest, we have Him presented as the mediator, God's messenger between Himself and Israel. While as the offering He is seen the innocent victim, a sweet savour to God, yet bearing the sin and dying for it." (Andrew Jukes, *The Law of Offerings,* pp. 44–45.) (See also *Blood; Scapegoat;* part 2: *Lamb.*)

Salt. 1) Salt, which retards the process of deterioration, is a symbol of incorruption and preservation. Concerning sacrificial offerings, the Lord revealed to Moses, "And every oblation of thy meat offering shalt thou season with salt; . . . with all thine offerings thou shalt offer salt" (Lev. 2:13). This divine dictum became "a covenant of salt for ever before the Lord" (Num. 18:19; 2 Chr. 13:5).

The Lord's covenant people, therefore, are appropriately called the "salt of the earth" and the "savor of men." Those who break the covenant, however, are like the salt that loses its savor, and are "good for nothing only to be cast out and trodden under the feet of men" (D&C 101:39–40; Matt. 5:13).

2) Salt renders lands barren and fruitless. It is at times sent as a judgment or a curse from man or God. Note, for instance, the context in which *salt* is found in Deuteronomy 29:23: "The whole land thereof is brimstone, and salt, and burning, that it is not sown, nor beareth, nor any grass groweth therein, like the overthrow of Sodom, and Gomorrah" (Deut. 29:23; Judg. 9:45; Jer. 17:6). The disciples of Jesus were warned to "remember Lot's wife" (Luke 17:32). It was the wife of Lot who was cursed to become "a pillar of salt" (Gen. 19:26).

Samuel. The mission and divine responsibilities of the prophet Samuel typified those of the Son of God. He was a prophet (1 Sam. 3:20), "faithful priest" (1 Sam. 2:35), and offerer of sacrifices (1 Sam. 7:9); and he "judged Israel all the days of his life" (1 Sam. 7:15). Also, he had the important role of anointing men to become kings (1 Sam. 10:1; 16:13). (See also *Prophet.*)

Sand. The word *sand* is employed in hyperbolic expressions to denote an immense number. Such statements as "the number of whom is as the sand of the sea" (Rev. 20:8) or "their numbers were great, even numberless as the sand upon the sea shore" (Moses 1:28) are not uncommon in the scriptures.

Sarah. Sarah (Hebrew, "princess"), as the mother of the faithful, typifies "the children of promise," those who accept the covenants and promises of Abraham and, through their faithfulness, are ensured eternal increase in the hereafter (Gal. 4:22–31; Heb. 11:11; 1 Pet. 3:6; D&C 132:19). (See also *Hagar.*)

Scapegoat. The scapegoat was "a sacrificial goat upon whose head the high priest placed the collective sins of the people. This was done each year on the Day of Atonement, after which the goat was sent out into the desert. The scapegoat was a symbol of Christ, who would take upon himself the sins of the world." (*Gospel Symbolism*, p. 271; see also Lev. 16:8–26.) (See also *Sacrifice*; part 2: *Lamb.*)

Scepter. A scepter, held by a king during a ceremonial occasion, is an insignia of authority and sovereignty. When possessed by a righteous ruler, the scepter represents justice, power, judgment, and kingship (D&C 85:7; Abr., facsimile 3:1). The scepter of the faithful is an "unchanging scepter of righteousness and truth" (D&C 121:46).

Scorpions. Scorpions are symbolic of the enemies of righteousness whose desire it is to sting, wound, torment, and kill (Ezek. 2:6; Rev. 9:3–10; Luke 10:19).

Seed. 1) Abinadi taught that "all those who have hearkened" unto the words of the prophets and "believed that the Lord would redeem his people" are the seed of Christ (Mosiah 15:11-14). They are "spiritually begotten" by Jesus, and are called "the children of Christ, his sons, and his daughters" (Mosiah 5:7-11).

2) *Seed* is often put for posterity (1 Ne. 2:23; Alma 46:23).

3) The word of God is like a seed which, when planted in the hearts of the humble, becomes a tree of life (Alma 32:28-43). (See also *Tree of Life.*)

Seed of Abraham. Those who wholeheartedly accept and are obedient to the ordinances and covenants of the gospel of Jesus Christ are the "children of Israel, and of the seed of Abraham" (D&C 103:17; Abr. 2:9-11; D&C 84:34). (See also *Abraham.*)

Serpent. 1) Lucifer possesses snakelike qualities. He "beguiles" (Moses 4:19), deceives (Rev. 12:9), poisons minds, generates fear, strikes quickly, and brings death with his venom. Further, of all the beasts of the field, he is the most subtle (Moses 4:5). For these and other reasons Satan is known as "that old serpent, who is the devil, who is the father of all lies" (2 Ne. 2:18; D&C 76:28). (See also *Adder; Asp; Cockatrice.*)

2) The brazen serpent "lifted up" by Moses in the wilderness was a type of Jesus Christ, who would be "lifted up" on the cross (John 3:14-15; Num. 21:6-9). Nephi, the son of Helaman, explained the significance of this action of Moses: "Yea, did [Moses] not bear record that the Son of God should come? And as he lifted up the brazen serpent in the wilderness, even so shall he be lifted up who should come. And as many as should look upon that serpent should live, even so as many as should look upon the Son of God with faith, having a contrite spirit, might live, even unto that life which is eternal." (Hel. 8:14-15; Alma 33:19.) (See also part 2: *Brazen Serpent.*)

Seven. The numbers seven and seventy are common in the scriptures. Examples include the "seven ewe lambs" (Gen. 21:28), "seven ears" of corn (Gen. 41:20-54), the "seven days" of Passover and of the feast of Tabernacles (Ex. 12:15; Deut. 16:13), "seven days" of purification (Lev. 13:21; 15:28; Num. 19:16), "seven altars" and "seven animals" of the sacrificial offering (Num. 23:1, 29), "seven days" of the creation, and seven days of the week (Ex. 20:11), the sabbatical or seventh year (Lev. 25:4-5), "sevenfold" avengement (Moses 5:48), compassing the city of Jericho "seven times" with "seven priests" bearing "seven trumpets" (Joshua 6:4-15), "seven women" (2 Ne. 14:1), "seven loaves" of bread (Matt. 15:34-37), forgiveness "seventy times seven" (Matt. 18:21-22), the Lord's appointed "seventy" (Luke 10:1; D&C 107:25), and their "seven presidents" (D&C 107:93).

Furthermore, the word *seven* occurs many times throughout the book of Revelation. For instance, there are the "seven churches" (Rev. 1:4), "seven servants" (JST, Rev. 1:4), "seven golden candlesticks" (Rev. 1:12), "seven stars" (Rev. 1:20), "seven lamps of fire" (Rev. 4:5), "seven seals" (Rev. 5:5), "seven horns and seven eyes" (Rev. 5:6), "seven angels" with their "seven trumpets" (Rev. 8:6), "seven thunders" (Rev. 10:3), "seven heads" and "seven crowns" (Rev. 12:3), "seven last plagues" (Rev. 15:1), "seven vials" (Rev. 17:1), "seven mountains" (Rev. 17:9), and "seven kings" (Rev. 17:10).

The root of the Hebrew word for seven (*sheva*) is identical to the Hebrew verb that means "to take an oath," thus connecting the word *seven* to covenants and covenant making. Further, the word *seven* denotes perfection and completion. (See also *Eight*.)

Sheaves. Agricultural imagery—sowing, reaping, harvesting—is often related by the prophets to missionary work. For instance, the great missionary Ammon rejoiced with his brethren, saying, "Behold, thousands . . . have been brought into the fold of God. Behold, the field was ripe, and blessed are ye, for ye did thrust in the sickle, and did reap with your might, yea, all the day long did ye labor; and behold the number of your sheaves! And they shall be gathered into the garners, that they are not wasted." (Alma 26:4-5.)

Anciently, grain was harvested, bundled together into sheaves, and carried to the threshing floor, where the wheat was then separated from the tares. Missionaries who are "laden with many sheaves" (D&C 75:5; 31:5; 33:9) are those whose harvest has been great, who are able to sit down and enjoy the fruit of their labors. (See also *Harvest; Wheat; Tares*.)

Sheep. Jesus Christ is the Shepherd; his disciples are his "little flock" (D&C 6:34; Ezek. 34:31). Sheep are a perfect likeness of the followers of the Lord (Ps. 79:13). They are gentle, submissive, mild, and meek—qualities possessed by Jesus' true disciples. However, as the scriptures indicate, sheep must beware of wolves, as the lambs are inclined to wander from the fold (Ps. 119:176; Matt. 10:6; Luke 15:6-9). (See also *Lamb; Shepherd; Wolf;* part 2: *Lamb*.)

Shepherd. 1) Christ is the "great shepherd," his disciples are the sheep (Heb. 13:20; 1 Pet. 2:25). (See also *Sheep*; part 2: *Shepherd.*)

2) Shepherds typify ecclesiastical leaders, guides, and pastors who oversee the flock of God (Ezek. 34; Jer. 23:1-4).

Shewbread. One temple ceremonial of the Mosaic system was directly associated with the emblems of the Lord's sacrament. Every Sabbath, twelve loaves of bread (called shewbread, which in the Hebrew means "the bread of his presence") were placed upon the table of shewbread. According to many biblical scholars, wine was also placed upon the table alongside of the bread. These were eaten by the priests, who were to partake with an eye upon the atoning sacrifice of the Lord. (See also *Bread; Wine.*)

Shield. 1) Signifies God himself, who is a protector and defender of his people (Gen. 15:1; Ps. 3:3). (See also part 2: *Shield.*)

2) The "shield of faith" is part of the armor employed by the Lord's warriors to ward off the "fiery darts of the wicked" (D&C 27:17; Eph. 6:16). (See also *Armor.*)

Sinai, Mount. Mount Sinai represents a temple *par excellence.* Sinai is the sanctuary which was created by the hands of the Lord (Ex. 15:17). Such motifs as the cosmic mountain, the waters of life, the sacred repast, sacrificial ordinances, religious laws, divine revelation, and others are found at this temple mount. It was at Sinai that Moses, Aaron, Nadab, Abihu, and seventy elders received a most sacred theophanic experience (Ex. 24:9-10). (See also *Mountain; Mount of Transfiguration; Temple.*)

Sleep. Sleep symbolizes death. Beginning with the day of birth and consummating at the hour of death, the physical body suffers innumerable hardships. After many years of toiling and laboring in the flesh, mortal man finds himself weary. Finally the moment arrives when the body is laid down to sleep in the dust (Dan. 12:2; 1 Thes. 4:14; 1 Cor. 15:6). The word *sleep,* then, is a euphemism for *death.* (See also *Bed.*)

Smoke. At times, fire and smoke accompany the presence of God. It is written that "God Almighty Himself dwells in eternal fire" (*Teachings,* p. 367), and that "God is a consuming fire" (Deut. 4:24). Smoke is often found in the Lord's sanctuaries — the temple in heaven (Rev. 15:8), Sinai (Ex. 19:18), and the temple of Isaiah's vision (Isa. 6:4). Smoke symbolizes the glory of God.

Sodom. See *Gomorrah.*

Solomon. As the king of Israel, as the ruler of many dominions, as the righteous judge, as the man of peace, as the king
revered by all kings, as the owner of a great name, as a savior of
the people, King Solomon is a type of the Lord (Ps. 72). (See also
King; part 2: *King of Kings.*)

Son. See *Daughter / Son.*

Stake. "In prophetic imagery, Zion is pictured as a great tent
upheld by cords fastened securely to stakes (Isa. 54:2-7). That
imagery finds its fulfillment in the ecclesiastical units called
stakes in the Church today (D&C 101:21)." (*Gospel Symbolism,* p. 272.)

Star. 1) Stars signify men, either evil or good. John wrote
about the premortal followers of Satan, referring to them as the
"stars of heaven" (Rev. 12:4). The "morning stars" mentioned
by Job were eminent persons (Job 38:7; D&C 128:23), morning
stars being spheres whose light continues for a period more
lengthy than the remaining stars of heaven. In connection with
this, Jesus, the "bright and morning star" (Rev. 22:16), is the
greatest. The eleven brothers of Joseph were compared to
eleven stars (Gen. 37:9). (See also part 2: *Star; Sun of Righteousness.*)

2) The brightness of the light of the stars has been compared to the glory that will exist in the telestial kingdom (D&C
76:98; 1 Cor. 15:40-41). By way of contrast, the light of the sun
is comparable to the glory found in the celestial kingdom. (See
also *Sun; Moon.*)

Stem of Jesse. "Christ is the *Stem of Jesse* (Isa. 11:1-5; D&C
113:1-2), by which is meant that our Lord came as a descendant of that noble Israelite who sired David the King. (Ruth
4:17.)" (*Mormon Doctrine,* p. 766.) (See also *Root;* part 2: *Stem
of Jesse.*)

Stiffneckedness. See *Neck.*

Stone. 1) The Saints of God are "lively [living] stones"
which, when united together, are "built up a spiritual house" or
a temple of God. In the same context, Jesus Christ is the "chief
corner stone" of this spiritual house (1 Pet. 2:5-6). Noteworthy
also is the fact that Jesus gave Peter, the chief Apostle of the
New Testament Church, the name Stone. Jesus said to Peter,
"Thou art Simon the son of Jona: thou shalt be called Cephas,
which is by interpretation, A stone" (John 1:42). (See also
Building; Stone; Rock; part 2: *Rock; Stone.*)

2) Those who overcome the world will be given a white
stone (Rev. 2:17). This stone "will become a Urim and Thum-

mim to each individual who receives one, whereby things pertaining to a higher order of kingdoms will be made known" (D&C 130:10).

Stumbling Block. Anything which causes hindrance and impedes a man's journey on his chosen path is called a "stumbling block." People most often stumble because of iniquity (Mosiah 7:29; Alma 4:10; 1 Cor. 1:23).

Sun. Lesser luminaries are made to signify the glories of the terrestrial and telestial kingdoms, but the sun is typical of the splendor, glory, and magnificence of the celestial kingdom (D&C 76:96; 1 Cor. 15:40–41). (See also *Star; Moon;* part 2: *Sun of Righteousness.*)

2) In an inspired dream had by Joseph of Egypt, the sun was a representation of his father Jacob (Gen. 37:9–10).

Sword. 1) The sword represents war. For instance, the expressions "Ye are visited by sword" (2 Ne. 1:18), "The sword of destruction did hang over them" (3 Ne. 2:19), and "They will take up the sword, one against another" (D&C 45:33) speak of fighting and warfare.

2) The word of God is "quick and powerful, sharper than a two-edged sword, to the dividing asunder of both joints and marrow" (D&C 6:2; Heb. 4:12; 1 Ne. 21:2). Related to this, "The sword of the Spirit . . . is the word of God" (Eph. 6:17; D&C 27:18).

Tabernacle. The tabernacle of Moses was a mobile temple, designed to be transported with the camp of Israel as they journeyed through the wilderness towards the promised land. Though the tabernacle was but a tent, it met all the qualifications of being one of the Lord's sanctuaries. (See also *Temple; Holy of Holies; Mountain.*)

Tares. Tares grow with wheat and are in many respects similar to it in appearance. These noxious weeds are typical of evil men, both within and without the Church. During the harvest of the world, tares will be bound into bundles and then burned (D&C 86; Matt. 13:24–43; D&C 88:94). (See also *Harvest.*)

Temple. 1) Sanctuaries made by the hands of man are but figures of the heavenly temple, the "true tabernacle, which the Lord pitched, and not man" (Heb. 8:9; 9:24; Rev. 11:19). Within these temples are found a miniature representation of the Garden of Eden, and the telestial, terrestrial, and celestial kingdoms. (See also *Mountain.*)

2) The tabernacle of clay, or the mortal body, is a "temple of God" (1 Cor. 3:16–17; Hel. 4:24). Paul asked, "What? know ye not that your body is the temple of the Holy Ghost which is in you, which ye have of God, and ye are not your own?" (1 Cor. 6:19; 2 Cor. 5:1–5.)

Jesus, prophesying of his death and resurrection, exclaimed, "Destroy this temple, and in three days I will raise it up," referring to "the temple of his body" (John 2:18–20; Rev. 21:22).

Thirty Pieces of Silver. Thirty pieces of silver, the price of a slave under the law of Moses (Ex. 21:32), signifies the price for which Judas betrayed Jesus (Matt. 26:14–16; Zech. 11:12). Elder Bruce R. McConkie has written, "Thirty pieces of silver! Such would they pay for the life of their God — no more and no less. And by so doing all men ever after would know that they esteemed him as the basest of men." (*Doctrinal New Testament Commentary*, 1:703.)

Thorns. Thorns typify the enemies of the house of Israel, which have the ability to cause injury by pricking and piercing (Num. 33:55; Ezek. 28:24).

Throne. Wherever the King of kings sets forth his judgments and decrees, advances his statutes and ordinances, and rules and reigns with kingly power, there his throne is found. Thus, heaven is called "God's throne" (3 Ne. 12:34; 1 Ne. 17:39), and in the millennial day, people "shall call Jerusalem the throne of the Lord" (Jer. 3:17). (See also *Mercy Seat.*)

2) Thrones of earthly monarchs symbolize kingship, sovereignty, and dominion (Gen. 41:40; 2 Sam. 3:10; 7:16; 1 Kgs. 1:47).

Thunder. 1) Thunder is one of the many judgments sent from God (1 Sam. 2:10; D&C 87:6), symbolically proceeding from the very throne of Deity (Rev. 4:5; 11:19). (See also *Earthquake; East Wind; Flood; Hail; Lightning.*)

2) At times the voice of a heavenly being is of such intensity and power that it is described as being like the "voice of thunder" (1 Ne. 17:45), the "noise of thunder" (Rev. 6:1), or the "voice of a great thunder" (Rev. 14:2).

Tongue. 1) The tongue represents the whole man (Mosiah 27:31; 3 Ne. 17:17) or the entire nation (Alma 45:16; 3 Ne. 26:4).

2) Also, the tongue symbolizes the speech of man (1 John 3:18; Prov. 25:15; Ps. 140:3).

Tree. 1) Green trees, which are "planted by the rivers of water" (Ps. 1:3), and whose fruits are good, represent righteous men. Thus Joseph and Hyrum Smith are identified as green trees (D&C 135:6), and the two prophets of the latter day who will prophesy in Jerusalem are "the two olive trees" spoken of by Zechariah and John (Zech. 4:8–14; Rev. 11:1–4).

Dry trees, on the other hand, which "bring forth evil fruit" (3 Ne. 14:17–18), represent wicked men (Luke 23:31). These will be hewn down at the last day and burned in the fire (Alma 5:52). (See also *Cedar; Oak; Fig Tree; Olive Tree; Fruit; Tree of Life.*)

2) On many occasions the prophets have likened the house of Israel unto an olive tree. (See also *Olive Tree.*)

Tree of Life. 1) The tree of life in Nephi's vision was "a representation of the love of God" (1 Ne. 11:25). We need to read this in connection with other statements made by the prophets, e.g., "God is love; and he that dwelleth in love dwelleth in God, and God in him" (1 John 4:16). That is to say, "the love of God" spoken of by Nephi relates readily to Jesus Christ, the great exemplar of love, and thus we may think of the tree as a symbol of the Savior. The context of this great vision seems to bear this out (1 Ne. 11:14–28).

Trees can be representative of men, but the tree of life typifies the greatest Man of all — the Son of God. By grasping the rod of iron, one approaches the tree of life (1 Ne. 15:23–24; Alma 32:40, 42). The fruit of this tree typifies the emblems of the sacrament — the bread and water (Alma 5:34) — to be enjoyed by those who have entered the waters of baptism (Alma 5:62). This fruit is "most precious and most desirable above all other fruits; yea, and it is the greatest of all the gifts of God" (1 Ne. 15:36). Those who partake will receive eternal life (Rev. 22:14). (See also *Tree; Fruit; Eden; Garden.*)

Trumpet. 1) Symbolizes the declaration of an important thing or event (Alma 29:1; Rev. 1:10; D&C 88:105–6). For example, the Lord's missionaries blow the trumpet by preaching the gospel: "And at all times, and in all places, he shall open his mouth and declare my gospel as with the voice of a trump" (D&C 24:12).

2) The sounding of a trump figuratively calls the outcasts of Israel to gather unto the Lord (Isa. 27:13; Matt. 24:31). It also calls forth the dead from the grave unto the bar of judgment (Morm. 9:13; 1 Cor. 15:52; 1 Thes. 4:16; Mosiah 26:24–25). Michael, the archangel, will blow his trump to awaken the dead (D&C 29:26).

3) Trumpets are blown in times of impending danger (both spiritual and physical danger) as a warning to the people (D&C 88:92; 77:12; Ezek. 33:3–6; Joel 2:1).

Urim and Thummim. The "earth, in its sanctified, immortal, and eternal state" (D&C 77:1), will become a giant Urim and Thummim (Hebrew words meaning "lights" and "perfections"). Joseph Smith once taught, "While at dinner, I remarked to my family and friends present, that when the earth was sanctified and became like a sea of glass, it would be one great urim and thummim, and the Saints could look in it and see as they are seen" (*History of the Church*, 5:279).

Veil. 1) The veil which Moses wore after his forty-day sojourn on Mount Sinai represented the veiling (or the removal) of the fullness of the gospel of Jesus Christ from the presence of the tribes of Israel. What remained unto the children of Israel were the "lesser priesthood . . . and the preparatory gospel . . . and the law of carnal commandments" (D&C 84:26–27). However, when Christ fulfilled the law of Moses, the veil of Moses was symbolically removed (2 Cor. 3:1–18).

2) The veil of the temple separates mankind from the presence of God. The rending of the veil at the time of the Crucifixion (Luke 23:45) verified the fulfillment of the law of Moses by the sacrifice of Jesus, demonstrating that man could now "enter into the holiest by the blood of Jesus" (Heb. 10:19). This veil is representative of the flesh of the Savior (Heb. 10:20; 9:3), showing that the crucified Lord stands between man and his gaining eternal life in the presence of God: "No man cometh unto the Father, but by me," Jesus declared (John 14:6).

3) Veils typify the covering or the concealing of something. The veil which covered the ark of the covenant (Ex. 35:12; 39:34; Num. 4:5) hid the ark from the eyes of the people. The expressions "veil of darkness" (D&C 38:8) and "dark veil of unbelief" (Alma 19:6) speak of a curtain which covers and veils the minds of people from the things of God. (See also *Curtain.*)

Vessels. 1) Anciently, temple officiants used sacred vessels and utensils in their performance of sacrificial rites and ordinances (Num. 4:14–16). Only those who were ritually pure were able to handle the temple instruments. From this practice came the scriptural idiom "Be ye clean that bear the vessels of the Lord" (D&C 133:5; 3 Ne. 20:41), an expression which instructs those who deal with priesthood ordinances and functions to be worthy of their office and calling.

2) The souls of men and women are considered to be vessels (Alma 60:23–24). Some are termed "chosen vessels of the Lord" (Moro. 7:31; Acts 9:15). Mary, the mother of Jesus, for example, was called a "precious and chosen vessel" (Alma 7:10). In con-

trast, those who warrant to be called "sons of perdition" are entitled "vessels of wrath" (D&C 76:33; Rom. 9:21-23).

Vine. 1) The vine is "a symbol of Christ, who said, 'I am the true vine' (John 15:1[; 1 Ne. 15:15]), meaning that he is the source of life to the branches (the Apostles) and that only as they are associated with him can they bring forth fruit (John 15:5)" (*Gospel Symbolism*, p. 275). (See also *Husbandman;* part 2: *Vine.*)

2) Hosea recorded that "Israel is an empty vine" (Hosea 10:1; see also Ps. 80:8-19; Jer. 2:21), meaning that Israel's fruits were valueless unto the surrounding nations due to Israel's extreme wickedness. (See also *Fruit.*)

Vineyard. 1) Isaiah employed a metaphor denoting that "the vineyard of the Lord of hosts is the house of Israel" (Isa. 5:7).

2) Prophetic imagery uses a vineyard to represent the world (Jacob 5, 6), where God's servants the missionaries are called to labor (D&C 33:3; 43:28). (See also *Harvest.*)

Virgin. Denotes a person or persons who are spiritually pure and undefiled, whose garments are not spotted with the blood and sins of the world (2 Cor. 11:2; Rev. 14:3-4).

Voice. 1) The word *voice* typifies the person by which a message is made known. For instance, the sentence "The voice of the Lord spake unto my father by night" (1 Ne. 16:9) means that "the Lord spake unto my father by night." And "I did obey the voice of the Spirit" (1 Ne. 4:18) conveys the same idea as "I did obey the Spirit."

2) The word *voice* also signifies the words of the speaker. Jesus explained that "my words . . . are my voice" (D&C 84:60; 18:34-35).

3) When people in a group are united in their opinion, they have "one voice" (Mosiah 5:2; Alma 43:49). Likewise, the expression "the voice of the people" (Mosiah 29:26; Alma 2:4) indicates a unity of thought among the people.

Water. 1) "Living water is the words of eternal life, the message of salvation, the truths about God and his kingdom; it is the doctrines of the gospel" (*Doctrinal New Testament Commentary,* 1:151; see also John 4:6-14; 7:37-39; Isa. 55:1). Jesus is the "fountain of living waters" (Jer. 2:13; 17:13; compare Isa. 33:21), or the divine source of all truth. (See also *Fountain.*)

2) "Many waters" is a metaphor for a multitude of persons (Rev. 17:1, 15; Jer. 47:2; Isa. 17:12–13). (See also *Flood.*)

Wilderness. Diametrically opposite to the promised land, the Garden of Eden, and Zion stands the wilderness or desert (Isa. 51:3; Joel 2:3; Isa. 35:6–7). Scriptural expressions set forth the desolate state of the wilderness — it is a "land of darkness" (Jer. 2:31), a "parched ground," a "thirsty land," and a "habitation of dragons" (Isa. 35:6–7). Further, "the wilderness" is a "land of deserts and of pits, . . . a land of drought, and of the shadow of death, . . . a land that no man passed through, and where no man dwelt" (Jer. 2:6). Divine curses and judgments transform rich lands and fruitful territories into deserts, due to the wickedness and abominations of the people which inhabit such areas (Joel 3:19; Jer. 17:5–6; 50:12–13). (See also *Promised Land.*)

Wind. 1) Wind is associated with the Holy Ghost (John 3:8; Acts 2:2–3) and the glory of God. During the dedicatory prayer offered at the Kirtland Temple, Joseph Smith entreated the Lord, "Let thy house be filled, as with a rushing mighty wind, with thy glory" (D&C 109:37).

2) At times, false doctrines are blown hither and thither as are the winds (Jude 1:12; Heb. 13:9). Paul explained that Apostles and prophets and other priesthood offices were set up in the Church for the purpose of the "perfecting of the Saints," for the "unity of the faith," and so that the Saints might "henceforth be no more children, tossed to and fro, and carried about with every wind of doctrine, by the sleight of men, and cunning craftiness" (Eph. 4:11–14). (See also *East Wind.*)

Wine. 1) Wine represents the blood of the wicked (2 Ne. 6:18).

2) Wine is an emblem of the blood of Jesus (Matt. 26:27–28; see also Deut. 32:14). The sacramental blessing states, "O God, the Eternal Father, we ask thee in the name of thy Son, Jesus Christ, to bless and sanctify this wine to the souls of all those who drink of it, that they may do it in remembrance of the blood of thy Son" (D&C 20:79; Moro. 5:2). (See also *Blood.*)

Winepress. The winepress typifies the judgments which God will send forth upon the wicked at the last days. Jehovah taught, "I have trodden the winepress alone; and of the people there was none with me: for I will tread them in mine anger, and trample them in my fury; and their blood shall be sprinkled upon my garments, and I will stain all my raiment" (Isa. 63:3).

"This picture is a familiar one in Israel. The wine is trampled from the grapes in great vats, staining the garments of the laborers as though with blood. But in this case the second coming of Christ is involved, the one harvesting the crop is the Lord himself, and the winepress is full of the wrath of God. . . . As the grapes are trodden in the winepress of wrath, so shall the wicked be trodden down at the last days. . . . How awful is the scene in this day of vengeance. The blood of the slain at the coming of the Lord will stain his garments as the red wine stains the raiment of those who tread on the grapes. He will tread on them as men trample on the fruit of the vine. Thus it shall be when the Son of Man harvests the earth." (*Millennial Messiah*, pp. 503–5.)

Wings. 1) The Spirit (2 Ne. 4:25), angels (Ex. 25:20; Isa. 6:2), beasts (Rev. 4:8), the wind (Ps. 104:3), and the earth (D&C 88:45) are depicted as possessing wings. Wings, in these instances, "are a representation of power," having the ability "to move, to act, etc." (D&C 77:4).

2) The expression "The children of men put their trust under the shadow of [God's] wings" (Ps. 36:7; 17:8) refers to the Lord's power and willingness to preserve his people. As a hen protects her young from predators by pulling them under her wings, Jesus Christ shelters the faithful under the wings of his love. (See also *Hen; Eagle.*)

Wolf. Speaking metaphorically, a wolf is a false prophet, faithless teacher, or any other enemy of the Church (Matt. 7:15; Alma 5:59–60; John 10:12; Acts 20:29). (See also *Dog; Fox.*)

Woman. A woman is made to represent a church.

1) The woman described by John in the twelfth chapter of Revelation symbolizes "the church of God" (JST, Rev. 12:7; see also D&C 101:81–85). (See also *Husband.*)

2) The church of the devil, also called the great and abominable church, is the "mother of abominations," the "whore of all the earth," the "mother of harlots" (1 Ne. 14:10, 16; Rev. 17:4–18). (See also *Harlot; Adultery.*)

World. The wicked of planet earth are denominated the "world" (JS–M 1:4; John 1:10–11; 15:18–19). Concerning this, John wrote: "Love not the world, neither the things that are in the world. If any man love the world, the love of the Father is not in him. For all that is in the world, the lust of the flesh, and the lust of the eyes, and the pride of life, is not of the Father, but is of the world." (1 John 2:15–16.) (See also *Earth; Edom.*)

Wormwood. Wormwood (the herb *artemisia* is used figuratively to denote a bitter condition, often in the form of a curse or judgment from God (Rev. 8:11; Lam. 3:15, 19; Deut. 29:18-19; Jer. 9:15; 23:15).

Yoke. Those who suffer physical or spiritual bondage are those who have a yoke of iron upon their neck (D&C 109:47; 1 Ne. 13:5; Gen. 27:40). These are they that "labour and are heavy laden." To them, Jesus said, "Take my yoke upon you . . . and ye shall find rest unto your souls. For my yoke is easy, and my burden is light" (Matt. 11:28-30). (See also *Chains.*)

Zion. 1) Zion describes a spiritual state or condition. The Prophet Joseph Smith recorded, "This is Zion—THE PURE IN HEART" (D&C 97:21).

2) Also, Zion is descriptive of places made sacred by the presence of God and holy men, such as the city of Enoch (Moses 7:18-19), Mount Zion (1 Kgs. 8:1), Jerusalem (Isa. 4:3-4), the New Jerusalem (D&C 45:66-67), and the heavenly Jerusalem (Heb. 12:22).

PART 2

SYMBOLS, NAMES, AND TITLES FOR DEITY

Symbols, Names, and Titles for Deity

"Names identify and describe. In biblical thought a name was an expression of the nature of its bearer. The Hebrew word for name is *shem*, meaning 'memorial.' To declare one's name was to reveal one's self. Nowhere is the importance of properly descriptive names more evident than in the names of Deity. When the Lord called Moses from the burning bush and commissioned him to bring his people out of Egypt, Moses' question was, 'When I come unto the children of Israel, and shall say unto them, The God of your fathers hath sent me unto you; and they shall say to me, What is his name? what shall I say unto them?' Knowing the importance of names, Moses could fully anticipate that his people would inquire by what name and in what authority he came. In response the Lord said, 'I AM THAT I AM,' that is, that Moses was to say that 'I AM' had sent him. Moses was further instructed that he was to say, 'The Lord God of your fathers, the God of Abraham, the God of Isaac, and the God of Jacob, hath sent me unto you: this is my name for ever, and this is my memorial unto all generations.' (Exodus 3:13–15.) This instruction is clarified in JST, Exodus 6:2–3, which reads, 'God spake unto Moses, and said unto him, I am the Lord: And I appeared unto Abraham, unto Isaac, and unto Jacob, I am the Lord God Almighty, the Lord JEHOVAH. And was not my name known unto them?'

"Within the two passages just quoted, the personality of Moses' God is distinctly expressed. *Jehovah* is the English rendering of the Hebrew tetragram *YHWH*. It is derived from the verb 'to be,' which implies his eternal nature. *I AM* is the first person singular form of the verb 'to be.' In the name Jehovah, or I AM, God manifests himself as a personal living being who labors in behalf of Israel and who will fulfill the promises made to the fathers. All of this conveys the idea of an unchanging, ever-living God, who through all generations is true to his word. 'God's personal existence, the continuity of His dealings with man, the unchangeableness of His promises, and the whole revelation of His redeeming mercy, gather round the name Jehovah' (Girdlestone, p. 38).

"Thus, to declare the name of the Lord was to testify of the Lord, a concept lost to both Jews and Christians alike by false traditions and faulty Bible translations. 'For this cause,' the Lord told Moses, 'have I raised thee up, for to shew in thee my power; and that my name may be declared throughout all the earth' (Ex. 9:16)." (*Gospel Symbolism*, pp. 176–77.)

This section lists over two hundred symbols, names, and titles for the Lord that occur in holy writ. Each symbol, name, or title witnesses to the nature of God, each stands as a testimony and witness of him, and each affirms anew the standards to which those who would be in his image and likeness, those desiring salvation, must arrive. We must, in the full and complete sense, take his name upon us; that is, we must emulate his character and attributes. Thus, as his name is Righteous, we must be righteous; as his name is Holy, we must be holy; as his name is Merciful, we must be full of mercy, and so on. Further, we must embrace as part of our faith those truths of which his names testify. We must accept him as our Salvation, as our Redeemer. We must know him as our Sanctuary, Comforter, and Hope. We must bow to him as King of kings and Lord of lords. We must serve him as our Master and testify of him as God's Begotten in the flesh, that he, having laid down his life and taken it up again, might thus grant us the promise of immortality and the hope of eternal life.

Adam. 1) Abraham tells us that the name Adam means "first father" (Abr. 1:3). Adam, who was created in the image and likeness of God, was a living symbol of the nature of God. In a very real sense, to know Adam was to know God. As Adam was the father of the human family, so God is the Father of the eternal family. God gave spirit birth to all, Adam made physical birth possible to all. Both Adam and the Father had a "perfect" son who was also in their "express image" (D&C 107:43; Heb. 1:3). In the symbolic sense, Eve (meaning "life") was taken from Adam's side, reminding us that all life comes from God. As Adam gave a name to all things, so God has given purpose to all things.

2) Christ is referred to as the second Adam or the "last Adam," because through the Resurrection he was the firstborn into immortal life (1 Cor. 15:45; see also *Gospel Symbolism*, pp. 146–47). (See also part 1: *Adam.*)

Advocate. Literally intercessor, helper, consoler, comforter. Christ, according to the law of advocacy or intercession, pleads the cause of the faithful Saints before the tribunals of eternity (D&C 29:5; 32:3; 62:1; 110:4; 1 John 2:1).

Almighty. Both the Father and the Son, being omnipotent, are designated by the name-titles Almighty (Gen. 49:25; D&C 121:33), Almighty God (Gen. 17:1; D&C 20:21), Lord Almighty (D&C 84:118; 2 Cor. 6:18), and Lord God Almighty (Rev. 4:8; D&C 109:77). These designations attest that these holy Beings have absolute and universal power. A deep sense of reverence is implicit in the use of such name-titles.

Almighty God. See *Almighty; Lord God Almighty.*

Alpha and Omega. The first and last letters of the Greek alphabet are used as a name-title for Christ. Figuratively, they represent the timeless and eternal nature of the attributes of Deity (D&C 76:4; Rev. 1:8, 17).

Amen. A term derived from a Hebrew word whose root suggests "so be it," "let it be done," "let it be granted." The word *amen* connotes the idea of that which has been unalterably confirmed (Num. 5:22), that which is sure, trustworthy, and faithful. In Revelation 3:14, Amen is used as a synonym for Christ, who affirms the divine purpose and who is the personification of truth.

Angel (Angel of His Presence). Literally "messenger of God." Jacob referred to Christ as "the Angel which redeemed me from all evil" (Gen. 48:16), and Abraham was spared death at the hands of the priests of Pharaoh by "the angel of his [the Almighty's] presence" (Abr. 1:15). In a revelation given to Joseph Smith, the "angel of his presence" is identified as the Savior (D&C 133:52–56). Christ is chief among all the messengers of his Father; he is the Messenger of Salvation, the "messenger of the covenant" (Mal. 3:1).

Anointed. The names Messiah and Christ signify "Anointed One." The anointing of prophets, priests, and kings made of each a type for the Christ. (See also part 1: *Anointing.*) Where the word *anointed* appears in our Old Testament texts, it could properly have been translated to read "Christ." In Psalm 2, in which David, in his perplexity, asks why the heathen rage and people imagine a vain thing, he is recorded as having responded to his own query by saying, "The kings of the earth set themselves, and the rulers take counsel together, against the Lord, and against his anointed" (Ps. 2:2). In a far superior translation, Eusebius renders the verse thus:

Why did the nations rage,
And the peoples imagine vain things?
The kings of the earth set themselves in array,
And the rulers were gathered together,
Against the Lord and against his Christ.
(Eusebius, *The Ecclesiastical History and the
Martyrs of Palestine*, 1:11.)

Apostle. Literally "he that is sent." Paul refers to Christ as
the great Apostle (Heb. 3:1). In the gospel of John, Christ is
quoted well over a hundred times as announcing that he is sent
of his Father, is come to do the will of the Father, and has no
other work to do save that of the Father who sent him. (See also
part 1: *Apostle*.)

Author. Christ is the author of salvation, having extended its
blessings to all men through his atoning sacrifice (see Heb.
12:2). In the full and perfect sense, the Father is the author of
the plan of salvation, a plan that was operative long before
Christ was chosen in the Grand Council to be God's Son "after
the manner of the flesh" and thus to become our Redeemer. Be
it remembered that when the Father asked, "Whom shall I
send?" our eldest brother responded, "Father, thy will be done,
and the glory be thine forever" (Moses 4:2; Abr. 3:27).

Baali. A Hebrew title meaning "my master" (Hosea 2:16).
(See also *Master*.)

Beginning. The Revelator refers to Christ as the "beginning
of the creation of God" (Rev. 3:14). Similarly, Paul calls him the
"firstborn of every creature" (Col. 1:15). Such expressions
could be interpreted to mean Christ's role as the Creator of a
new system of things or of the new covenant which replaced the
Mosaic system. Perhaps both meanings were intended. (See
also *Firstborn*.) Christ is also referred to as the "beginning and
the ending" (see Rev. 1:8). (See also *Alpha and Omega*.)

Begotten of the Father. See *Only Begotten*.

Being. In referring to Deity as a Being (Mosiah 4:19), King
Benjamin reminds us that God is not a conglomeration of laws
—he is not a bodiless, partless, passionless spirit essence filling
the immensity of space. God is an individual, a person, an exalted, resurrected, and glorified man (D&C 130:22). Joseph
Smith explained: "*If the veil were rent today, and the great
God who holds this world in its orbit, and who upholds all
worlds and all things by his power, was to make himself vis-*

*ible, —I say, if you were to see him today, you would see him
like a man in form —like yourselves in all the person, image,
and very form as a man; for Adam was created in the very
fashion, image and likeness of God, and received instruction
from, and walked, talked and conversed with him, as one
man talks and communes with another."* (*Teachings*, p. 345;
italics in original.)

Beloved Son. Christ is the Beloved Son, a designation consis-
tently used by the Father to introduce him (see Matt. 3:17; 17:5;
Mark 1:11; Luke 3:22; D&C 93:15; 3 Ne. 11:7; 21:20: JS-H
1:17). The name signifies Christ's favored or preferential status
among all the Father's spirit children. It also attests to his
divine sonship. Christ is spoken of as the "Beloved and Chosen"
(Moses 4:2), and as being "in the bosom of the Father" (D&C
76:25).

Bishop. This title, meaning "overseer," emphasized Christ's
right, or the right of those properly called in his name, to rule
over the affairs of the Church (1 Pet. 2:25). (See also part 1:
Bishop.)

Blessed. Paul appropriately refers to him from whom all
blessings flow as "the blessed" (1 Tim. 6:15). The scriptures
commonly use the verb *bless* in association with the word *sanctify.* For instance, in the sacramental prayers, the bread and
wine (water) are "blessed and sanctified" (D&C 20:77, 79).
Thus, these sacred symbols are consecrated, or hallowed, to the
memory of Christ and his atoning sacrifice. In its root, *bless*
means "to consecrate with blood."

Branch. A prophetic name used in reference to the promised
Messiah by the prophets of ancient Israel. It was intended to
point attention to the divine assurance that the Messiah would
be an Israelite —a branch or descendant of David. Through
Jeremiah, the Lord said: "Behold, the days come, saith the
Lord, that I will raise unto David a righteous Branch, and a King
shall reign and prosper, and shall execute judgment and justice
in the earth. In his days Judah shall be saved, and Israel shall
dwell safely: and this is his name whereby he shall be called,
THE LORD OUR RIGHTEOUSNESS." (Jer. 23:5-6; see also Jer.
33:15-17; Isa. 11:1-5; Zech. 3:8-10; 6:12-15.) (See also part 1:
Branch.)

Brazen Serpent. The brazen serpent Moses lifted up in the
wilderness was a type for the crucifixion of Christ (Num. 21:6-9;
John 3:14-15). As commentary on this story, Nephi said, "He
[God] sent fiery flying serpents among them; and after they

were bitten he prepared a way that they might be healed; and the labor which they had to perform was to look; and because of the simpleness of the way, or the easiness of it, there were many who perished" (1 Ne. 17:41; Num. 21:6–9; Hel. 8:15; John 3:14–15). (See also part 1: *Serpent.*)

Bread. A metaphor for the Word of God. Jesus spoke of himself as the "bread of God" and the "bread of life" (John 6:33, 48). As manna from heaven was to the physical salvation of Israel in the wilderness, so the acceptance of Jesus as the Christ is to our eternal salvation. The ordinance of the sacrament is the symbolic eating and drinking of the body of Christ (D&C 20:77, 79). To partake of the sacrament is to announce that we have accepted Christ as the staff, or source, of eternal life. It is also to renew our covenant to stand as a witness of him at all times and in all places, seeking to do as he would do and act as he would act. (See also part 1: *Bread.*)

Bridegroom. Christ is the Bridegroom (Matt. 9:15; Mark 2:19; Luke 5:34; John 3:29). The Church, meaning the Saints who have manifested their willingness to take upon themselves his name (D&C 20:77), is his bride in waiting. A frequent characteristic of Hebrew prophecy was to describe apostasy through the metaphor of adultery, and Israel's covenant with God as a marriage (Jer. 2:30–37; Ezek. 16; Hosea 1–3). "Though the term is used with various shades of meaning, 'to know God' in the purest scriptural sense is to have an intimate or covenant relationship with him. The Old Testament references to knowing God and to a man knowing his wife, meaning conceiving a child with her, both use the same Hebrew word (i.e., *yada*). As a man was to leave father and mother and cleave unto his wife and thus become one flesh with her, so he was to leave the things of the world and cleave unto his God and become one with him. As faithfulness in marriage was essential to the nurturing of love, so faithfulness in keeping gospel covenants was understood to be necessary in obtaining a knowledge of God. As love of spouse was strengthened in sacrifice and devotion, so the knowledge of God was obtained in living those covenants with exactness and honor." (Joseph Fielding McConkie, *Prophets and Prophecy,* pp. 171–72.) (See also part 1: *Bridegroom; Bride.*)

Bright and Morning Star. The star of Bethlehem was the sign of the Messiah, linked with the theme of a light being lifted up over the nations. Moses spoke of the coming of the Messiah as a "Star out of Jacob" (Num. 24:17). Job spoke of the righteous host of heaven prior to birth into mortality as the "morning stars" (Job 38:7)—a metaphor which helps explain the symbolism used by John the Revelator in describing Jesus as the "bright and morning star" (Rev. 22:16). In the galaxy of God's spirit offspring, Jesus is the brightest star. (See also *Star of Jacob; Sun;* part 1: *Star.*)

Brightness of His Glory. Christ is the manifestation of his Father. "He that hath seen me hath seen the Father" (John 14:9) was Jesus' response to Philip's request to show the disciples the Father. Joseph Smith said that the Savior "exactly resembled" the Father in "features and likeness" (*History of the Church,* 4:536). Paul, teaching this same truth—that in all things the Son was like the Father—described him as being "the brightness of his [the Father's] glory, and the express image of his person" (Heb. 1:3).

Captain. Presumably it was Jehovah who appeared to Joshua and introduced himself as the "captain of the Lord's host" (Josh. 5:15). With this title, Christ designates himself as the chief soldier or commanding officer in his own army, of which Joshua was the earthly head. Though the scriptures have not done so, it would not be inappropriate for us to give this same designation to Michael, or Adam, who stands at the head of the army of the Lord serving "under the . . . direction of the Holy One" (see Rev. 12:7-9; D&C 78:16). Paul referred to Christ as "the captain of their salvation" (Heb. 2:10), simply meaning that he is the agent of salvation to all who believe and obey the law of God.

Chief Cornerstone. The cornerstone is a long, well-squared stone resting upon the foundation of a building at the terminus of two walls. Its purpose requires that it be carefully chosen. It must be sound—in the case of sandstone, free from weakening cavities; and in the case of limestone, without any white streaks of spar that might lead to cleavage under pressure. As such, the chief cornerstone is a natural type. The Psalmist spoke of Christ as "the stone which the builders refused," which would ultimately become "the head stone of the corner" (Ps. 118:22). The analogy is descriptive of the Jewish rejection of Christ in the name of loyalty to the law of Moses and might also be applied to those today whose loyalty to the Bible blinds them to the greater light of Restoration scriptures about the Savior. Christ applied the prophecy to himself in his mortal ministry (see Matt. 21:42; Luke 20:17).

The book of Isaiah contains this same imagery: "Therefore thus saith the Lord God, Behold, I lay in Zion for a foundation a stone, a tried stone, a precious corner stone, a sure foundation: he that believeth shall not make haste" (Isa. 28:16). Christ is our "tried" and "sure foundation." Hence Paul's imagery of the Church being built "upon the foundation of the apostles and prophets, Jesus Christ himself being the chief corner stone" (Eph. 2:20).

It is Lehi's son Jacob who gives us our most perfect commentary on these ancient texts. "I, Jacob, am led on by the Spirit unto prophesying; for I perceive by the workings of the Spirit which is in me, that by the stumbling of the Jews they will reject the stone upon which they might build and have safe foundation. But behold, according to the scriptures, this stone shall become the great, and the last, and the only sure foundation, upon which the Jews can build." (Jacob 4:15–16.) Then, as an explanation as to how Christ is to become the chief cornerstone, Jacob retells Zenos's allegory (see Jacob 5). (See also part 1: *Cornerstone; Rock; Stone.*)

Chosen One. Similar in meaning to "mine elect" as in Isaiah 42:1 (see also Matt. 12:18), the epithet "Chosen" (Moses 4:2) has reference to our Eternal Father's choice of Christ from among all his spirit children to be our Savior.

Christ. Greek *Christos*, meaning "to anoint"; Hebrew *Meshiah*, meaning "anointed one." Jesus was the Savior's given name; Christ was a surname or title which attested that he was the Messiah or Anointed One for whom Israel had been waiting.

In Old Testament times, anointing was the principal and divinely appointed ceremony in the inauguration of prophets, priests, and kings. The anointing was a ritual consecration, or setting apart, to sacred purposes. It centered in the pouring of pure olive oil upon the head of the one being anointed as a symbolic representation of the Spirit of the Lord that was to be poured out upon the designated leader and, through him, upon the entire nation. All prophets, priests, and kings were intended to be living types or prophecies of what the Christ, the great Prophet, Priest, and King, would be. (See also part 1: *Anointing.*)

Christ Jesus. See *Jesus Christ.*

Christ of God. See *Christ.*

Commander. Isaiah described Christ as the "leader and commander to the people" (Isa. 55:4). (See also *Captain; Lord of Hosts; Lord of Sabaoth.*)

Consolation of Israel. Christ is the "consolation of Israel" (Luke 2:25), for in and through him they have reason for hope. He alone can bring a lasting relief from distress and misery. (See also *Hope of Israel.*)

Cornerstone. See *Chief Cornerstone.*

Counselor. The Eternal Father designates himself as Man of Counsel; Christ, his Son, bears the name-title Counsellor (see Isa. 9:6–7). The name attests to their exalted position as the source of all knowledge, light, and truth.

Covenant. See *Messenger of the Covenant.*

Covert. Isaiah likened Christ to a "covert from the tempest" (Isa. 32:2), that is, a place of shelter and safety. (See also *Refuge*; part 1: *Refuge.*)

Creator. Both the Father and the Son bear the title Creator (*Teachings*, p. 190; Moses 1:33). We are the spirit offspring of the Eternal Father; all other acts of creation are the labor of the son acting by the power and under the direction of the Father (Moses 1:32–33; John 1:1–3; Heb. 1:1–3; D&C 76:22–24). In the creation of the earth, it appears that the Son was assisted by many of the noble and great spirits destined to inhabit it (see Abr. 3:22–24).

Creator of Israel. Only by the providence of Jehovah's hand did the nation of Israel exist anciently, and only by that providence will there be a restoration of that ancient kingdom in the last days (see Isa. 43:14–15; Acts 1:6).

David. Only Moses was more prominent in the story of the Old Testament than David. As with Moses, the events of David's life constituted a remarkable type for the Messiah. Both were known as the son of Jesse, both were born in Bethlehem, both were good shepherds, both would have willingly laid down their life for their sheep, both were the "beloved" of God (that being the meaning of the name David), both were anointed of God, and both were to rule as Israel's king in the day of her triumph and glory.

David, having established for Israel the day of her greatness and glory, is a natural type for Christ during the millennial reign. Thus, the millennial kingdom is spoken of as the kingdom of David, and Christ is described as sitting on the throne of David. Jeremiah wrote of that day, saying: "Behold, the days come, saith the Lord, that I will raise unto David a righteous Branch, and a King shall reign and prosper, and shall execute judgment and justice in the earth. In his days Judah shall be saved, and Israel shall dwell safely: and this is his name

whereby he shall be called, THE LORD OUR RIGHTEOUS-
NESS." (Jer. 23:3-6.) In that future day, gathering Israel would
serve "the Lord their God, and David their king," Jeremiah
prophesied (Jer. 30:9).

Through the pen of Ezekiel the Lord again described the
millennial day: "David my servant shall be king over them; and
they all shall have one shepherd: they shall also walk in my
judgments, and observe my statutes, and do them. And they
shall dwell in the land that I have given unto Jacob my servant,
wherein your fathers have dwelt; and they shall dwell therein,
even they, and their children, and their children's children for
ever: and my servant David shall be their prince for ever."
(Ezek. 37:24-25.)

Not only was David a type for Christ in the sense that Christ
would reign on his throne forever, but also in the sense that
through Christ would come the resurrection which, in spite of
David's sins, would eventually redeem his soul from hell. "I will
make an everlasting covenant with you," the Lord said, "even
the sure mercies of David," which mercies are that the resurrection will pass even upon the wicked. "Behold, I have given him
for a witness to the people" is the promise. (Isa. 55:3-4.) "In
other words, if David, who committed adultery and on whose
hands was found the blood of Uriah, will be resurrected, then all
men should rest in the hope that they shall rise from the grave."
(*Promised Messiah*, p. 452.) (See also *Son of David*; part 1:
David.)

Dayspring. Foreshadowing the birth of Christ, Zacharias,
father of John, prophetically spoke of Christ as the "dayspring
from on high" (Luke 1:78). The dayspring is the dawning of a
new day. Such imagery depicts the birth of Christ as the beginning of a new day, the dawning of a new light, and the coming of
the hope of Israel.

Daystar. Christ is the daystar from on high; he is the bright
and shining light to those who sit in darkness. Peter spoke of the
necessity of those in the Church to enjoy a "more sure word of
prophecy . . . until the day dawn, and the day star arise in your
hearts" (2 Pet. 1:19)—that is, until the second coming of the
Lord, or until the millennial day when Christ will reign personally on earth. Prior to that day when Christ will walk again
among us, the faithful are entitled to the manifestation of his
presence, and that of his Father. Joseph Smith explained, "The
more sure word of prophecy means a man's knowing that he is
sealed up unto eternal life, by revelation and the spirit of proph-

ecy, through the power of the Holy Priesthood" (D&C 131:5). (See also part 1: *Star.*)

Deliverer. Christ is the Deliverer (2 Sam. 22:1–4; Ps. 18:1–3; 40:17; 70:5), a designation akin to Savior or Redeemer. By his protecting hand, Christ has preserved many from harm or injury. Such instances are but the symbolic representation of the greater or spiritual deliverance that is granted to all through his atoning sacrifice, whereby we are delivered from the bondage of death and the grave and whereby our deliverance from the bondage of sin is made possible (Isa. 59:20–21; Rom. 11:25–26). (See also *Redeemer; Savior.*)

Desire of all Nations. Christ is the desire of all nations. "For thus saith the Lord of hosts; Yet once, it is a little while, and I will shake the heavens, and the earth, and the sea, and the dry land; and I will shake all nations, and the desire of all nations shall come" (Hag. 2:6–7). Haggai's prophecy refers to the second coming of Christ. From Nephi's dream we learn that before Christ returns there will be righteous Saints numbered among all nations. It will be these Saints, numbered among the host of the wicked, who will devoutly desire the return of Christ. (1 Ne. 14:12–14.)

The idea of Christ as the desire of all nations does not find expression in modern Bible translations.

Dew. Often dew is mentioned as a type for things that are transitory and passing (see Morm. 4:18; Hosea 6:4); however, Hosea also uses it to represent the powers of Christ to bring a renewal of life (Hosea 14:4–5). The Psalmist uses it to describe the vivacity and vigor of Christ in his earthly ministry (Ps. 110:3). Joseph Smith twice uses it to represent the quiet and unobtrusive manner in which the truths of heaven are revealed to the souls of men (see D&C 121:45; 128:19). (See also part 1: *Dew.*)

Door; Door of the Sheep. Christ is the door, or the "door of the sheep" (John 10:7, 9). The doctrine conveyed here is that Christ is the "way, the truth, and the life" and that no one can approach the Father, either in this world or in the world to come, save by and through him (John 14:6). (See also part 1: *Door; Sheep.*)

Eagle. Moses, writing of Jehovah's great love for Jacob, refers to him as the apple of the Lord's eye. Describing the protective hand of providence as it rested upon this favored son, he wrote: "As an eagle stirreth up her nest, fluttereth over her young, spreadeth abroad her wings, taketh them, beareth them on her wings: So the Lord alone did lead him, and there was no strange god with him" (Deut. 32:10–12). Anciently, and even into the mid-nineteenth century, it was thought that some birds carried their young upon their wings. While none of the imagery in this passage should be taken literally, it is still a beautiful and graphic way for Moses to have portrayed the majesty of God and his love for our ancient father. (See also part 1: *Eagle.*)

Elect. As the faithful of the house of Israel are referred to as the elect of God, so the chief citizen of that house is quite properly designated by that title. "Behold my servant, whom I uphold; mine elect, in whom my soul delighteth; I have put my spirit upon him: he shall bring forth judgment to the Gentiles," wrote Isaiah (Isa. 42:1). Reference to Christ as "mine elect" serves to remind us of his exalted status in our first estate. (See also *Chosen.*)

Endless. Used as a noun and not as an adjective, Endless is one of the names of Deity and signifies his unending, eternal continuance as the supreme, exalted ruler of heaven and earth. "Behold, I am the Lord God Almighty, and Endless is my name," Jehovah told Moses, "for I am without beginning of days or end of years; and is not this endless?" (Moses 1:3; cf. 7:35.) "Endless is my name," the Lord announced anew to Joseph Smith. By combining the name Endless with other terms, the Lord has revealed significant truths: endless life is more than life without end; it is the kind and quality of life that God lives; and endless punishment is not punishment that never ceases, but rather the just and perfect punishment dispensed by God (see D&C 19:4–12).

Ensign. Ensigns (flags, banners, or ornamental standards) are traditionally used to identify military units in their order of march and as rallying points on the field of battle. In their wilderness march, each of the tribes of Israel had their own ensigns in order that all might find their proper place of march or encampment. Since those of all dispensations must rally or gather to Christ and his gospel, it is natural that he, the messenger of salvation, and his standard bearers, the prophets, should be referred to as ensigns. (See Isa. 5:26; 11:10, 12; 18:3; 30:17; Zech. 9:16.) (See also part 1: *Ensign.*)

Eternal Father. "On very formal occasions, as in the revealed sacramental prayers, Deity is addressed as 'God, the *Eternal Father.*' (D&C 20:77–79.) This exalted and sacred name-title combines in one expression the concept of God as an Eternal, exalted Being and his position as the personal Father of the spirits of all men. In the sense in which Christ is called the *Everlasting Father* (Isa. 9:6), he is also the *Eternal Father*, for he is both Eternal and (in special ways) the Father." (*Mormon Doctrine*, p. 236.)

Eternal God. "Both the Father and the Son carry the exalted name-title *Eternal God.* Both are exalted Beings and as such are Eternal; both are from everlasting to everlasting, with all that this phrase connotes; both are beyond finite comprehension in power, dominion, godly attributes, and eternal glory. (D&C 121:32.) By their eternal grace men have been created, redeemed, and placed as possible heirs of all things." (*Mormon Doctrine*, pp. 236–37.)

Eternal Head. This designation of Deity, like the names Eternal God and Eternal Father, emphasizes the endless duration of God's divine supremacy. God will never cease to be God, the Eternal Father will never cease to be the Eternal Father, and the Most High God (Alma 26:14) will never cease to reign as the Eternal Head (Hel. 13:38). Among the weeds of heresy that occasionally find expression in Latter-day Saint circles is the idea that God was elected by and serves at the pleasure of certain intelligences who will impeach him should he displease them. The idea is absolute nonsense; it is without so much as a shred of scriptural or prophetic justification, and is fully contrary to the intent and meaning of such name-titles of Deity as Eternal Father, Eternal God, Eternal Head, Eternal Judge, Eternal Life, Everlasting Father, Everlasting God, and Everlasting Light.

Eternal Judge. See *Judge.*

Eternal King. See *King.*

Eternal Life. See *Life.*

Everlasting Father. "One of Isaiah's great messianic prophecies names Christ as 'The *everlasting Father*' (Isa. 9:6), an expression having reference both to our Lord's everlasting godhood and to the special senses in which he stands as the Father. Since God the Father is both an everlasting Being and the Father of the spirits of men, he also may be properly called the *Everlasting Father.*" (*Mormon Doctrine*, p. 243.)

Everlasting God. "Both the Father and the Son are known by the sacred name-title Everlasting God. (Gen. 21:33; Isa. 9:6; 40:28; Jer. 10:10; Rom. 16:26; D&C 133:34.) Carrying as it does a connotation of eternal continuance and unending existence, this designation of Deity points up the sharp contrast between the living Gods and the false and temporary gods of the world." (*Mormon Doctrine*, p. 243.)

Everlasting Light. See *Light.*

Express Image. Christ represents the Father in both a symbolic and a literal sense. To have heard the doctrine of one is to have heard the doctrine of the other. To have witnessed the actions of one in a given circumstance is to know precisely what the other would have done in the same situation. Thus Christ responded to Philip's request to see the Father, "He that hath seen me hath seen the Father" (John 14:9). Paul tells us that the Son was the "express image" of his Father (Heb. 1:3); Joseph Smith said they "exactly resembled each other in features and likeness" (*History of the Church*, 4:536).

Faithful Witness. See *Witness.*

Father. God is the Father of our spirits; he gave us spirit birth in the same manner as he did to the premortal Christ. Thus we find the resurrected Christ telling Mary, "I ascend unto my Father, and your Father; and to my God, and your God" (John 20:17). Frequently in the scriptures Christ is also spoken of as the Father. Christ is the Father in four senses: 1) He is the creator, under the direction of the Father, of the earth and all that is upon it (see Heb. 1:2; D&C 93:9-10). 2) We are spiritually adopted by Christ through the making of sacred covenants with God. In such covenants we take upon ourselves the name of Christ and thus become his sons and daughters (see Mosiah 5:7-8). 3) Christ has been empowered of God to speak in the first person for him (John 5:43; 17:6-26; D&C 50:43). 4) As our redeemer from death and hell, Christ grants us a newness of life. He broke the bands of death for us, making the resurrection a reality to all men and extending the promise of eternal life to those who are obedient to the laws and ordinances of the gospel. (See 2 Ne. 9:7-13, 15; D&C 76:50-70.)

Father of Heaven. Nephi refers to Christ as the "Father of heaven" in the context of his entering into a covenant with Abraham (see 1 Ne. 22:9). As Abraham was the father of the faithful, so Christ is the father of all who do the works of Abraham (see D&C 132:32), that is, all who make the same covenants that Abraham made and who, like Abraham, prove themselves willing to place their all upon God's altar.

Father of Heaven and of Earth. See *Creator.*

Fatted Calf. In the parable of the prodigal son, the fatted calf that was killed that all might rejoice may be seen as a symbolic representation of Christ and his atoning sacrifice. Having directed the calf to be killed, the father said of the son that was lost, "For this my son was dead, and is alive again" (Luke 15:23-34). The apparent analogy is that we are all prodigals, that we are all lost, and that if we will humble ourselves and return to the Father, seeking his mercy, we can live again through the death of Christ.

First and the Last. See *Alpha and Omega.*

First Begotten of the Dead. As the first to be resurrected — that is, as the first of this earth's inhabitants to come forth from the grave with body and spirit inseparably connected — Christ is referred to as "the first begotten of the dead" (see Rev. 1:5; Col. 1:18).

Firstborn. Christ is the Firstborn, meaning that he was the first spirit child born to God the Father in the premortal existence (see D&C 93:21). John Taylor taught that it was Christ's premortal birthright as the firstborn, provided he was worthy, to be chosen as our Redeemer (see John Taylor, *The Mediation and Atonement*, pp. 136-37). In the nativity story, Luke tells us that Jesus was also Mary's "firstborn son" (Luke 2:6-7). Mary and Joseph subsequently became the parents of both sons and daughters (see Matt. 13:55). (See also part 1: *Firstborn.*)

Firstborn from the Dead. See *Firstborn.*

Gift of God. Jesus Christ is the gift of God (see John 4:10). "God so loved the world," testified the Apostle John, "that he gave his only begotten Son, that whosoever believeth in him should not perish, but have everlasting life" (John 3:16). Indeed, it is beyond the power of words born of a mortal tongue to measure the value of the Atonement. Appropriately, Paul referred to Christ as the "unspeakable gift" (2 Cor. 9:15).

Glory. Christ is "the Lord of glory" (1 Cor. 2:8).

God. The Supreme and Absolute Being, he who is omnipotent, omnipresent, and omniscient, he who is Creator, Ruler, and Preserver of all things, is known to us as God. In him the fulness of all perfection is found; and "in him every good gift and every good principle dwell" (*Lectures on Faith*, 2:2). "There is a God in heaven," modern revelation attests, "who is infinite and eternal, from everlasting to everlasting the same unchangeable God, the framer of heaven and earth, and all things which are in them" (D&C 20:17). "He comprehendeth all things, and all things are before him, and all things are round about him; and he is above all things, and in all things, and is through all things, and is round about all things; and all things are by him, and of him, even God, forever and ever. And again, verily I say unto you, he hath given a law unto all things, by which they move in their times and their seasons; and their courses are fixed, even the courses of the heavens and the earth, which comprehend the earth and all the planets." (D&C 88:41–43.)

God Blessed. God is the source of all good things (see Rom. 9:5); this is attested to in such expressions as the following: *godsend,* meaning "a message sent from God"; *Godspeed,* meaning "God speed you in your journey" or "God prosper you"; *good-bye,* meaning "God be with you"; *good day,* meaning "may God be with you during the day"; *good night,* meaning "God give you a good night"; and so forth (see Eric Partridge, *Origins: A Short Etymological Dictionary of Modern English,* p. 259).

God of Abraham, Isaac, and Jacob. "1. Christ is the *God of our Fathers,* the *God of Abraham, Isaac, and Jacob.* (D&C 136:21–22; Ex. 3:1–16.) It was he who appeared to and covenanted with Abraham (Abr. 2:6–11), who was the one by whom salvation should come (1 Ne. 6:4), and who was destined in due course to come into the world and be crucified for the sins of the world. (1 Ne. 19:7–17.)

"2. Since Abraham, who had the fulness of the gospel, worshiped both the Father and the Son, Peter and others have taken occasion, quite properly, to refer to the Father also as the *God of our Fathers, the God of Abraham, Isaac, and Jacob.* (Acts 3:13; 5:30; 22:14.)" (*Mormon Doctrine,* p. 322.)

God of Heaven. See *Father in Heaven.*

God of Israel. This name is an expression of Christ's special love for the house of Israel into which he was born. Those who are truly of Israel are those with believing blood, those who have covenanted to take upon themselves the name of Christ (3 Ne. 21:6). Those who have suffered shame and persecution in his holy name are especially loved by him. Upon such he bestows the fulness of his mercy, love, and kindness (D&C 133:52–53). These are his chosen people, his anointed servants, those called to take the gospel of salvation to all the nations of the earth (Abr. 2:9, 11).

God of Miracles. "For behold, I am God; and I am a God of miracles; and I will show unto the world that I am the same yesterday, today, and forever; and I work not among the children of men save it be according to their faith" (2 Ne. 27:23). True religion is always a religion of miracles; it is not earthbound, nor does it seek verification at the hands of mortal men.

The principles and practices of true religion are always rooted in the powers of heaven.

God of Nature. Christ is the "God of nature" (1 Ne. 19:12), for it is in and through his almighty power that all things are created, upheld, governed, and controlled. The undeniable evidence of order throughout the universe has caused many who are without faith in the God of miracles to acknowledge nature as their god. In so doing they have chosen to pay homage to the law rather than the Lawgiver. Law is without body, parts, and passions; it is incapable of love, unaffected by faith, and without the power to exalt so much as a single soul.

God of the Whole Earth. As God is the Creator of all things, so he seeks the salvation of all things. His love is not constricted by the bounds of the nation of Israel. Indeed, the purpose for which he created a nation to be known as his chosen people was that there might be some expressly charged with the responsibility to declare his love and concern (i.e., the plan of salvation) among all the peoples of the earth. (See Isa. 54:5.) This name-title also distinguishes the God of heaven from the countless local gods ignorantly worshipped by so many in ancient times.

God of Truth. See *Truth.*

God Omnipotent. See *Omnipotent.*

God with Us. See *Immanuel.*

Good Master. See *Master.*

Good Shepherd. See *Shepherd.*

Governor. When Herod inquired of the chief priests and scribes where the king of the Jews would be born, they quoted the prophecy of Micah: "But thou, Beth-lehem Ephratah, though thou be little among the thousands of Judah, yet out of thee shall he come forth unto me that is to be ruler in Israel" (Micah 5:2). In the King James Version of Matthew, the Micah text reads, "And thou Bethlehem, in the land of Juda, art not the least among the princes of Juda: for out of thee shall come a Governor, that shall rule my people" (Matt. 2:6). Thus *ruler* in the Micah text is rendered *governor* in the Matthean account. The Greek word being translated, *governor*, means "to lead, i.e., *a.* to go before; *b.* to be a leader; to rule, command; to have authority over" (Thayer, *The New Thayer's Greek-English Lexicon of the New Testament*, p. 276a). Thus a number of modern translations have chosen to have the phrase "shall rule my people" rendered "shall be shepherd of my people." This shifts the meaning of the text from Christ's millennial rule when he will reign in power to that of his mortal ministry, which centered in his role of guiding, guarding, folding, and feeding the Lord's flock.

That Christ will indeed reign in power as a governor over the Lord's people there can be no doubt. "The government," Isaiah said, "shall be upon his shoulder: and his name shall be called Wonderful, Counsellor, The mighty God, The everlasting Father, The Prince of Peace. Of the increase of his government and peace there shall be no end, upon the throne of David, and upon his kingdom, to order it, and to establish it with judgment and with justice from henceforth even for ever. The zeal of the Lord of hosts will perform this." (Isa. 6–7.)

Gracious. Those who leave the world and come to Christ come to know that he is kind, benevolent, and full of divine grace. Of such Peter said, "Ye have tasted that the Lord is gracious" (1 Pet. 2:3).

Great Creator. See *Creator.*

Great I Am. See *I Am.*

Great Mediator. See *Mediator.*

Great Physician. See *Physician.*

Great Shepherd. See *Shepherd.*

Guide. He who said "Come follow me" is our sure guide who marks the path all must follow to obtain salvation (see Ps. 48:14). "If we can find a saved being," Joseph Smith asserted, "we may ascertain without much difficulty what all others must be in order to be saved. We think that it will not be a matter of dispute, that two beings who are unlike each other cannot both be saved; for whatever constitutes the salvation of one will constitute the salvation of every creature which will be saved; and if we find one saved being in all existence, we may see what all others must be, or else not be saved. We ask, then, where is the prototype? or where is the saved being? We conclude . . . that it is Christ." (*Lectures on Faith* 7:9.)

Head. Regarded, with the heart, as the chief member of the body, the word *head* implies a preeminent and authoritative position. It is used symbolically of Jesus in several ways.

1) "The head of every man is Christ" (1 Cor. 11:3). "At the name of Jesus every knee should bow" (Philip. 2:10), and even among those who inherit the telestial kingdom, we are told that "every tongue shall confess to him who sits upon the throne forever and ever; for they shall be judged according to their works" (D&C 76:110–11). All must acknowledge Christ as the Creator, Preserver, Ruler, and Savior. "For by him were all things

created, that are in heaven, and that are in earth, visible and invisible, whether they be thrones, or dominions, or principalities, or powers: all things were created by him, and for him: and he is before all things, and by him all things consist" (Col. 1:16-17).

2) "The head of the body, the church" (Col. 1:18). In all things preeminence rests with Christ. We become members of his Church by taking upon ourselves his name, and we work out our salvation by becoming one with him. "Whatsoever ye shall do, ye shall do it in my name; therefore ye shall call the church in my name; and ye shall call upon the Father in my name that he will bless the church for my sake. . . . therefore ye shall call whatsoever things ye do call, in my name; therefore if ye call upon the Father, for the church, if it be in my name the Father will hear you; and if it so be that the church is built upon my gospel then will the Father show forth his own works in it." (3 Ne. 27:7-10.)

3. "The head of the corner" (Matt. 21:42). (See *Chief Cornerstone*.)

Heir of all things. The Son of God is a rightful heir of his divine Father, and through obedience he became equal with the Father in power, might, and dominion. Paul testified to those of his day that "God, who at sundry times and in divers manners spake in time past unto the fathers by the prophets, hath in these last days spoken unto us by his Son, whom he hath appointed heir of all things, by whom also he made the worlds; who being the brightness of his glory, and the express image of his person, and upholding all things by the word of his power, when he had by himself purged our sins, sat down on the right hand of the Majesty on high" (Heb. 1:1-3).

Help. "Our soul waiteth for the Lord: he is our help and our shield" (Ps. 33:20; 40:17).

Heritage. To Abraham's family, meaning those of the believing blood, has come a legacy of spiritual riches. Their inheritance is one of faith and spiritual power. To all such, God is their heritage (see Isa. 58:14).

Highest. One of the name-titles given the Father to designate his exalted rank even in the Godhead is that of the Highest. Christ testified, saying, "My Father is greater than I" (John 14:28). Announcing the birth of the Messiah, Gabriel declared that the Christ "shall be great, and shall be called the Son of the Highest" (Luke 1:32), or, as rendered in Today's English Version, "He will be great and will be called the Son of the Most High God" (Luke 1:32). The revelation on the degrees of glory states that those who obtain the celestial kingdom will enjoy the glory of the sun, "even the glory of *God, the highest of all*" (D&C 76:70; italics added).

High Priest. By divine decree, the higher or Melchizedek Priesthood "administereth the gospel and holdeth the key of the mysteries of the kingdom, even the key of the knowledge of God" (D&C 84:19). From the days of Moses to those of Christ it was the rightful duty of the high priest in the lesser priesthood to instruct the nation of Israel in the doctrine of sin and its expiation and to officiate in the making of national covenants. The high priest was the source through which spiritual life was communicated to the Lord's people. His annual entrance into the Holy of Holies on the Day of Atonement was a prophetic representation of Christ's ascension into heaven and his intercessory role with the Father. The daily work of the priests at the altar of the temple was symbolic of the efficacy of the blood of the Lamb of God who, through the willing sacrifice of his own life, would make the atonement that was infinite and eternal. Thus Christ, the perfect anti-type of all priesthood functions, and whom Paul properly calls the "great high priest," was both mediator and sacrifice. (Heb. 4:14; 3:1.) (See also part 1: *High Priest.*)

Holy. In this designation for Christ, *Holy* is being used as a noun rather than as an adjective. That which is holy is sacred rather than secular; it is that which has been "set apart," "consecrated," or "dedicated" to God. Obviously, the purpose of the name is to convey the concept of the supreme holiness and perfection embodied in the Son of Man of Holiness (see Moses 6:57). (See also *Holy One.*)

Holy Child Jesus. See *Holy Servant.*

Holy God. See *God.*

Holy Messiah. Christ is called by the name Holy Messiah, when the purpose is to bring to mind both his holy and perfected state and his position as Deliverer and King (see 2 Ne. 2:6, 8). (See *Messiah.*)

Holy One. The expression "the Holy One" or "the Holy One of God" is used several times in the New Testament to designate the Lord. We find it first on the lips of the demoniac who, recognizing Jesus of Nazareth, asked, "Art thou come to destroy us? I know thee who thou art, the Holy One of God." (Mark 1:24; Luke 4:34.) The next time the title is ascribed to him is when Peter, striving to find words to answer the Lord's question as to whom the Twelve would go if they intended to abandon him: "Lord, to whom shall we go? thou hast the words of eternal life.

And we believe and are sure that thou art that Christ, the Son of the living God." (John 6:68-69.) Peter would later testify against those who put Christ to death, saying that they had "disowned the Holy and Righteous One" (New American Standard Bible, Acts 3:14); and John wrote that the Saints had received "an anointing" from the "Holy One" (1 John 2:20, 27).

Holy One of Israel. "O then, my beloved brethren, come unto the Lord, the Holy One. Remember that his paths are righteous. Behold, the way for man is narrow, but it lieth in a straight course before him, and the keeper of the gate is the Holy One of Israel; and he employeth no servant there; and there is none other way save it be by the gate; for he cannot be deceived, for the Lord God is his name." (2 Ne. 9:41.) The appellation Holy One of Israel signifies that Christ, who is without sin, was chosen and consecrated of God, as was Israel, to be the servant of the Father and to be the source of salvation to all the nations of the earth.

Holy One of Jacob. See *Holy One of Israel.*

Holy Servant. Peter, as recorded in the King James Version, refers to Christ as the "holy child Jesus" (Acts 4:27, 30). This is a mistranslation, and is rendered "Holy Servant" in virtually all other translations. (See also *Servant.*)

Hope of Glory. As used in the scriptures, hope is the desire of faithful people to be saved in the kingdom of God (see Alma 5:10). Thus it becomes an appropriate appellation for him through whom hope and salvation are possible — the Lord Jesus Christ (see Col. 1:27). Lehi's son Jacob wrote, "For this intent have we written these things, that they may know that we knew of Christ, and we had a hope of his glory many hundred years before his coming; and not only we ourselves had a hope of his glory, but also all the holy prophets which were before us" (Jacob 4:4).

Horn of Salvation. The expression "an horn of salvation" in the song of Zacharias refers to the promised Messiah (Luke 1:69). *Horn* is frequently used in the scriptures as a symbol of power and strength. Since a horn in animals is used as a weapon of attack rather than of defense, it is held by some to be a symbol of aggressive strength. Thus "horn of salvation" implies "strength of salvation" or "power of salvation." (See also part 1: *Horn.*)

Husband. In scriptural imagery, Christ is the Bridegroom who claims his bride (the Church), celebrates their marriage supper, and then becomes the Husband of his wife. "As a Husband he shall deal intimately, with tenderness and compassion, toward the remnant of his people who have returned to enjoy millennial rest with him" (*Mormon Doctrine*, p. 370). (See also part 1: *Husband.*)

I Am. To the religious leaders who disputed Christ's claim that he was the Son of God and proceeded from his Father came an astounding declaration: "Verily, verily, I say unto you, Before Abraham was, I am" (John 8:58). Thus he announced himself to the nation of the Jews as Jehovah, the very name he had used when he appeared before the likes of Abraham, Isaac, Jacob, and Moses (see JST, Ex. 6:3). It is in the person of Jesus that all that Jehovah promised his covenant people finds realization:

"I am the bread of life" (John 6:35).
"I am the light of the world" (John 8:12; 9:5).
"I am the door of the sheep" (John 10:7).
"I am the good shepherd" (John 10:11).
"I am from above . . . I am not of this world" (John 8:23).
"I am the resurrection, and the life" (John 11:25).
"I am the way, the truth, and the life" (John 14:6).
"I am the true vine" (John 15:1, 5).
"I am the root and the offspring of David" (Rev. 22:16).

To those of our dispensation, the Lord said: "Hearken and listen to the voice of him who is from all eternity to all eternity, the Great I AM, even Jesus Christ" (D&C 39:1). Thus the great doctrine of God's presence among his people, that marvelous assurance that "from eternity to eternity he is the same" (D&C 76:4) is proclaimed anew. That God who spoke to Abraham speaks to us; that God who covenanted with Isaac and Jacob covenants with us; that God who endowed Moses with power from on high and led the children of Israel through the wilderness will endow us with that same power and lead us to our land of promise. (See also *Jehovah.*)

Image of God. Paul referred to Christ as the "image of [God's] person," meaning that he was a revelation of his Father (Heb. 1:3). "If ye had known me, ye should have known my Father also," Christ explained to his chosen disciples at the Last Supper, "and from henceforth ye know him, and have seen him. Philip saith unto him, Lord, shew us the Father, and it sufficeth us. Jesus saith unto him, Have I been so long time with you, and yet hast thou not known me, Philip? he that hath seen me hath seen the Father." (John 14:7-9.) This is simply to say that because the Son says and does that which the Father would say and do in the same situation, to have seen the one is to have seen the other.

In the case of the Father and the Son, they also share a perfect physical resemblance. Describing their appearance in an account of the First Vision, Joseph Smith said they "exactly resembled each other in features and likeness" (*History of the Church*, 4:536).

Immanuel. Literally "God is with us." Immanuel is a symbolic name given to the child whose birth was foretold by Isaiah as the sign to Ahaz and his court that God would deliver them from their enemies (Isa. 7:14; 8:8). Matthew applies the name to Jesus (Matt. 1:23).

Ishi. A Hebrew title meaning "my husband" (Hosea 2:16). (See also *Husband*.)

JAH. "Sing unto God, sing praises to his name: extol him that rideth upon the heavens by his name JAH, and rejoice before him" (Ps. 68:4). The name Jah is a contraction for Jehovah and means "the self-existent" or "eternal."

Jehovah. Jehovah is the covenant or proper name of the God of Israel. Considerable confusion shrouds the name because of the false traditions of the Jews. These traditions have found expression in the preservation of the texts of the Bible to the extent that the proper name of Deity has become a stumbling block to many Bible readers and a matter of contention between various religious sects.

Manifesting himself to Abraham, the Lord said, "My name is Jehovah, and I know the end from the beginning; therefore my hand shall be over thee" (Abr. 2:8). This was followed by the making of what we know as the Abrahamic covenant, which includes the promise that Abraham's seed would have claim upon the priesthood and were to assume the responsibility to declare the gospel of salvation among all the nations of the earth—and this in the name of the Lord Jehovah (see Abr. 2:6-11).

The following verses in the book of Exodus have been the source of confusion: "And God spake unto Moses, and said unto him, I am the Lord: and I appeared unto Abraham, unto Isaac, and unto Jacob, by the name of God Almighty, but by my name JEHOVAH was I not known to them" (Ex. 6:2-3). Thus the text states that Abraham, Isaac, and Jacob did not know the Lord by the sacred name Jehovah. Yet we know that the name Jehovah was in use even long before the days of Abraham. For instance, Genesis 2:4, which reads "Lord God," should have been rendered "Jehovah Elohim." Similarly, Abraham expressly addressed the Lord by the name Adoni (Lord) Jehovah (Gen. 15:2), and God reveals himself to Abraham by that name, saying, "I am the Lord that brought thee out of Ur of the Chaldees" (Gen. 15:7). It will also be remembered that Abraham named the place where he was called upon to offer Isaac as a sacrifice "Jehovah-jireh" (Gen. 22:14). For a Latter-day Saint, however, the matter is simply resolved. Joseph Smith corrected the Exodus text in his inspired translation of the Bible. There the text simply reads: "And I appeared unto Abraham, unto Isaac, and unto Jacob. I am the Lord God Almighty; the Lord JEHOVAH. And was not my name known unto them?" (JST, Ex. 6:3).

The pronunciation of this name by which God was known to the Hebrews has been lost, the Jews themselves scrupulously avoiding every mention of it. The Jewish tradition, which had its origin in reverence, degenerated into a superstition. The commandment against blaspheming the name of the Lord was incorrectly rendered to state that anyone, be he stranger or native, that named the name of the Lord, be put to death (LXX, Lev. 24:16; see also the New English Bible, which states that "whosoever utters the Name of the Lord shall be put to death").

That proper reverence was due the holy name is beyond question. From a revelation given to Joseph Smith we learn that anciently the Priesthood was known as *"the Holy Priesthood, after the Order of the Son of God.* But out of respect or reverence to the name of the Supreme Being, to avoid the too frequent repetition of his name, they, the church, in ancient days, called that priesthood after Melchizedek, or the Melchizedek Priesthood." (D&C 107:3-4.) It is the excessive reverence which the Jews entertained for the sacred name which has resulted in a loss of clarity and understanding in the Bible text. Forbidden to pronounce the name, they would, in reading, substitute either Adonai, meaning "Lord," or Elohim, meaning "God," according to the vowel points by which it was accompanied. In the King James Version, the Jewish custom has been followed, and the name is generally denoted by "Lord" or God" printed in a capital letter followed by small capitals.

Most scholars believe that the name Jehovah (this is the Anglicized form of the name Yahweh) is derived from an old form of the Hebrew verb meaning "to be" or "to become." The word stresses existence, with the meaning being that expressed in Exodus 3:14: "I AM." This has been understood to emphasize the unchanging nature of God, particularly his changeless commitment to the faithful.

But the name suggests more, especially in the context of its introduction to Israel. This came as Moses, standing before the burning bush, hesitated to accept God's commission. "Moses said unto God, Who am I, that I should go unto Pharaoh, and that I should bring forth the children of Israel out of Egypt?" He was then assured that God would be with him. Again he asked, "Behold, when I come unto the children of Israel, and shall say unto them, The God of your fathers hath sent me unto you; and they shall say to me, What is his name? what shall I say unto them?" The divine response was "I AM THAT I AM," and God said, "Thus shalt thou say unto the children of Israel, I AM hath sent me unto you." Moses was further instructed to say that "the Lord God of your fathers, the God of Abraham, the God of Isaac, and the God of Jacob, hath sent me unto you: this is my name for ever, and this is my memorial unto all generations." (Ex. 3:11–15.)

Shortly thereafter, God revealed to Moses that he had been known to the ancient fathers by the name Jehovah and that by that name he had delivered them, entered into covenants with them, and granted them a land of promise. Thus the name Jehovah becomes God's affirmation that he is an ever-present God rather than the God of history or of the prophetic future. Jehovah is his personal name, a name reaching beyond the appellations of Lord and God, for it is a manifestation of his nature and his involvement with his covenant people.

Jesus. Jesus is the Greek equivalent for the Hebrew name Joshua, which means "Jehovah is salvation." Moses' successor, Joshua, is represented in the New Testament by the name Jesus (Acts 7:45; Heb. 4:8). Both Mary and Joseph were commanded by the angel of the Lord to name the Christ child Jesus (Luke 1:31; Matt. 1:21). Thus it is the personal name by which the Lord is known in the Gospels and the Acts, but generally in the Epistles it appears in combination with "Christ" or other appellatives.

"JE—This first syllable Je, or Jeho, or Jah-Jehovah—this name of God, speaks of the divine authority that Jesus came as the great I AM. The syllable tells us of His eternal Godhead, of

His covenant relations, and of His mighty powers and condescending love. All the virtues dimly seen in the Jehovah of old became manifest in Him who came from heaven.

"SUS—This other syllable is associated with the name *Oshea, Hosea,* or *Houshaia,* meaning 'help,' which was the name of one of the spies sent out by Moses, but which he changed to *Jehosua,* signifying 'Jehovah our Saviour,' or 'Deliverer,' or 'The help of Jehovah' (Numbers 13:16). . . . Thus in this second part of [the name] Jesus, we are assured of pardon and peace, of deliverance from sin and hell." (Herbert Lockyer, *All the Divine Names and Titles in the Bible,* p. 174.)

Jesus Christ. The personal name given the Son of God for the purpose of his mortal ministry was Jesus. Christ, the Savior's surname, is the Greek equivalent of the Hebrew Messiah, which means "anointed." Thus, to anoint a prophet, priest, or king was to make of him a type of what the Christ would be as Israel's Prophet, Priest, and King. By force of usage, the name or title Christ is also used as a personal name for the Savior. (See also *Jesus.*)

Judge. Christ is Judge of the living and the dead (see Acts 10:42). To him the Father "hath committed all judgment" (John 5:22). Having redeemed us from death with the cost of his own blood, and from sin with the price of his own suffering, Christ is rightfully our judge, having bought us with a price (1 Cor. 6:20). It is his right to command obedience and to punish its counterpart.

His judgment is administered with perfect justice (Isa. 9:7); and "with righteousness shall he judge the poor, and reprove with equity for the meek of the earth" (Isa. 11:4). "As I hear, I judge," he said, "and my judgment is just; because I seek not mine own will, but the will of the Father which hath sent me" (John 5:30). In the coming day of judgment, when he judges whose judgment is just, perfect justice will be administered to all men. "Shall not the Judge of all the earth do right?" (Gen. 18:25; Ps. 94:1-2). (See also part 1: *Judges.*)

Judge of Israel. See *Judge.*

Just One. The word *just* comes from the Latin *jus,* which means "law" or "right." The Just One or Righteous One is a common description of Christ in the New Testament (Acts 22:14; 1 John 2:1; 1 Pet. 3:18). Christ's righteousness in his judicial reign means that in covenant faithfulness he saves his people. The "justified" are those who have rightful claim upon the promise of salvation, having kept their covenants with exactness and honor. Thus Christ is the Just One, signifying that perfect justice, equity, judgment, impartiality, and righteousness are embodied in his person. (See also *Righteous.*)

Keeper of the Gate. "The keeper of the gate," Jacob testified, "is the Holy One of Israel; and he employeth no servant there." Further, there is no other way one can enter the heavenly kingdom, "for he cannot be deceived, for the Lord God is his name" (2 Ne. 9:41).

The gate symbolized entrance into a new life, the passage from one state or world to another. "Whoso cometh in at the gate and climbeth up by me," Christ said, "shall never fall" (Moses 7:53). Anciently, kings sat in judgment at gates, "probably as sacred places of divine power" (Cooper, *An Illustrated Encyclopaedia of Traditional Symbols*, p. 73). (See also *Door of the Sheep;* part 1: *Gate.*)

King. "I am Messiah, the King of Zion," the premortal Christ proclaimed to Enoch (Moses 7:53). Millenniums later, David, exulting that Mount Zion was "the joy of the whole earth," acclaimed it also as "the city of the great King, . . . the city of the Lord of hosts, . . . the city of our God." (Ps. 48:1–8.) "Rejoice greatly, O daughter of Zion; shout, O daughter of Jerusalem," wrote Zachariah. "Behold, thy King cometh unto thee: he is just, and having salvation; . . . he shall speak peace unto the heathen: and his dominion shall be from sea even to sea, and from the river even to the ends of the earth." (Zech. 9:9–10.) Heralding Christ's birth, Gabriel declared: "He shall reign over the house of Jacob for ever; and of his kingdom there shall be no end" (Luke 1:33).

Christ is Israel's King, the Church his earthly kingdom. The meridian Saints regarded themselves as the vassals of their divinely anointed King. Under his regal sway they had been delivered from the power of darkness (Col. 1:13) and would yet enjoy a complete triumph over all that is ungodly and unjust, for their king is destined to "reign in righteousness" (Isa. 32:1). To those of faith, Christ is the Ruler, Lawgiver, and Sovereign in whom all power rests. (See also part 1: *King.*)

King of Glory. This name-title for Christ signifies both his status as King and the transcendent glory that attends him. Only those who are clean and pure, those worthy to enter the temple, those able to stand on holy ground, can endure the glory of God. Declaring these truths, the Psalmist asked, "Who shall ascend into the hill of the Lord? or who shall stand in his holy place?" And in response he declares: "He that hath clean hands, and a pure heart; who hath not lifted up his soul unto vanity, nor sworn deceitfully. He shall receive the blessing from the Lord, and righteousness from the God of his salvation. This is the generation of them that seek him, that seek thy face, O Jacob. Selah. Lift up your heads, O ye gates; and be ye lift up, ye everlasting doors; and the King of glory shall come in." (Ps. 24:3-7.)

King of Heaven. Christ and God are our Kings and will so rule and reign throughout the endless eternities. To the extent that the heavenly order finds expression on our mortal earth, it is representative of the divine monarchy. Indeed, salvation consists in our being ordained both priests and kings, priestesses and queens, that we too might rule endless creations in like manner. "And to him who overcometh, and keepeth my commandments unto the end, will I give power over many kingdoms; and he shall rule them with the word of God; and they shall be in his hands as the vessels of clay in the hands of a potter; and he shall govern them by faith, with equity and justice, even as I received of my Father." (JST, Rev. 2:26-27; Rev. 1:5-6.)

King of Israel. See *King.*

King of Kings. When Christ, the suffering servant, he who descended below all things, returns in glory and power to rule and reign, he will come as "KING OF KINGS, AND LORD OF LORDS" (Rev. 19:16). His power will be supreme; he will have complete dominion over all the earth. Those who rule will do so at his pleasure and in his name. Though the title King of kings embraces all such things, it reaches far beyond them. All who gain exaltation are ordained kings and queens, priests and priestesses, in which positions they shall exercise power and authority in the Lord's eternal kingdoms throughout an endless eternity.

King of the Jews. "Though rejected and crucified by them, Christ was and is the *King of the Jews.* Messianic prophecies had foretold the glorious reign of a great King, the King of Israel. (Zech. 9:9-10.) The Jews were looking forward to a temporal reign in which all nations of the earth would go up from year to year 'to worship the King, the Lord of hosts,' in Jerusalem (Zech. 14:16-21), an event which in reality is to occur during the Millennium when Christ, the King, reigns personally on earth. (A of F 1:10.)

"Accordingly, when our Lord came ministering among the Jews and proclaiming his divine Sonship, the great query in the minds of the people was whether this was the promised King. He was believed to be of the lineage of David. (Matt. 1:1-16; Luke 3:23-38.) On one occasion the people sought to make him king by force. (John 6:15.) On another the multitudes hailed him publicly as the King of Israel. (Matt. 21:1-11; Luke 19:28-40; John 12:12-16.) Pilate asked him: 'Art thou the King of the Jews?' to which query he received an affirmative answer, with the qualifying explanation: 'My kingdom is not of this world' (John 18:33-37; Luke 23:1-4), a doctrine that our Lord had also taught previously. (Luke 22:24-30.) Then Pilate, when the Jews chanted, 'We have no king but Caesar,' ordered the crucifixion and the placing of a writing above our Lord's head reading: 'JESUS OF NAZARETH THE KING OF THE JEWS.' (John 19:14-22.)

"At the Second Coming the Jews shall be converted, recognize him whom they crucified, and 'lament because they persecuted their king.' (D&C 45:51-53; Zech. 12:10-14; 13:6.)" (*Mormon Doctrine*, p. 424.)

King of Zion. In the Millennium, after the return of Enoch's city, Christ will reign personally on earth as "the King of Zion" (Moses 7:53, 63-64; Rev. 20:4). To those attempting to establish a modern day Zion the Lord said, "Verily I say unto you that in time ye shall have no king nor ruler, for I will be your king and watch over you. Wherefore, hear my voice and follow me, and you shall be a free people, and ye shall have no laws but my laws when I come, for I am your lawgiver, and what can stay my hand?" (D&C 38:21-22; 45:59.)

Lamb. The ordinance of animal sacrifice was first taught to Adam in the Garden of Eden. From that moment through the long millennia until Christ became the "great and last sacrifice," many millions of sheep were sacrificed in the Israelite communities. Each of these sacrifices became "a similitude of the sacrifice of the Only Begotten of the Father" (Moses 5:7; D&C 138:13). The sacrifice of the lamb was a prophecy of and a type for the atoning sacrifice of Christ.

In six ways the sacrifical lamb was a type for Jesus Christ. 1) No bones of the lamb were to be broken (Ps. 34:20; Ex. 12:46; John 19:36). 2) The lamb must be perfect (Mal. 1:7-14; 3 Ne. 12:48). 3) The lamb must be without blemish (Ex. 12:5; Heb.

7:26–27; 1 Pet. 2:22). 4) The flesh of the lamb was to be eaten (Ex. 12:8; John 6:53–55). 5) The lamb must be the firstborn (Ex. 13:2; D&C 93:21). 6) The lamb must be a male (Ex. 12:5; Matt. 1:21).

Above all, as the blood of the lamb saved the ancient Israelites from temporal death during the first Passover, even so will Christ, "our passover" (1 Cor. 5:7), save those of righteous Israel from spiritual death (Heb. 9:20–22). (See also part 1: *Lamb.*)

Lawgiver. Jesus Christ is "our lawgiver" (Isa. 33:22; D&C 45:59). The Lord has stated: "Wherefore, hear my voice and follow me, and you shall be a free people, and ye shall have no laws but my laws when I come, for I am your lawgiver" (D&C 38:22); "I am the law" (3 Ne. 15:9).

Leader. Speaking messianically, Isaiah referred to Christ as the leader and commander of the people (Isa. 55:4). As a leader (or a shepherd), Jesus directs his sheep to the green pastures and leads them "beside the still waters" (Ps. 23:2). He "calleth his own sheep by name, and leadeth them out" (John 10:3). According to the Book of Mormon, he "shall lead them, even by the springs of water shall he guide them" (1 Ne. 21:10).

As the "captain of [our] salvation" (Heb. 2:10), the Lord states, "I will lead you along" (D&C 78:18); more specifically, the injunction is "Be thou humble; and the Lord thy God shall lead thee by the hand" (D&C 112:10; see also Abr. 1:18).

Christ is not the leader of individuals alone, but he directs and leads the nation of Israel as well. In Doctrine and Covenants 38:33, the Lord states, "For Israel shall be saved, and I will lead them whithersoever I will."

Life. Jesus is "the life" of the world (John 1:4) in three principal ways:

1) The scriptures often describe Jesus Christ as "the light and the life of the world" (D&C 12:9; 10:70; 34:2; 39:2; 45:7; 3 Ne. 11:11; 9:18). It is this "light of Christ" which is "given to every man" (Moro. 7:15–18) which provides life to all things. Jesus is "the light which is in all things, which giveth life to all things" (D&C 88:13). This "light proceedeth forth from the presence of God to fill the immensity of space" (D&C 88:12). In this way the Lord "giveth life unto the world" (John 6:33). He is the "Word of life" (1 John 1:1) and the "Prince of life" (Acts 3:15); and "in him was the life of men" (D&C 93:9).

2) Through the Atonement, Christ made eternal life available to those who are obedient to the commandments. The

Apostle John wrote, "He that believeth on the Son hath ever-lasting life: and he that believeth not the Son shall not see life" (John 3:36). Elsewhere John wrote that "eternal life" is in the Son and that "he that hath the Son hath life; and he that hath not the Son of God hath not life" (1 John 5:11-12). Accordingly, Jesus tells his listeners, "I give unto them [those souls who are righteous] eternal life" (John 10:28). Paul's epistle to the Romans includes this concise and relevant statement: "The wages of sin is death [spiritual death]; but the gift of God is eternal life through Jesus Christ our Lord" (Rom. 6:23).

3) Through the Atonement, the Lord made it possible for the resurrection to come about, partly because he was given power from the Father "to have life in himself" (John 5:26). Thus Jesus said unto Martha, "I am the resurrection, and the life: he that believeth in me, though he were dead, yet shall he live" (John 11:25).

In sum, we see that Jesus is life, that he has life, and that he gives both physical and spiritual life through his atonement.

Light. Jesus is "the light of the sun, . . . the light of the moon, . . . the light of the stars," (D&C 88:7-9) and "the light of the world" (John 8:12). He is the "true Light, which lighteth every man that cometh into the world" (John 1:9; D&C 93:2; Moro. 7:16-19). During the great millennial day, mankind will "need no candle, neither light of the sun," for the Lord will be their light (Rev. 22:5; Isa. 60:19).

With words which are to be had only through revelation, in a declaration not understood by the greatest of the world's scholars, scientists, and intellectuals, the Lord revealed to the Prophet Joseph Smith his role as the light: "And the light which shineth, which giveth you light, is through him who enlighteneth your eyes, which is the same light that quickeneth your understandings; . . . the light which is in all things, which giveth life to all things, which is the law by which all things are governed, even the power of God who sitteth upon his throne" (D&C 88:11-13). (See also part 1: *Light.*)

Lion. Since the lion was the emblem of the tribe of Judah (Gen. 49:8-12), and since Jesus Christ "sprang out of Juda" (Heb. 7:14), we find John the Revelator referring to Jesus as the "Lion of the tribe of Juda" (Rev. 5:5). At first glance it may seem peculiar to refer to the Lord as a lion, but the scriptures make it evident that this majestic animal has many characteristics that are similar in nature to those of Christ. For instance, a lion is valiant (2 Sam. 17:10) and fearless (Nahum 2:11). He is noted for his fierceness (Job 10:16; 28:8) and, as the king of beasts, his majesty (Prov. 30:29–30). The lion is superior in strength to all other beasts (Prov. 30:30) and to man (Judg. 14:18). Christ, the King of kings, has all of these characteristics. Also, a lion is known to hide in "secret places" (Ps. 17:12; Lam. 3:10), as does the Lord, meaning that God's dwelling place is unknown to man. (See also part 1: *Lion.*)

Living God. Jesus Christ is an active God—not the God of history but the God of the present. He is not an unknown god whom his saints "ignorantly worship" (Acts 17:23). Neither is he a golden idol formed by a "smith with the tongs," or a wooden statue carved by "the carpenter [who] stretcheth out his rule" (Isa. 44:12–13). Rather he is "the true and living God" (1 Ne. 17:30; D&C 20:19; Alma 7:6; 11:27) with "a body of flesh and bones as tangible as man's" (D&C 130:22). We learn that the Father also is a "living God," for Nephi refers to Jesus Christ as the "Son of the living God" (2 Ne. 31:16).

Living Stone. Jesus is referred to as a stone and a rock. However, unlike the dead, lifeless stones known to be found upon the hillsides and on the valley floors, he is the "living stone" (1 Pet. 2:4). (See also *Rock; Stone.*)

Lord. The title Lord is the most frequently used name for Jesus Christ in holy writ. In the Bible, this English word is regularly employed by the King James translators in place of three Hebrew words and four Greek words. Thus, in the Old Testament record, "Lord" replaces *Adonnay* at least 300 times, *Yahweh* on at least 5,300 occasions, and *Yah* approximately 50 times. In the New Testament record, this divine title was used once in place of *rabboni*, five times for *despotes*, once for *megistanes*, and some 700 times for *kyrios.*

It is helpful to see the New Testament uses of the title Lord with the name-titles accompanying them:

Lord (1 Cor. 12:3)
Lord Almighty (2 Cor. 6:18)
Lord and Christ (Acts 2:36)
My Lord and my God (John 20:28)
Lord and Master (John 13:13–14)
Lord and Saviour (2 Pet. 3:2)
Lord and Saviour Jesus Christ (2 Pet. 1:11)
Lord Christ (Col. 3:24)
Lord from heaven (1 Cor. 15:47)
Lord God Almighty (Rev. 11:17)
Lord God omnipotent (Rev. 19:6)

Lord Jesus (Acts 1:21)
Lord Jesus Christ (Acts 11:17)
Lord Jesus Christ our Saviour (Titus 1:4)
Lord Jesus Christ, the Son of the Father (2 John 1:3)
Lord of all (Acts 10:36)
Lord of glory (1 Cor. 2:8)
Lord of the harvest (Matt. 9:38)
Lord of lords (Rev. 17:14)
Lord of peace (2 Thes. 3:16)
Lord of the Sabbath (Luke 6:5)
Lord of the dead and living (Rom. 14:9)
Lord thy God (Matt. 4:7)

Lord God. The English title Lord God (D&C 109:77; 121:4; Moses 3:4; 2 Ne. 1:5), a translation from the Hebrew *Yahweh Elohim* (literally "Jehovah Gods"), is a superlative appellation denoting the plurality of Deity's attributes. He is the most merciful, the most loving, the most just, the most righteous, the most truthful of all beings—just to name a few of his attributes. Under this title, Jesus has been called "the Lord God of Abraham" (Gen. 28:13), "the Lord God of Israel" (Ex. 32:27), "the Lord God of Elijah" (2 Kgs. 2:14), the "Lord God of our fathers" (2 Chr. 20:6), "the Lord God of hosts" (1 Kgs. 19:10), and "Lord God Almighty" (Rev. 4:8; 11:17).

Lord God Almighty. In a vocative statement not unlike other poetic scripture, Jacob referred to Jesus Christ as the "Lord God Almighty." He stated: "Holy, holy are thy judgments, O Lord God Almighty—but I know my guilt" (2 Ne. 9:46). The word *Almighty* suggests the supreme power and might of the Lord. (See also *Almighty.*)

Lord God of Hosts. See *Lord of Hosts; Lord of Sabaoth.*

Lord God Omnipotent. King Benjamin referred to Jesus Christ as the "Lord Omnipotent" (Mosiah 3:5, 17–18; 5:2) and the "Lord God Omnipotent" (Mosiah 3:21; 5:15). The word *omnipotent* denotes "all power" or "unlimited power" and is an apt description of Deity, for he has "all power" (D&C 19:3), "almighty power" (D&C 19:14), and "all power, both in heaven and on earth" (D&C 93:17). Jeremiah described God's omnipotence in this manner: "Ah Lord God! behold, thou hast made the heaven and the earth by thy great power and stretched out arm, and there is nothing too hard for thee." (Jer. 32:17.)

Lord Jehovah. Although the name Jehovah is found more than 5,300 times in the Hebrew scriptures, it is translated as such only four times in the King James Version of the Bible (Ex.

6:3; Ps. 83:18; Isa. 12:2; 26:4). In all other instances, the translators employed the title Lord. In Isaiah 12:2, however, this divine name is combined with the title Lord, and is thus read "Lord JEHOVAH." Here the King James translators apparently chose to use the name Jehovah rather than have the verse read "Lord Lord." (See also Jehovah.)

Lord Jesus. See *Jesus.*

Lord Jesus Christ. See *Jesus Christ.*

Lord of All. Luke called Jesus the "Lord of all" (Acts 10:36). Paul's epistle to the Romans explained: "For there is no difference between the Jew and the Greek: for the same Lord [is] over all" (Rom. 10:12). Indeed, Jesus Christ is the "Lord both of the dead and living" (Rom. 14:9). Nephi summarized Christ's role as Lord of all in these words: "And he inviteth them all to come unto him and partake of his goodness; and he denieth none that come unto him, black and white, bond and free, male and female; and he remembereth the heathen; and all are alike unto God, both Jew and Gentile" (2 Ne. 26:33).

Lord of Glory. Jesus Christ, while yet an innocent child and sinless youth, did not receive of a fulness of glory from the Father. "He received not of the fulness at first," testified John, "but continued from grace to grace" (D&C 93:13), or "glory to glory," as Paul describes this process (see 2 Cor. 3:18). However, after Jesus was baptized, "he received a fulness of the glory of the Father" (D&C 93:6–20). From this point on, and forevermore, Jesus is referred to as "the Lord of glory" (James 2:1; 1 Cor. 2:8).

Doctrine and Covenants 84:102 records that during the millennial reign of the King of kings, people will sing:

> Glory, and honor,
> and power, and might,
> be ascribed to our God;
> for he is full of mercy,
> justice, grace and truth,
> and peace,
> Forever and ever, Amen.

Lord of Hosts. The title Lord of Hosts is found 267 times in the Old Testament, more than 50 times in the Book of Mormon, 12 times in the Doctrine and Covenants, and once in the Pearl of Great Price—but never in the New Testament. This title is also found as "Lord God of hosts" (Hosea 12:5) and "God of hosts" (Amos 3:13).

Jesus is the Lord God of Hosts in the sense that he is the God of the host of Israel, the Lord of the host of the righteous, and the King who leads his armies in righteous battle against the wicked. (See also *Lord of Sabaoth.*)

Lord of Lords. Jesus Christ is the "Lord of lords" (Rev. 17:14), a title which is descriptive of his supremacy, lordship, majesty, royalty, and kingship. Clearly, this phrase has reference to Christ's lordship over other deities and gods. It has nothing to do with the lords of the world, such as barons, wealthy landowners, ecclesiastical governors, presidents, kings, and the like. The scriptures reflect the supremacy of Jesus. Moses, a king himself (Deut. 33:4-5), wrote, "For the Lord your God is God of gods, and Lord of lords, a great God, a mighty, and a terrible" (Deut. 10:17). The Apostle Paul wrote to Timothy that "our Lord Jesus Christ . . . is the blessed and only Potentate, the King of kings, and Lord of lords; who only hath immortality, dwelling in the light which no man can approach unto; . . . to whom be honour and power everlasting" (1 Tim. 6:14-16). At the final return of the Lord, when Jesus comes to the earth in all his glorious power, he will be riding a mighty "white horse," wearing "many crowns" upon his head, and "clothed with a vesture dipped in blood." "On his vesture and on his thigh" will be written the titles "KING OF KINGS, AND LORD OF LORDS." (Rev. 19:11-16.)

Lord of Sabaoth. The titles Lord of Sabaoth and Lord of Hosts have identical meanings—*sabaoth* is a Hebrew word translated as "hosts" or "armies" (for "Lord of Sabaoth" used in the context of war, see D&C 87:7). Jesus is the "Lord of Sabaoth" (Rom. 9:29; James 5:4; D&C 88:2) in four ways.

1) He is the God of the "heavenly host" the myriad of angelic and heavenly beings which exist in the celestial worlds (see Luke 2:13; 2 Kgs. 6:17).

2) He is the Creator and Lord of all celestial and terrestrial spheres, such as "the sun, and the moon, and the stars, even all the host of heaven" (Deut. 4:19). Perhaps this is what the Prophet Joseph Smith was referring to when he wrote of the "Lord of Sabaoth, which is by interpretation, the creator of the first day, the beginning and the end" (D&C 95:7).

3) All those of the tribe of Levi were called the "host" (Num. 4:3), and their sanctuary service and duties was referred to as "warfare." Thus, all the Levites who entered into the temple were "to war the warfare, to do the work in the tabernacle of the congregation" (Hebrew translation of Num. 4:23—similarly with the same phraseology in Num. 4:30, 35, 39, 43; 8:24-25;

Dan. 8:11, 13). Jehovah was the Lord of Hosts, referring to the Levite hosts.

4) God is the Lord of Sabaoth, meaning he is the Deity of the hosts or armies of Israel. In connection with this, the writer of the book of 1 Samuel quoted David as saying to Goliath, the Philistine giant, "Thou comest to me with a sword, and with a spear, and with a shield: but I come to thee in the name of the Lord of Hosts, the God of the armies of Israel" (1 Sam. 17:45). (See also part 1: *Army.*)

Lord of Sabbath. The English term "Sabbath" is a transliteration from the Hebrew *shabbat*. Both words are names for the religious day of the week of two major religions: the Christian Sabbath is the first day of the week, and the Jewish *shabbat* is the seventh day of the week. The Hebrew denominative verb of the same root, *shabat*, means "to cease from one's labor" or "to rest." Thus the Sabbath is the day for people to cease from their temporal labors and the tasks which are performed on the other six days of the week, and also the day to worship and revere covenants. Jesus is the Lord of the Sabbath (see Mark 2:23–28) because he created this holy day; he himself used this day to rest from the labors of creation (Gen. 2:2–3); he became the firstfruits of the resurrection on the Sabbath; and he is the Author of all rules and regulations which are to be observed on this holy day (D&C 59:2–20; Ex. 20:8–11). (See also part 1: *Sabbath.*)

Lord of the Vineyard. Symbolically, the house of Israel is compared to a vineyard. Isaiah wrote, "For the vineyard of the Lord of hosts is the house of Israel" (Isa. 5:7). And Jesus Christ, as the God of Israel, is the "lord of the vineyard" (see Matt. 20:1–16; see also Jacob 6:1–11), meaning he is the Lord of the house of Israel. (For the Father as the Lord of the Vineyard, see Matt. 21:33–46.) (See also *Vine*; part 1: *Vine; Vineyard.*)

Lord Omnipotent. See *Lord God Omnipotent.*

Lord Our Righteousness. See *Righteousness.*

Lord's Christ. Jesus is "the Lord's Christ" (Luke 2:26), or, as a word-for-word translation from the Greek reads, Jesus is the "Christ of the Lord." The English title Lord (Greek *Kyrios*) refers to both God the Father and to the Son. In this particular instance the title Lord refers to God the Father. Thus, this phrase could be read "Christ (anointed one) of the Father," meaning that Jesus is the Father's Anointed One. In a related passage, the Psalmist stated, "Therefore God, thy God, hath anointed thee with the oil of gladness above thy fellows" (Ps. 45:6–7; see also Isa. 60:1). (See also *Christ; Messiah.*)

Maker. Christ is referred to as the "Maker" (D&C 30:2; Hosea 8:14; see also Jer. 51:15; D&C 117:6), a title which describes his role as the creator of "all things . . . that are in heaven, and that are in earth, visible and invisible, whether they be thrones, or dominions, or principalities, or powers: all things were created by him, and for him" (Col. 1:16).

Man. Though Jehovah was a god in the heavens, he condescended to live as a man upon the earth (1 Ne. 11:16-26; 2 Ne. 4:26). He was the "man approved of God" (Acts 2:22), "the one man" (Rom. 5:15), "a man of war" (Ex. 15:3), and "a man of sorrows" (Isa. 53:1-12; Luke 22:44; John 19:30). Paul noted that Adam was the "first man," but the "second man is the Lord from heaven" (1 Cor. 15:47). He is the personage whom the Nephites witnessed when they "cast their eyes up again towards heaven; and behold, they saw a Man descending out of heaven" (3 Ne. 11:8).

How was Jesus a man?

1) He was perceived as being a man by his contemporaries. Many made such exclamations as: "Come, see a man, which told me all things that ever I did; . . . this is indeed the Christ" (John 4:29, 42) and "What manner of man is this, that even the wind and the sea obey him?" (Mark 4:41.) Before Christ's crucifixion, Pilate presented him to the "chief priests and officers," saying, "Behold the man!" (John 19:5-6.) And several scriptures refer to "the man Jesus Christ" (Rom. 5:15; see also 1 Tim. 2:5).

2) He was born of a human mother (Luke 2:5, 7), and he grew as a child (Luke 2:40) and "increased in . . . stature" (Luke 2:52).

3) He was tempted as men are (Matt. 4:1-11) and suffered as men do (Heb. 2:10).

4) He possessed human qualities: he was hungry, thirsty, sorrowful, angry, weary, compassionate, and so on (see Matt. 26:38); he possessed a body (Luke 24:39).

5) He suffered bodily pain, bled from every pore, and died.

6) God the Father is known as the "Man of Holiness" (Moses 6:57) and "Man of Counsel" (Moses 7:35), and his son is called the "Son of Man," an abbreviated form of "Son of Man of Holiness" (Moses 6:57). Jesus was in the "express image" of his Father, who also is a "Man."

7) Jesus had to qualify for his own salvation, as do all men (D&C 93:12-17).

Master. Six different Greek words and one Hebrew word were translated to the English "master" by the King James translators. These are *despotes*, meaning "sovereign" (1 Tim. 6:1-2); *didaskolos*, "teacher" (Matt. 8:19); *epistates*, "overseer" (Luke 5:5); *kathegetes*, "leader" (Matt. 23:8); *kurios*, "Lord" (Eph. 6:9); *kubernetes*, "pilot" or "shipmaster" (Acts 27:11); and *rabbi*, "teacher" (Matt. 26:25).

Jesus often spoke of himself as "Master" (Matt. 10:24-25; 26:18; Mark 14:14; Luke 6:40; 22:11; John 13:14). He said, "Ye call me Master and Lord: and ye say well; for so I am" (John 13:13); and on another occasion, "But be not ye called Rabbi: for one is your Master, even Christ; and all ye are brethren. . . . Neither be ye called masters: for one is your Master, even Christ." (Matt. 23:7-10.)

Others referred to the Lord as "Master" (Matt. 9:11; 17:24; Mark 5:35; Luke 5:5; 8:24; John 11:28; 13:13). "They said unto him, Rabbi, (which is to say, being interpreted, Master,) where dwellest thou?" (John 1:38.) The Apostle Paul, after the ascension of Jesus, called the Lord the "Master in heaven" (Eph. 6:9; Col. 4:1).

Master in Heaven. See *Master.*

Mediator. A mediator is a person who serves as a go-between or middleman between two parties. Moses was the mediator of the old covenant and Jesus of the new. "Moses . . . was ordained by the hand of angels to be a mediator of this first covenant, (the law.) Now this mediator was not a mediator of the new covenant . . . , who is Christ. . . . Christ is the mediator of life." (JST, Gal. 3:19-20.)

The Apostle Paul taught the New Testament Saints that "there is one God, and one mediator between God and men, the man Christ Jesus" (1 Tim. 2:5). We read that Jesus is "the way" unto the Father. "No man cometh unto the Father, but by me," declared the Savior (John 14:6).

It is through the Lord that "we both have access by one Spirit unto the Father" (Eph. 2:18). Jesus' role as the Mediator leads directly to the salvation of all those who come unto him. Paul explained to the Hebrews that "for this cause he is the mediator of the new covenant, that . . . they which are called might receive the promise of eternal inheritance" (JST, Heb. 9:15). Just men are made perfect "through Jesus the mediator of the new covenant, who wrought out this perfect atonement through the shedding of his own blood" (D&C 76:69).

Mediator of the New Covenant. See *Mediator.*

Merciful. God's mercy is a constant theme throughout the scriptures. Many have testified that "his mercy endureth for ever" (1 Chr. 16:34, 41; 2 Chr. 5:13; 7:3, 6; Ezra 3:11; Ps.

118:1-4) and that he is "merciful and gracious" (D&C 109:53; Ex. 34:6; Ps. 103:8; Joel 2:13; Jonah 4:2). The Psalmist exulted, "The Lord is merciful and gracious, slow to anger, and plenteous in mercy" (Ps. 103:8); "He is ever merciful" (Ps. 37:26). Nehemiah proclaimed, "Thou art a God ready to pardon, gracious and merciful" (Neh. 9:17). Moses wrote, "The Lord, the Lord God, merciful and gracious, [is] longsuffering, and abundant in goodness and truth, keeping mercy for thousands, forgiving iniquity and transgression and sin" (Ex. 34:6-7). And Alma, the American prophet, testified that "God is merciful unto all who believe on his name" (Alma 32:22). The Psalmist added that the Lord's mercy is manifest in all his doings (see Ps. 136).

Messiah. The title Messiah is the English transliteration of the Hebrew word *meshiach*, which means "anointed one." The equivalent word in Greek is *christos*, or "Christ." John makes this connection in his Gospel, referring to "the Messias [Messiah], which is, being interpreted, the Christ" (John 1:41); and he tells us "that Messias cometh, which is called Christ" (John 4:25). The expressions *Messiah, Christ,* and *Anointed One* thus have identical meanings.

The scriptures take great pains to make certain we know who the Messiah is. Nephi identifies him as being the "Savior of the world" (1 Ne. 10:4), the "Redeemer of the world" (1 Ne. 10:5), and "the Lamb of God" (1 Ne. 12:18), all titles referring to Jesus Christ. Nephi testified to his people that Jesus was the "true Messiah, their Lord and their Redeemer" (1 Ne. 10:14), and that "the Son of God was the Messiah who should come" (1 Ne. 10:17). More specifically, Nephi identified the Messiah by prophesying, "His name shall be Jesus Christ, the Son of God" (2 Ne. 25:19).

Jesus Christ himself testified of his messiahship. To Enoch he said, "I am Messiah, the King of Zion, the Rock of Heaven" (Moses 7:53). And Matthew testified that Jesus was ordered, "Tell us whether thou be the Christ [Messiah]," to which he responded, "Thou hast said" (Matt. 26:63-64).

Every Israelite priest (Lev. 8:30; 10:7), high priest (Ex. 30:30), and king (1 Kgs. 1:34) was a messiah, meaning each was anointed with the holy anointing oil. As such, they were figures or types for Jesus, the Messiah. (See also part 1: *Anointing; Cyrus; Olive Oil.*)

Messiah the Prince. Jesus is "Messiah the Prince" (Dan. 9:25), a title which denotes his royal lineage, his regal status, and his divine sonship. Since the words *Messiah, Christ,* and

Anointed One have identical meanings, this deific title could also be written "the Anointed Prince."

Mighty God. Jesus Christ is the "mighty God" (Isa. 9:6), the "Mighty One of Israel" (1 Ne. 22:12), and the "mighty One of Jacob" (Isa. 49:26), titles which express his omnipotence and greatness. The scriptures describe the mightiness of Deity by saying he is "mighty in deed and word" (Luke 24:19) and "mighty in work" (Jer. 32:19; 10:6). All of his doings are "mighty works" (Matt. 11:20; 13:54) or "mighty works of God" (D&C 88:108-9). God has "mighty power" (Eph. 1:19). He is "mighty to save" (Isa. 63:1), for the "spirit of . . . might" (Isa. 11:2) is with him. Of all the souls who have resided upon this planet, the Lord is the "most mighty" (Ps. 45:3). Even John the Baptist, of whom it is said that "among those that are born of women there is not a greater prophet" (*Teachings*, p. 275), declared that Jesus is "mightier than I" (Matt. 3:11).

Mighty One of Israel. See *Mighty God.*

Mighty One of Jacob. See *Mighty God.*

Minister. During the days of the Mosaic tabernacle and of Solomon's temple, every high priest acted unto the people as a minister "ordained to offer gifts and sacrifices" (Heb. 8:3). Jesus also served as "a minister of the sanctuary," but his was "a more excellent ministry" (Heb. 8:2, 6), with a gift and sacrificial offering consisting of his own life (Rom. 6:23). As Jesus himself said, "The Son of man came not to be ministered unto, but to minister, and to give his life a ransom for many" (Matt. 20:28).

Most High. "Most High" (D&C 59:10) is an abbreviated form of "Most High God," a phrase which signifies the supreme eminence of God. (See also *Most High God.*)

Most High God. The title Most High God, ascribed to both the Father and the Son (Mark 5:7; D&C 59:10), is a superlative description which expresses their matchless exaltation. God is at the greatest height of all gods. His position is lofty, elevated, and towering above all else — he is Lord of all. As Most High God he is King of kings, God of gods, and Lord of lords. "Hosanna to the Lord, the most high God," exulted Nephi, "for he is God over all the earth, yea, even above all" (1 Ne. 11:6).

Nazarene. The messianic prophecy "He shall be called a Nazarene" (Matt. 2:23) has reference to Jesus Christ. The Lord, who lived in the city of Nazareth for almost thirty years of his life, said of himself, "I am Jesus of Nazareth" (Acts 22:8).

Others often referred to the Savior as "Jesus of Nazareth" (Acts 2:22; 6:14; 26:9).

Only Begotten. The title "Only Begotten" (Moses 6:57) is an apocopated and abbreviated form of the longer title "the Only Begotten of the Father" (D&C 93:11). (See also *Only Begotten of the Father.*)

Only Begotten of the Father. Jesus is referred to as the "Only Begotten of the Father" (D&C 93:11) and the "Only Begotten Son of the Father" (D&C 76:35), two expressions which describe his familial relationship with God the Father.

Only Begotten Son. See *Only Begotten of the Father.*

Passover. The ancient Passover was enacted annually during the Jewish month of Abib, commemorating the occasion when the destroying angel "passed over" the obedient children of Israel. In many ways this Passover of the Old Testament was a type for the Great Passover of the New Testament, which was fulfilled in Jesus Christ. Paul referred to Jesus as "Christ our passover" (1 Cor. 5:7) because, as the Passover Lamb, Jesus fulfilled the role of the ancient Passover lamb. Consider the parallels:

1) The ancient Passover gave temporal deliverance to those who smeared the lamb's blood on their doorposts (Ex. 12:7, 12, 13). The new Passover gives spiritual deliverance to those who accept the blood of Jesus Christ (Matt. 1:21; Luke 4:18).

2) The ancient lamb was "without blemish" (Ex. 12:5; Lev. 22:21). Jesus Christ was without blemish (1 Pet. 1:19).

3) No bone of the Passover lamb was to be broken in the performance of the sacrifice (Ex. 12:46). No bone of the Lord was broken during the crucifixion (John 19:33, 36).

4) The Passover lamb was to be slain by the "whole assembly" (Ex. 12:6). Jesus, the New Testament fulfillment of the Passover lamb, was slain by a whole nation (Luke 23:1, 10, 13, 23, 35).

5) The Israelites were told to "eat the flesh" of the Passover lamb (Ex. 12:8; 2 Chr. 30:18). The sacramental bread is the emblem of the flesh of Jesus Christ (Matt. 26:26–28). (See also part 1: *Passover.*)

Physician. Jesus was a "physician" (Luke 4:23; Matt. 9:12) during his mortal life in that he was often found "healing the sick, raising the dead, causing the lame to walk, the blind to receive their sight, and the deaf to hear, and curing all manner of diseases" (Mosiah 3:5). In short, he was the quintessential Physician to those with physical deformities and illnesses.

However, in a far more important sense, Jesus was, is, and always will be the divine Physician to those who are spiritually sick—those people whose ears cannot hear the whisperings of the Holy Ghost, whose eyes cannot perceive the things of God, whose spiritual senses need repair, and whose souls require the healing powers that only Jesus, through his atonement, can provide. Christ's role as a spiritual physician has been summarized by Moroni: "Listen to the words of Christ, your Redeemer, your Lord and your God. Behold, I came into the world not to call the righteous but sinners to repentance; the whole need no physician, but they that are sick" (Moro. 8:8). (See also part 1: *Physician.*)

Plant of Renown. The Lord is known as the "seed of David" (2 Tim. 2:8), the "rod out of the stem of Jesse" (Isa. 11:1), the "BRANCH" (Zech. 3:8), the "vine" (John 15:1), and the "stem" (D&C 113:1–2), all designations that describe him as the "plant of renown" (Ezek. 34:29) and "a tender plant" (Isa. 53:2; Mosiah 14:2). A plant is a perfect figure of Christ. It is set firmly in the ground. It produces flowers, which are pleasant to look upon, sweet smelling, and generally enjoyable to mankind. Most plants replace deadly carbon monoxide with lifesaving oxygen. And many plants produce fruit which typically is delicate, delicious, and sweet, which provides nutrition, and which gives vitality and physical strength to its partakers. Jehovah, as the "plant of renown," gives fruit to Israel, so that "they shall be no more consumed with hunger in the land" (Ezek. 34:29). (See also part 1: *Plant.*)

Potentate. All earthly kings, potentates, and princes have temporary and limited power and authority, which is both localized and limited to the extent of their kingdom. But there is one King who holds unlimited power, whose boundaries know no limits, and whose authority is from everlasting to everlasting; this is Jesus Christ, who is "the blessed and only Potentate, the King of kings, and Lord of lords" (1 Tim. 6:15).

Power of God. Jesus Christ is "the power of God who sitteth upon his throne, who is in the bosom of eternity, who is in the midst of all things" (D&C 88:13; see also Alma 19:17).

Priest. Both the Levitical and Nephite priests offered all manner of sacrifices before God, representing each member of the Israelite community. The services of these authorized functionaries were essential to the salvation of the community of believers. Further, the ordinances and sacrifices performed by the priests pointed to Christ, and in many ways were types and similitudes of his ministry.

Jesus, as the "priest for ever after the order of Melchizedek" (Ps. 110:4; Heb. 7:17), also offered a "great and last sacrifice" (Alma 34:10) on behalf of all people. His sacrifice consisted of "the sacrifice of himself" (Heb. 9:26). (See also part 1: *Priest.*)

Prophet. An important and well-known messianic prophecy was revealed to the prophet Moses. The Lord told him, "I will raise them up a Prophet from among their brethren, like unto thee" (Deut. 18:18; see also 18:15-18). Although this prediction is of a dual or manifold nature, its principal fulfillment was satisfied with Jesus Christ, who was the chief prophet of all time. During his mortal ministry, both his disciples and his enemies recognized him as a prophet. Matthew recorded that the enemies of the Lord "took him for a prophet" (Matt. 21:46), and his followers, upon seeing his marvelous works and miracles, exclaimed, "This is of a truth that prophet that should come into the world" (John 6:14).

Jesus referred to himself as a prophet when he stated, "A prophet is not without honour, but in his own country" (Mark 6:4). Jesus had a testimony and an assurance that he was the Messiah and the Savior of the world, the same testimony that all true prophets have concerning him (Rev. 19:10). Of this he constantly bore witness.

Furthermore, as a prophet, Jesus personally uttered many prophecies which were fulfilled during his lifetime. For instance:

Prophecy	Fulfillment
His betrayal (Matt. 20:18)	(Matt. 26:14-16, 45-49)
Being forsaken by his disciples (John 16:32)	(Matt. 26:56)
Peter's denial (John 13:38)	(Luke 22:60-62)
Jesus' resurrection (John 2:19-21)	(Luke 24:5-6)
Jesus' ascension (John 20:17)	(Acts 1:9-10)

Every true prophet of God, regardless of what historical age in which he lives, is a type for the greatest of the prophets, who is Jesus. (See also part 1: *Prophet.*)

Prophet of Nazareth. See *Prophet.*

Propitiation. Jesus Christ is the "propitiation for our sins" (1 John 2:2; 4:10). It is he "whom God hath set forth to be a propitiation through faith in his blood, to declare his righteousness for the remission of sins that are past, through the forbearance of God" (Rom. 3:25). It is he who propitiates or appeases justice for the purpose of reuniting God and man.

Purifier. Like a master goldsmith who separates the dross from the gold, thus purifying the precious metal, the Lord sits "as a refiner and purifier" (Mal. 3:3) of souls. Specifically, God purifies those found "obeying the truth" (1 Pet. 1:22) and those found "yielding their hearts unto God" (Hel. 3:35). Purification occurs through the agency of faith (Acts 15:9) and by the "blood of Christ" (Heb. 9:13-14). Paul testified that Christ "gave himself for us, that he might redeem us from all iniquity, and purify unto himself a peculiar people" (Titus 2:14). (See also *Refiner;* part 1: *Gold; Dross; Furnace.*)

Rabbi. During his mortal ministry, Jesus was called Rabbi, an honorific Hebrew title of great respect meaning "my master." Jesus, by virtue of his lordship, is rightly the only one who can be called Master. To the multitude he said, "But be not ye called Rabbi: for one is your Master, even Christ; and all ye are brethren" (Matt. 23:8; see also John 1:38).

Rabboni. The title Rabboni, the Aramaic equivalent of the Hebrew title Rabbi, has the basic meaning of "my master." This title of great respect is found only once in the New Testament in John 20:16. In addition, the word *Lord* in Mark 10:51 is translated incorrectly and should also be *Rabboni.*

Redeemer. The Hebrew word for redeemer, *goel,* is defined as one who "ransoms," "redeems," or "revenges." In the Hebrew scriptures, any man can act as a *goel* for a kinsman (Lev. 25:25; Num. 5:8; 35:12; Ruth 2:20). However, the *Goel* who acts on behalf of the entire nation of Israel is the God of the Old Testament, who is called Jehovah. He is the Redeemer (Isa. 41:14; 43:14; 44:6, 24), and his people are the *geulim,* or the "redeemed ones" (Isa. 35:9; 51:10; 62:12). "By me redemption cometh," said the Lord to those in the New World (3 Ne. 9:17). Without a Redeemer, there could be no redemption, resurrection, or exaltation (Alma 12:25; 21:9; Hel. 5:10-11; D&C 29:42-45; Alma 9:27). (See also part 1: *Boaz.*)

Redeemer of Israel. See *Redeemer of the World.*

Redeemer of the World. The Son of God has been called the Redeemer (Job 19:25) and "the Redeemer of Israel" (1 Ne.

21:7). But he is much more than that—he is "the Redeemer of the world" (1 Ne. 11:27). Concerning his calling as Redeemer of the entire world, Jesus declared, "Behold, I have come unto the world to bring redemption unto the world, to save the world from sin" (3 Ne. 9:21).

Refiner. At the time of the Second Coming the Lord will "sit as a refiner and purifier of silver" (Mal. 3:3) and will "purify the sons of Levi" as a goldsmith purifies gold. In other words, the Lord will refine the souls of the Levites, separating the dross from the precious metal. In a general sense, Jesus is the Refiner of the heart of every righteous soul, removing the sinful nature of man from the godly nature that is inherent within him. (See also part 1: *Gold; Dross; Furnace.*)

Resurrection. Jesus testified, "I am the resurrection" (John 11:25). Note that he did not declare, "I was resurrected," identifying resurrection as his own personal condition, nor did he state, "I raise the dead," meaning that he restores the spirit to the body in a temporary state of mortality, as he did with Lazarus. Rather, his statement teaches the important fact that his atonement will enable all who have ever lived to be resurrected (Alma 11:41-42; 1 Cor. 15:21-22). Jehovah summarized his mission as the Resurrection when he taught, "I will ransom them from the power of the grave; I will redeem them from death: O death, I will be thy plagues; O grave, I will be thy destruction" (Hosea 13:14).

Reverend. Reverend means worthy to be revered, worthy of great honor. Regarding the Lord, David composed a psalm which stated, "Holy and reverend is his name" (Ps. 111:9). A literal translation from the Hebrew may be rendered, "His name is to be had in reverence and holiness."

Righteous. The Apostle John called his Master "Jesus Christ the righteous" (1 John 2:1), a perfect designation for the only sinless one who has ever dwelled upon the earth. Before John's ministry, "Enoch saw the day of the coming of the Son of Man, even in the flesh, and his soul rejoiced, saying: The Righteous is lifted up, and the Lamb is slain from the foundation of the world" (Moses 7:47). Other prophets have called Christ the "righteous servant" (Isa. 53:11) and the "righteous judge" (2 Tim. 4:8; see also Moses 6:57).

Everything about Jesus is righteous—his judgments (Hel. 14:29), his purposes (D&C 17:9), his paths (2 Ne. 9:41), and his character (1 Pet. 2:22-23).

Righteous Judge. Only Deity can be a wholly righteous

judge, because certain godly qualifications are essential. Jesus is the "righteous Judge" (Moses 6:57; 2 Tim. 4:8; Acts 17:31) because:

1) He has experienced mortal life and temptation as we have (Heb. 2:14–18; Alma 7:11–13); therefore, he is able to show empathy.

2) He has perfect knowledge and intelligence (D&C 38:1–2). One cannot judge righteously if he does not know all of the circumstances.

3) The "Father . . . hath given him authority to execute judgment . . . because he is the Son of man" (John 5:26–27), that is, the Son of Man of Holiness. (See also *Son of Man*.)

Righteousness. Both the Father and the Son are called Righteousness. The Son is designated "THE LORD OUR RIGHTEOUSNESS" by the prophet Jeremiah (Jer. 23:6), and Nephi refers to him as "the Son of righteousness" (2 Ne. 26:9), demonstrating that he is the Son of one called Righteousness. God has the name Righteousness because every trait, characteristic, and feature which belong to him pertains to justice, virtue, and purity.

Righteous Servant. See *Servant.*

Rock. Jesus Christ, who was known in Old Testament times as Jehovah, was given the figurative title of the Rock by many of the prophetic writers. In a simple statement, Moses wrote, "He is the Rock" (Deut. 32:4). The Psalmist spoke of the "Lord my rock" (Ps. 28:1; see also 42:9; 78:35) and recorded that "he only is my rock" (Ps. 62:2). Paul explained to the Corinthian Saints that Moses and the Israelites "did all drink the same spiritual drink: for they drank of that spiritual Rock that followed them: and that Rock was Christ" (1 Cor. 10:1–4).

These metaphorical expressions are intended to demonstrate that the Lord has many of the same characteristics as a rock. A rock is often thought to be immovable, steadfast, and sure. It serves as a foundation for building structures, is towering and monumental, and is unchangeable — the same throughout the ages.

David repeatedly emphasized the idea that Jehovah is a rock. He wrote that the Lord was "my rock and my fortress" (Ps. 31:3); he wrote, "He only is my rock and my salvation; he is my defence; I shall not be greatly moved" (Ps. 62:2). Those who fortify themselves with the Rock will not be "greatly moved" by the landslides of evil or the winds of false doctrines. (See also *Stone*; part 1: *Rock; Stone.*)

Rock of Heaven. The Lord declared to Enoch, "I am Messiah, the King of Zion, the Rock of Heaven, which is broad as eternity" (Moses 7:53-55).

Rock of Israel. Interestingly, in the "rock in Horeb" pericope recorded by Moses, three symbols of Christ—the rock, the rod, and the water—come together to bless the Israelites. With each element, the figurative and the actual both play their part in saving thirsty Israel (Ex. 17:1-7; Num. 20:1-13). Thus, David, "the sweet psalmist of Israel," refers to "the God of Israel" as being the "Rock of Israel" (2 Sam. 23:1-3). (See also *Rock.*)

Root of David. To John, the Lord said, "I am the root and the offspring of David" (Rev. 22:16), referring to his lineal descent through King David. In more simple terms, Jesus is called the "son of David" (Matt. 1:1), and King David is referred to as "his father David" (Luke 1:32).

However, Jesus as the Root may have a deeper meaning. An Old Testament passage explains of Jesus Christ, "He shall grow up . . . as a tender plant, and as a root out of a dry ground" (Isa. 53:2; Mosiah 14:2). Botanists explain that the life of any plant is found in the root—first, because water and nutrients come through the roots, and secondly, because the trunk, branches, leaves, and fruit all spring from and exist because of the roots. In short, the entire plant depends upon the roots for its life. Thus, Jesus is the Root, and every Saint is a "branch" which is dependent upon Christ for both spiritual and physical existence (John 15:1-7). (See also part 1: *Root.*)

Ruler. There are many ways in which the Lord is described as Ruler (see Micah 5:2). He is the Potentate, Prince, Sceptre, Rod and Staff, Captain, Commander, Deliverer, Governor, Guide, King, Lawgiver, and Master. As the Ruler, Jesus Christ will "reign over the house of Jacob for ever; and of his kingdom there shall be no end" (Luke 1:33). "He ruleth high in the heavens," taught Nephi (1 Ne. 17:39), both "in the heavens above and in the earth beneath" (2 Ne. 29:7). He is the "Lord, who ruleth over all flesh" (D&C 133:61).

To the Corinthians, Paul wrote, "Then cometh the end, when he [Jesus] shall have delivered up the kingdom to God, even the Father; when he shall have put down all rule and all authority and power. For he must reign." (1 Cor. 15:24-25.) "I will be your ruler when I come," declared the Lord (D&C 41:4). (See also part 1: *King.*)

Salvation. Although the Greek name Jesus means "salvation," the noun *salvation* rarely appears as a title referring to Christ. Isaiah declared, "Behold, thy salvation [speaking of the

Lord] cometh; behold, his reward is with him, and his work before him" (Isa. 62:11). Luke records, "And Jesus said unto [Zacchaeus], This day is salvation come to this house. . . . For the Son of man is come to seek and to save that which was lost" (Luke 19:9–10). And Nephi referred to Jesus as "the Lamb, and my rock and my salvation" (1 Ne. 13:36; also see 1 Ne. 15:15).

Jesus as Salvation is an appropriate title, since this word is synonymous with the words *exaltation* and *eternal life.*

Sanctuary. The Lord explained to Ezekiel that to the dispersed of Israel "will I be . . . as a little sanctuary in the countries where they shall come" (Ezek. 11:16). He was reassuring them that even in far-flung areas, the Saints of God are able to find peace and refuge in Christ in a manner similar to those who discover peace at the holy temple of God. The Psalmist spoke of this when he recorded, "Lord, thou hast been our dwelling place in all generations" (Ps. 90:1); "I will say of the Lord, He is my refuge and my fortress: my God; in him will I trust" (Ps. 91:2); and "Only with thine eyes shalt thou behold and see the reward of the wicked. Because thou hast made the Lord, which is my refuge, even the most High, thy habitation" (Ps. 91:8–9).

According to the prophet Isaiah, the Lord is as a "sanctuary" unto the righteous, and "a stone of stumbling and . . . a rock of offence" unto the wicked (Isa. 8:14). Thus, to the wicked, Christ becomes offensive, like a huge stone blocking the roadway. To the righteous, he remains a source of refuge and protection. (See also part 1: *Temple; Tabernacle.*)

Savior. Jesus is the Savior (1 Ne. 10:4; D&C 20:1; Moses 1:6). "Beside him there is no Savior" (D&C 76:1). He has the exclusive assignment to save, or to bring salvation to as many souls as will accept him. "I came . . . to save the world" (John 12:47), Christ testified. Specifically, it is sinners who need a Savior; thus, he "came into the world to save sinners" (1 Tim. 1:15). He will not save people in their sins, but he "shall save his people from their sins" (Matt. 1:21). Recorded in Alma is the explanation that he has power "to save every man that believeth on his name and bringeth forth fruit meet for repentance" (Alma 12:15). Jesus saves men from death, hell, and the grave.

Savior Jesus Christ. Of all the fraudulent men in all the ages of the world who have claimed to be the saviors of mankind, who is the true Savior of the world? As all the holy prophets have testified, the sole and only Savior is the "Savior Jesus Christ" (3 Ne. 5:20; 2 Tim. 1:10).

Savior of the World. John, who was the "Beloved," the "Revelator," and an Apostle of the Lord, gave this apostolic witness of the Lord: "We have seen and do testify that the Father sent the Son to be the Saviour of the world" (1 John 4:14; see also 1 Ne. 13:40).

Servant. Jesus is the "servant" (Isa. 42:1; Matt. 12:18), or "righteous servant" (Isa. 53:11) in that he serves the Father (Ps. 40:8; John 8:29) and serves all mankind (Matt. 20:26–28). Paul said of the mortal Lord that he "took upon him the form of a servant" (Philip. 2:7).

Shepherd. The scriptures refer to Jesus Christ as the "Shepherd of Israel" (Ps. 80:1), the "good shepherd" (John 10:11), the "great shepherd" (Heb. 13:20), and the "chief Shepherd" (1 Pet. 5:4). All these designations distinguish Christ from common or typical shepherds. Jesus is an extraordinary shepherd; he is a shepherd to the souls of men (Mark 6:34; Luke 12:32).

Many similarities exist between the Good Shepherd and the ordinary herdsman. Both have the responsibility of protecting their sheep from wild beasts and robbers. Both are constantly on the lookout for pasture and sufficient water. Both care for sick sheep and carry tired lambs (Gen. 33:13; Isa. 40:11; Luke 15:4–7). Both know their own sheep, and the sheep recognize the voice of their master.

Dissimilarities also exist between them, since some shepherds are unfaithful and wicked:

Good Shepherd	Unfaithful Shepherd
1. Giveth his life (John 10:11)	1. Flees in danger (John 10:12)
2. Feeds his flock (Isa. 40:11)	2. Feeds himself (Ezek. 34:8; Zech. 11:16)
3. Gathers the flock (Isa. 40:11)	3. Divides the sheep (Ezek. 34:8; Zech. 11:16; Jer. 23:1)
4. Is tender (Isa. 40:11)	4. Is cruel (Ezek. 34:8; Zech. 11:14–17)

Since sheepherding was a common occupation in the biblical world, many of the prophets were literal shepherds. Abel was a "keeper of sheep" (Gen. 4:2), as were Abraham, Jacob, Moses, Amos, Job, David, and Zechariah. As shepherds of lambs, and also shepherds of men, these prophets were types of the Great Shepherd. (See also part 1: *Sheep; Shepherd.*)

Shield. Magen, the Hebrew word for shield, is a derivative from the verb *ganen,* which means "to defend" or "to protect." Thus, a shield is an instrument that protects man from the arrows, spears, or swords of the enemy. The Lord is a shield by protecting man from both physical and spiritual harm. Thus, Jehovah told Abraham, "Fear not, Abram: I am thy shield" (Gen. 15:1), and to his latter-day disciples he promised, "I will be their shield" (D&C 35:14). "The Lord is my strength and my shield," (Ps. 28:7), wrote the Psalmist. "He is a shield unto them that put their trust in him" (Prov. 30:5). (See also part 1: *Armor; Shield.*)

King David sang a song in which he personified God as a protector (2 Sam. 22:2-4; see also D&C 3:8).

> The Lord is my rock, and my fortress, and my deliverer;
> The God of my rock; in him I will trust:
> he is my shield, and the horn of my salvation,
> my high tower, and my refuge, my saviour;
> thou savest me from violence.
> · · · · · · · · · · · · · · · ·
> I [will] be saved from mine enemies.

Shiloh. An ancient prophecy in Genesis relates that "the sceptre shall not depart from Judah, nor a lawgiver from between his feet, until Shiloh come" (Gen. 49:10), or as the Joseph Smith Translation renders it, "Messiah who is called Shilo" (JST, Gen. 50:24). The Hebrew *Shiloh* means "he whose right it is," or "that which belongs to him." Thus, the power and authority to rule and to reign belong to Shiloh, who is Jesus. Ezekiel was probably referring to this ancient prophecy when he stated, "Until he come whose right it is; and I will give it [the diadem and the crown] him" (Ezek. 21:26-27).

Son. Authority and power accompany the name Son, a shortened form of "Son of God" or "Son of Man." Adam was told, "Wherefore, thou shalt do all that thou doest in the name of the Son, and thou shalt repent and call upon God in the name of the Son forevermore" (Moses 5:8). (See also *Son of Man.*)

Son Ahman. In the pure language of Adam, God is called *Ahman,* Jesus is called *Son Ahman,* and men are referred to as *Sons Ahman* (see Orson Pratt, *Journal of Discourses,* 2:342). The definitions of these terms is unknown. However, the title Son Ahman is used twice in the Doctrine and Covenants: "your Redeemer, even the Son Ahman" (D&C 78:20); and "Son Ahman; or, in other words, Alphus; or, in other words, Omegus; even Jesus Christ your Lord" (D&C 95:17).

Son of Abraham. The Lord is the "son of Abraham" (Matt. 1:1), meaning that he descended through the loins of this righteous and chosen patriarch. (See also part 1: *Abraham.*)

Son of David. Mary, the literal mother of Jesus, and Joseph, his stepfather, were both of the house of David (Matt. 1:1–17; Luke 1:26–38; 2:4). Jesus was referred to as the "Son of David" (Matt. 1:1; 9:27) several times during his mortal ministry, meaning that he was born through the lineage of King David, or he was "of the seed of David" (2 Tim. 2:8). (See also part 1: *David.*)

Son of God. Jesus was not the "son of Joseph" (Luke 3:23; John 1:45), as some had supposed. Unlike those born of a mortal father, he was begotten by a Heavenly Being, even God the Father. The scriptures testify that "the Son of God was the Messiah" (1 Ne. 10:17) and that "Jesus Christ [is] the Son of God" (2 Ne. 25:19).

Son of Joseph. During his mortal ministry, Jesus Christ was called the "son of Joseph" (Luke 3:23; John 1:45) by many who did not fully understand his divine sonship. In truth, however, Jesus was the Son of God. (See *Son of God*; part 1: *Joseph.*)

Son of Man. Although the Lord is referred to as Son of Man in the New Testament scriptures, this divine name was first known to Adam. Recorded in the book of Moses is the explanation that "in the language of Adam" the Father is called "Man of Holiness . . . , and the name of his Only Begotten is the Son of Man, even Jesus Christ" (Moses 6:57). Thus Jesus is the Son of Man, a shortened form of Son of Man of Holiness.

Son of Mary. Jesus was the "son of Mary" (Mark 6:3; Matt. 1:18–25; Mosiah 3:8), a title which reverenced and gave honor to his saintly mother. Mary was "the mother of the Son of God, after the manner of the flesh" (1 Ne. 11:18), recorded Nephi.

Son of Righteousness. God the Father is called Righteousness, a term that describes his piousness, holiness, and rectitude. Most appropriately, Jesus Christ, who possesses all of the attributes of his Father, is referred to as "the Son of Righteousness" (3 Ne. 25:2; 2 Ne. 26:9).

Son of the Blessed. See *Blessed.*

Son of the Eternal Father. Similar to all mortal beings, Jesus was born of a mortal mother, but unlike all humans, he was begotten by an Infinite Being. He is "the Son of the Eternal Father" (1 Ne. 11:21). (See also *Only Begotten Son.*)

Son of the Everlasting God. During the time that Nephi

"was caught away in the Spirit of the Lord" to an "exceedingly high mountain," an angel of the Lord identified Jesus Christ as being "the Son of the Eternal Father" (1 Ne. 11:1, 21). A short time later, Nephi spoke of the Lord as "the Son of the everlasting God" (1 Ne. 11:32).

Son of the Highest. Luke recorded in his testimony that the newborn Jesus was "the Son of the Highest" (Luke 1:32), an expression which describes his relationship with his exalted Father.

Son of the Living God. To those of this dispensation the Lord declared, "Behold, I am Jesus Christ, the Son of the living God" (D&C 14:9; 42:1; 55:2). That is to say, his divine Father is not a god of stone, wood, or iron. Neither is he an ephemeral being, made of the rays of the sun or the wisps of the air. Rather, the "living God" is a being who is alive, intelligent, having a body composed of flesh and bones (D&C 130:22); and Jesus is his Son.

Son of the Most High God. The title "Son of the most high God" (1 Ne. 11:6) is a simple but beautiful expression which describes the Lord's relationship with God the Father. The Father is the Most High God, and Jesus is his Son.

Spirit of Truth. Revealed through the Prophet Joseph Smith was the divine declaration of Jesus, "I am the Spirit of truth" (D&C 93:26). Also, Jesus is "the light and the Redeemer of the world; the Spirit of truth" (D&C 93:9). Associated with these statements are the declarations of the Lord: "My voice is Spirit; my Spirit is truth; truth abideth and hath no end; and if it be in you it shall abound" (D&C 88:66); and "The words that I speak unto you, they are spirit, and they are life" (John 6:63).

Star. In one brief season of the history of the earth, one prominent "new star" appeared in the heavens, conspicuous and noticeable to those living upon two continents—those dwelling in ancient Palestine and those living in the land of Bountiful (Matt. 2:2, 7, 9-10; 3 Ne. 1:21). This distant sun was so singular and unique as to cause the Lamanite prophet Samuel to declare to the Nephites that this "new star" was "such an one as ye never have beheld" (Hel. 14:5). This star was a "sign" (Hel. 14:5-6) of the birth of the Lord. It was a symbol of Jesus, who is called the "star out of Jacob" (Num. 24:17), and "the bright and morning star" (Rev. 22:16).

Jesus is the star in the sense that, like other stars, he lends to the spiritual night beauty, wonderment, and light. And as stars exhibit the greatness of God's power and glory (Ps. 8:3;

Isa. 40:26), Jesus stands preeminent in showing to the world the glory of the Father. (See also *Sun of Righteousness*; part 1: *Star; Sun.*)

Stem of Jesse. The Prophet Joseph Smith received this important revelation: "Who is the Stem of Jesse spoken of in the 1st, 2d, 3d, 4th, and 5th verses of the 11th chapter of Isaiah? Verily thus saith the Lord: It is Christ." (D&C 113:1-2.) Jesus is the Stem of Jesse, meaning that he is a descendant through the lines of Jesse, father of David. (See also part 1: *Stem of Jesse.*)

Stone. The scriptures often represent Jesus as being the "stone" (Jacob 4:15), the "stone of Israel" (D&C 50:44; Gen. 49:24), or the "chief corner stone" (Eph. 2:20), expressions which describe an important aspect of Christ's mission. In what ways is Jesus Christ like a stone? Jacob explained that the stone gives "safe foundation" to the building, and that Jesus is the "stone [which] shall become the great, and the last, and the only sure foundation" (Jacob 4:15-16). Similarly, Paul likened Jesus unto the "chief corner stone" of the structure. Although Christ and his Apostles are all foundation stones (Eph. 2:20), the cornerstone is the principal and most fundamental part of the building. Jesus is "a tried stone, a precious corner stone, a sure foundation" (Isa. 28:16).

Peter, while quoting and paraphrasing Isaiah, explained that Jesus is a stone to both the righteous and the wicked. To the righteous he is "a chief corner stone, elect, precious," but to the wicked he is "a stone of stumbling, and a rock of offence" (1 Pet. 2:6-8). (See also *Rock*; part 1: *Rock; Stone.*)

Stone of Israel. See *Stone.*

Strength of Israel. Jehovah is "the Strength of Israel" (1 Sam. 15:29), a title which demonstrates God's role as protector of Israel and as the power behind all of Israel's successes. Nephi praised God by exclaiming, "My God shall be my strength" (1 Ne. 21:5); "The Lord Jehovah is my strength" (2 Ne. 22:2). The phrase "The Lord is my strength," or its equivalent, is found throughout the Old Testament (Ex. 15:2; Ps. 18:1-2).

Strong Lord. The Psalmist inquired, "O Lord God of hosts, who is a strong Lord like unto thee?" (Ps. 89:8.) Although there is no recorded answer to this question, the answer is understood by all: "There is none like unto the Lord" (Ex. 8:10). He alone is "the mighty God" (Isa. 9:6), "the Strength of Israel" (1 Sam. 15:29), "the Mighty One of Israel" (1 Ne. 22:12).

Sun of Righteousness. In the scriptures, stars are commonly used symbolically to denote men. But the star nearest to the earth, known as the sun, represents the Son of God. Many of the prophets have compared the Son of God to this giant celestial orb. Malachi referred to the Lord as "the Sun of righteousness" (Mal. 4:2). Similarly, the Psalmist stated, "For the Lord God is a sun and shield" (Ps. 84:11). Matthew and John employed such similes when, speaking of Jesus, they wrote that "his face did shine as the sun" (Matt. 17:2), and that "his countenance was as the sun shineth in his strength" (Rev. 1:16). Both the Apostle Paul and the Prophet Joseph Smith, after seeing the resurrected, glorified Lord, described his appearance as being "above the brightness of the sun" (Acts 26:13; JS–H 1:16). Lehi saw Jesus "descending out of the midst of heaven, and he beheld that his luster was above that of the sun at noonday" (1 Ne. 1:9).

Furthermore, Jesus is called the Star, the Dayspring (meaning "the dawn"), and the Light. A modern revelation says of Christ, "He is in the sun, and the light of the sun, and the power thereof by which it was made" (D&C 88:7). Finally, when John the Revelator viewed the celestial city, he recorded that "the city had no need of the sun, neither of the moon, to shine in it: for the glory of God did lighten it, and the Lamb is the light thereof" (Rev. 21:23).

In what way is Jesus like the sun?

—As far as this earth is concerned, there are many stars (men), but only one sun (Jesus Christ).

—The planets and the moons and other celestial orbs derive their light from the sun.

—The sun is considered the head of all the heavens.

—Men cannot look directly at the sun, as they will become blind.

—The sun shines upon all, both upon the righteous and the unrighteous.

—The sun always shines; its motions are both regular and predictable.

—The sun generates life.

—The sun dispels darkness; it exposes what the night hides.

—The sun rises in the east, as Jesus will in his second coming.

—The sun burns as well as builds, just as Jesus will at his second coming. (See also *Star*; part 1: *Star; Sun*.)

Supreme Being. The title "Supreme Being," found twice in holy scripture (D&C 107:4; Alma 11:22), describes the supremacy and exaltation of God.

Supreme Creator. Jesus Christ is "the creator of Israel" (Isa. 43:15), "the great Creator" (2 Ne. 9:5), the "Maker" (D&C 134:6), and the "Supreme Creator" (Alma 30:44). Alma explained to the anti-Christ Korihor, "The scriptures are laid before thee, yea, and all things denote there is a God; yea, even the earth, and all things that are upon the face of it, yea, and its motion, yea, and also all the planets which move in their regular form do witness that there is a Supreme Creator" (Alma 30:44).

Surety. A surety is someone who makes sure, or gives assurance against loss, damage, or default. He makes himself responsible for another person, or stands as a guarantor of another's obligations. In the Bible, Judah became a surety to his father on behalf of his younger brother Benjamin. "I will be surety for him; of my hand shalt thou require him: if I bring him not unto thee, and set him before thee, then let me bear the blame for ever" (Gen. 43:9; see also Gen. 44:32). Also, Job appealed unto God to be his surety (Job 17:3); and in the New Testament, Paul agreed to be a surety to Philemon on behalf of Onesimus (Philem. 1:18, 19).

Since the idea of one person becoming a surety for another during the biblical period was a common event, it was a natural thing for the Apostle Paul to refer to Jesus Christ as a surety. To the Hebrews he wrote, "By so much was Jesus made a surety of a better testament" (Heb. 7:22).

Testator. In a legal sense, a testator is one who, having goods to bestow upon friends, relatives, or legal heirs, prepares a will and testament. The testator is often one anticipating death. He has full authority and power to bequeath his valuables according to his desires. To legitimize his testament, witnesses are present, that they may later testify as to the surety of the event. Testaments are always sealed with the signature of the testator. Furthermore, a testator has the authority to disannul any will created previously under his direction.

In a scriptural sense, Jesus is a testator, and the will that he left is the "new testament" or "new covenant." In establishing his new covenant, Christ disannuled Moses' old testament or covenant (Heb. 9:15–17). Several witnesses testify concerning the validity of Jesus' testament: God the Father, the Holy Ghost (John 15:26), the Twelve Apostles, and the scriptures. Jesus made certain that his new covenant would be published to the world (Matt. 28:19–20).

The Apostle Paul summed up Christ's role as testator in a few short sentences: "And for this cause he is the mediator of

168

A Guide to Scriptural Symbols

the new testament, that by means of death, for the redemption
of the transgressions that were under the first testament, they
which are called might receive the promise of eternal inheritance. For where a testament is, there must also of necessity be
the death of the testator. For a testament is of force after men
are dead: otherwise it is of no strength at all while the testator
liveth." (Heb. 9:15–17.)

Of course a testator must have heirs, or receivers of the gifts.
Paul explained that "we are the children of God: and if children,
then heirs; heirs of God, and joint-heirs with Christ" (Rom.
8:16–17; Gal. 4:7).

True. Jesus is called "True" (Rev. 19:11; 3:7), an adjective
which describes one aspect of his character. Everything concerning the Lord is true. Perfect truth resides with him. He has
been described as "him that is true" (1 John 5:20; see also Rev.
3:7; 6:10). "Jesus Christ is just and true" (D&C 20:30). He is the
"true God" (1 John 5:20), the true witness (John 8:14–18), "the
true Light" (John 1:9; 1 John 2:8; D&C 88:50), "the true bread"
(John 6:32), "the true vine" (John 15:1), and "the true
Messiah" (1 Ne. 10:14). Several have testified, "Master, we
know that thou art true" (Matt. 22:16).

True and Living God. See *True; Living God.*

True Shepherd. See *Shepherd.*

True Vine. See *Vine.*

Truth. Jesus said of himself, "I am . . . the truth" (John
14:6), "I am . . . the truth of the world," (Ether 4:12), and "I am
the Spirit of truth" (D&C 93:26). Others referred to him as the
"God of truth" (Deut. 32:4) and the "Lord God of truth" (Ps.
31:5). "He is full of . . . truth" (D&C 93:11); indeed, "he received
a fulness of truth, yea, even of all truth" (D&C 93:26). John recorded that Christ was born into the world to "bear witness
unto the truth" (John 18:37).

Everything concerning Christ is truth. His "law is the truth"
(Ps. 119:142), his "works are truth" (Dan. 4:37), his "word is
truth" (John 17:17), his "commandments are truth" (Ps.
119:151), and his scriptures are truth (D&C 17:6). He is the perfect embodiment and the quintessential representation of truth.
All truth centers in him and emanates from him.

Vine. Jesus taught his followers, "I am the true vine, and
my Father is the husbandman. . . . Ye are the branches." (John
15:1, 5.) Deep and profound meanings are found in these simple
words. A husbandman is one who plants, plows, and cultivates

the plants. This is the role of the Father. Jesus, who is the vine, supplies the branches (the Saints) with water and nutrients (with life). They "receive the strength and nourishment from the true vine," states Nephi (1 Ne. 15:15; see also Alma 16:17). Furthermore, "the branch cannot bear fruit of itself, except it abide in the vine" (John 15:4). Those who do not abide in the vine and produce fruit are cut off by the husbandman and are "cast forth as a branch, and [are] withered; and men gather them, and cast them into the fire, and they are burned" (John 15:6). But those who "abide in the vine . . . , the same bringeth forth much fruit" (John 15:4-5). The focal passage of this section is found in verse 5: "For without me ye can do nothing." Without Christ, there would be no link to the Father. Without Christ, there would be neither spiritual nor physical life. Without Christ, man would be unable to bear fruit. (See also part 1: *Fruit; Vine; Vineyard; Tree of Life.*)

Wall of Fire. In miraculous ways, God often employs the use of fire to protect his servants from danger (2 Kgs. 1; Hel. 5:23-49). In such a manner, Jesus, in a future day, will protect the city of Jerusalem. "For I, saith the Lord, will be unto her a wall of fire round about, and will be the glory in the midst of her" (Zech. 2:5). Elsewhere, we read, "For the Lord thy God is a consuming fire" (Deut. 4:24; Heb. 12:29). (See also part 1: *Fire.*)

Way. "Jesus saith . . . , I am the way" (John 14:6). What is the way of the Lord?

1) His is the narrow way. "Strait is the gate, and narrow is the way, which leadeth unto life, and few there be that find it" (Matt. 7:14).

2) His is the way to God (Matt. 11:27; John 6:44-45; Eph. 2:18). "I am the way . . . : no man cometh unto the Father, but by me" (John 14:6).

3) His is "the way of eternal life" (2 Ne. 10:23) and "the way of salvation" (Acts 16:17). "He that believeth in me, though he were dead, yet shall he live: and whosoever liveth and believeth in me shall never die" (John 11:25-27).

4) His is the way to heaven (Heb. 9:8).

5) His is the new way. Moses, for a period of time, was the "right way" (Jacob 7:7), but "in the gift of his Son hath God prepared a more excellent way" (Ether 12:11). Paul called him the "new and living way" (Heb. 10:20).

6) His is the only way. King Benjamin testified: "There shall be no other name given nor any other way nor means whereby

salvation can come unto the children of men, only in and through the name of Christ, the Lord Omnipotent" (Mosiah 3:17). (See also part 1: *Highway.*)

Wisdom of God. Jesus is the "wisdom of God" (1 Cor. 1:24) and "the hidden wisdom, which God ordained before the world unto our glory: which none of the princes of this world knew: for had they known it, they would not have crucified the Lord of glory" (1 Cor. 2:7–8).

Isaiah prophesied that the "spirit of wisdom" (Isa. 11:2) would be with the Lord. At a much later date, Luke recorded that as a child, Jesus "grew, and waxed strong in spirit, filled with wisdom" (Luke 2:40). Jesus' listeners, after hearing his teachings, were heard to exclaim, "Whence hath this man this wisdom?" (Matt. 13:54.) Paul testified that in God "the Father, and Christ . . . are hid all the treasures of wisdom and knowledge" (Col. 2:2–3).

So "great is his wisdom" (D&C 76:2) that his "wisdom is greater than the cunning of the devil" (D&C 10:43). Even "the foolishness of God is wiser than men" (1 Cor. 1:25).

Witness. Seven centuries before the birth of Christ, Isaiah had prophesied that Jesus would be "a witness to the people" (Isa. 55:4). During his mortal ministry, Jesus testified to Pilate: "To this end was I born, and for this cause came I into the world, that I should bear witness unto the truth" (John 18:37). After the crucifixion of the Lord, the Revelator testified that Jesus had been "the faithful and true witness" (Rev. 3:14; see also Rev. 1:5).

Wonderful. Speaking of the Messiah who was to be born of a virgin, Isaiah prophesied that "his name shall be called Wonderful" (Isa. 9:6). Jesus is Wonderful in that he demonstrates grace, mercy, and justice; and especially in that he gave his life for the sake of all humanity.

Word. The only biblical writer to refer to Jesus Christ as the Word was the Apostle John. He recorded, "And his name is called The Word of God" (Rev. 19:13); "and our hands have handled, of the Word of life" (1 John 1:1); and "there are three that bear record in heaven, the Father, the Word, and the Holy Ghost: and these three are one" (1 John 5:7).

Jesus was the Word in the sense that he was the one from whom the revelations came. He was and always will be the Word to the prophets and Apostles of all ages. According to the Doctrine and Covenants, "He was the Word, even the messenger of salvation" (D&C 93:8). The Apostle John, in an inspired play on words, interchanged the terms *word* (meaning the words of the scriptures) and *Word* (meaning Jesus Christ). "In the beginning was the gospel preached through the Son. And the gospel was the word, and the word was with the Son, and the Son was with God, and the Son was of God. . . . And the same word was made flesh, and dwelt among us." (JST, John 1:1, 14.)

Jesus Christ (the Word), gave the gospel message (the word) to all mankind, through the prophets. Furthermore, Joseph Smith recorded in the Doctrine and Covenants that the words of the scriptures are the voice of Jesus; and those who read these words have the promise. "Wherefore, you can testify that you have heard my voice, and know my words" (D&C 18:33–36).

Word of God. Jesus Christ, when he returns to the earth in all his majesty and glory, will be "clothed with a vesture dipped in blood: and his name is called The Word of God" (Rev. 19:13).

Word of God's Power. Through the word of Jesus Christ all things were created. Several scriptural passages explain this principle.

—"I have created by the word of my power" (D&C 29:30).

—"And by the power of his word man was created of the dust of the earth" (Morm. 9:17).

—"By the power of his word man came upon the face of the earth, which earth was created by the power of his word" (Jacob 4:9).

—"And the stars also were made even according to my word" (Moses 2:16).

—"Spiritually were they created and made according to my word" (Moses 3:7; see also 2:5).

Thus, when we speak of the "word of [God's] power," which is a reference to Jesus Christ (Moses 1:32), we are speaking of the creative process of the Father and the Son. All things were created by the word of Jesus Christ. (See also *Word.*)

Yesterday, Today, and Forever. The prophets describe God as being "the same yesterday, today, and forever" (2 Ne. 27:23; 1 Ne. 10:18; Heb. 13:8; Alma 31:17; D&C 20:12), meaning that his character, goals, and purposes are unchanging throughout the eternities. Concerning this, Mormon wrote, "For do we not read that God is the same yesterday, today, and forever, and in him there is no variableness neither shadow of changing?" (Morm. 9:9.) And Joseph Smith explained, "Listen to the voice of the Lord your God, even Alpha and Omega, the beginning and the end, whose course is one eternal round, the same today as yesterday, and forever" (D&C 35:1).

PART 3

SYMBOLIC
AND
THEOPHORIC
NAMES

Symbolic and Theophoric Names

"Names are verbal symbols: they announce existence, herald one's reputation, and express character; they are, in some instances, a scepter of authority or even a crown of glory. Biblical names generally were descriptive of the one bearing them. They might identify position, memorialize a significant event in someone's life, express a hope entertained by those giving the name, or even represent a prophesied destiny. To 'call one's name' over something signified ownership, possession, and protection — for example, of David over a city (see 2 Samuel 12:28), of seven women seeking the name of a man to take away their reproach (see Isaiah 4:1), of God over the nations (see Amos 9:12) and over Israel (see Isaiah 63:19). To 'cut off the name' was the equivalent of liquidating the person (see Deuteronomy 7:24). 'In modern usage, names are convenient labels by which we differentiate one thing from another, one person from another. But in the ancient world Shakespeare's question "What's in a name?" would have been taken very seriously. For a person's self was expressed and contained in his name. Analogously, God's self, his real person, is concentrated in his name.' (Anderson, 'Names of God,' in *Interpreter's Dictionary of the Bible*, 2:408.)" (Robert L. Millet and Joseph Fielding McConkie, *In His Holy Name*, p. 11.)

Ancient Israelites were mononymous people — each child received only one name at birth. Personal names were often given in connection with a particular circumstance or event. Thus, we can identify:

- —Names connected with a physical characteristic of the newborn child. The name Esau means "shaggy" or "hairy."
- —Names describing the personality or temperament of the person. For instance, the name Nabal means "fool."
- —Names that indicate the events surrounding the birth of the child. The name Haggai signifies "born on a day of a festival."

—Individuals named after fruits, plants, or trees. Tamar is named after the palm tree; Habakkuk means "basil, mint."

—Individuals named after animals. Hamor means "ass," Arieh is a "lion."

—Names given as symbols. Isaiah's son was named Maher-shalal-hash-baz, meaning "Speedy-spoil-quick-booty."

Many Old Testament characters and places were given theophoric names (compound words composed of either a noun, pronoun, adjective, or verb, combined with a name of Deity). Some four hundred such names are listed in the Old Testament. These religious names spoke of the attributes, character, personality, and virtues of the deity being described.

"Names play a significant part in the scriptural story. This is true of both place-names and personal names, and is illustrated by the countless instances in which the Bible pauses in its narrative to explain the meaning of names. Place-names are often a form of verbal archaeology, describing an area or setting. Personal names were considered of such importance that on occasion they were announced by heavenly messengers or some other form of revelation. It was so important that the name and the person match that in other instances names were changed by divine decree. Personal names served as miniature biographies, descriptions of character, testimonies or expressions of praise to God, reminders of significant events, and divine warning. In short, Bible names served as memorials, symbols, and prophecies." (*Gospel Symbolism*, p. 173.)

In the space after each name in the following list of symbolic and theophoric names, we have made a brief comment suggesting a possible interpretation. Our remarks should be considered observations only.

Theophoric Names Containing the Name El (God)

Abdeel (Jer. 36:26). "Servant of God." True disciples are servants of the Master.

Abiel (1 Sam. 9:1). "God is my father." God is the Father of all spirits; his Son is the Father of those who believe.

Adiel (1 Chr. 4:36). "God has adorned himself." That is, with robes of righteousness and the crown of glory.

Adriel (1 Sam. 18:19). "Flock of God." The Lord is the Shepherd; his followers are therefore called sheep. (See also part 1: *Sheep; Shepherd.*)

Ammiel (Num 13:12). "My kinsman is God." The righteous are kindred spirits with the Lord.

Ariel (Isa. 29:1). "Lion of God." (See also part 1: *Lion.*)

Asahel (Ezra 10:15). "God has made." He is the Creator of all things.

Asareel (1 Chr. 4:16). "God has bound." "I, the Lord, am bound when ye do what I say" (D&C 82:10).

Asriel (Josh. 17:2). "Vow of God." The Lord is a God of covenants and vows.

Azareel (Neh. 11:13). "God has helped." (See also part 2: *Help.*)

Azriel (Jer. 36:26). "My help is God." (See also part 2: *Help.*)

Barachel (Job 32:2). "God blesses." The righteous receive blessings; the wicked, curses.

Daniel (Dan. 1:6). "God is my judge." (See also part 2: *Judge.*)

Deuel (Num. 1:14). "Knowledge of God." Essential in order to receive exaltation.

Eladah (1 Chr. 7:20). "God has adorned." (See also *Adiel.*)

Eldaah (Gen. 25:4). "God has called." Many have been called to the gospel of Jesus Christ.

Eldad (Num. 11:26). "God has loved." (See also *Elidad.*)

Elead (1 Chr. 7:21). "God has testified." (See also part 2: *Testator.*)

Eleasah (1 Chr. 2:39). "God has made." (See also *Asahel.*)

Eleazar (Ex. 6:23). "God has helped." (See also part 2: *Help.*)

Elhanan (2 Sam. 21:19). "God has shown favor." "He that is righteous is favored of God" (1 Ne. 17:35).

Eliab (1 Sam. 16:6). "My God is father." (See also *Abiel.*)

Eliada (2 Sam. 5:16). "God knows." Signifies his omniscience.

Eliahba (2 Sam. 23:32). "God hides." His heavenly dwelling place is concealed from mortal eyes.

Eliakim (Isa. 22:20). "God sets upright." He establishes the upright upon the sure Foundation. (See also part 2: *Foundation.*)

Eliam (2 Sam. 11:3). "God is kinsman." (See also *Ammiel.*)

Eliasaph (Num. 1:14). "God has added." (See also *Josiphiah.*)

Eliashib (1 Chr. 3:24). "God restores." He restores gospel truths, priesthood keys and powers, and sacred ordinances.

Eliathah (1 Chr. 25:4). "God has come." Pertains to the condescension of the Lord (1 Ne. 11).

Elidad (Num. 34:21). "My God has loved." He is the perfect standard of love.

Eliel (1 Chr. 5:24). "My God is God." In contrast to the false gods and deities of the ancient Israelite period, El (God) was the true and living God.

Eliezer (Gen. 15:2). "God is help." (See also part 2: *Help.*)

Elihu (1 Sam. 1:1). "He is my God." (See also *Eliel.*)

Elijah (1 Kgs. 17:1). "Yah is my God." An affirmation that Jehovah is God.

Elimelech (Ruth 1:2). "God is my king." (See also *Malchijah.*)

Eliphaz (Gen. 36:4). "God is fine gold." He symbolizes that which is pure, incorruptible, and of great value. (See also part 1: *Gold.*)

Eliphelet (2 Sam. 23:34). "God is deliverance." From death, hell, and the devil.

Elisha (1 Kgs. 19:16). "God is salvation." (See also part 2: *Salvation.*)

Elishama (Num. 1:10). "God has heard." (See also *Ishmael.*)

Elishaphat (2 Chr. 23:1). "God has judged." (See also part 2: *Judge.*)

Elisheba (Ex. 6:23). "God is an oath." A metaphor describing God as a covenant maker.

Elishua (2 Sam. 5:15). "God is salvation." (See also part 2: *Salvation.*)

Eliud (Matt. 1:14). "My God is majesty." A personification related to his divine kingship.

Elizaphan (Num. 3:30). "God has protected." He acts as a refuge and sanctuary unto those who seek him.

Elizur (Num. 1:5). "God is a rock." He is steadfast and sure. (See also part 2: *Rock.*)

Elkanah (Ex. 6:24). "God has created." (See also *Asahel.*)

Elnaam (1 Chr. 11:46). "God is pleasantness." He is all things good.

Elnathan (2 Kgs. 24:8). "God has given." (See also *Joash.*)

Elpaal (1 Chr. 8:11). "God has acted." Pertains to the Lord's dealings with mankind.

Eluzai (1 Chr. 12:5). "God is my strength." (See also part 2: *Strength of Israel*.)

Elzabad (1 Chr. 12:12). "God has given." (See also *Joash*.)

Ezekiel (Ezek. 1:3). "May God make strong." He strengthens those with weak knees and feeble hearts.

Gabriel (Dan. 8:16). "God is strong." He is omnipotent. (See also part 2: *Strong Lord*.)

Gaddiel (Num. 13:10). "My fortune is God." Eternal riches are obtained after one receives a hope in Christ.

Gamaliel (Num. 1:10). "My reward is God." (See also *Gaddiel*.)

Geuel (Num. 13:15). "Majesty of God." (See also *Eliud*.)

Hanameel (Jer. 32:7). "God has shown favor." (See also *Elhanan*.)

Hanniel (Num. 34:23). "Favor of God." (See also *Elhanan*.)

Hazael (1 Kgs. 19:15). "God has seen." (See also *Jahaziel*.)

Haziel (1 Chr. 23:9). "Vision of God." A vision reserved for the faithful.

Hiel (1 Kgs. 6:34). "Brother of God." (See also *Joah*.)

Immanuel (Isa. 7:14). "With us is God." He is omnipresent through the power of his Holy Spirit.

Ishmael (Gen. 16:11). "God hears." He hears our supplications and petitions.

Israel (Gen. 32:28). "God contends." He is a "man of war" (Ex. 15:3).

Ithiel (Prov. 30:1). "God is with me." (See also *Immanuel*.)

Jaasiel (1 Chr. 27:21). "God has done." (See also *Asahel*.)

Jabneel (Josh. 15:11). "God causes to be built." (See also *Benaiah*.)

Jahaziel (Ezra 8:5). "God sees." His eye is an "all-searching eye" (2 Ne. 9:44) which penetrates all things.

Jahdiel (1 Chr. 5:24). "God rejoices." His life is an existence of unparalleled joy.

Jahleel (Num. 26:26). "Wait for God." The righteous expect his instructions and revelations and anticipate his blessings.

Jathniel (1 Chr. 26:2). "God is constant." He is unchanging and enduring, the same throughout the eternities.

Jediael (1 Chr. 7:6). "God knows." He is omniscient.

Jehalelel (1 Chr. 4:16). "He will praise God." Because of the perfect mercy, justice, and love which resides in Deity, the faithful continually praise God.

Jehiel (Ezra 8:9). "May God live." (See also *Izrahiah.*)

Jekabzeel (Neh. 11:25). "May God gather together." Pertains to the gathering of the house of Israel.

Jerahmeel (Jer. 36:26). "May God have pity." (See also part 2: *Merciful.*)

Jeruel (2 Chr. 20:16). "Foundation of God." That is, the prophets and Apostles, with Jesus Christ as the chief cornerstone.

Jesimiel (1 Chr. 4:36). "God establishes." (See also *Eliakim.*)

Jezreel (Josh. 15:56). "God sows." He sows wheat seed, or plants the righteous.

Jiphthah-el (Josh. 19:14). "God opens." The portals of heaven are open unto the faithful.

Joel (1 Sam. 8:2). "Yah is God." An affirmation that Jehovah is God.

Kadmiel (Neh. 12:8). "God is before me." He is both a harbinger and a vanguard unto the faithful of his army.

Lael (Num. 3:24). "Who belongs to God." The faithful of every dispensation are the Lord's possession.

Lemuel (Prov. 31:1). "Who belongs to God." (See also *Lael.*)

Malchiel (Gen. 46:17). "My king is God." (See also *Malchijah.*)

Mehetabel (Gen. 36:39). "God does good." He is the epitome of all things good.

Mehujael (Gen. 4:18). "God causes to live." He is the Resurrection.

Meshezabeel (Neh. 3:4). "God saves." Through the atoning sacrifice, man is saved from death, hell, and the devil.

Michael (Num. 13:13). "Who is like God." (See also *Micaiah*; part 1: *Michael; Adam.*)

Mishael (Ex. 6:22). "Who belongs to God." (See also *Lael.*)

Nethaneel (Num. 1:8). "God has given." (See also *Joash.*)

Othniel (Josh. 15:17). "Gatekeeper of God." (See also part 2: *Keeper of the Gate.*)

Paltiel (Num. 34:26). "God is my deliverance." (See also part 2: *Deliverer*.)

Pedahel (Num. 34:28). "God ransoms." (See also *Pedaiah*.)

Pethuel (Joel 1:1). "Youthfulness of God." Speaks of the eternal agelessness of Deity.

Raphael (D&C 128:21). "God has healed." (See also *Rephaiah*.)

Reuel (Ex. 2:18). "Friend of God." True disciples are called friends. (See also part 1: *Friend*.)

Samuel (1 Sam. 1:20). "Name of God."

Shealtiel (Hag. 1:1). "I have asked God." Pertains to prayer.

Shelumiel (Num. 1:6). "God is my peace." He is known as the Prince of Peace. (See also part 2: *Prince of Peace*.)

Tabeel (Ezra 4:7). "God is good." A simple yet profound epigram states that "all things which are good cometh from God; and that which is evil cometh of the devil" (Moro. 7:12).

Uriel (1 Chr. 6:24). "My light is God." The light by which mortal man discerns truth from error.

Uzziel (Ex. 6:18). "God is my strength." (See also part 2: *Strength of Israel*.)

Zabdiel (1 Chr. 27:2). "Gift of God." (See also *Kushaiah*.)

Theophoric Names Containing the Name Yahweh (Lord)

Abijah (1 Kgs. 14:1). "Yah is my father." (See also *Abiel*.)

Adaiah (2 Kgs. 22:1). "Yah has adorned himself." (See also *Adiel*.)

Adonijah (2 Sam. 3:4). "Yah is my Lord." A testimonial, a declaration of the divinity of Jehovah.

Ahijah (2 Kgs. 9:9). "Brother of Yah." (See also *Joah*.)

Amariah (Ezra 7:3). "Said by Yah." (See also part 2: *Word*.)

Amaziah (2 Kgs. 12:21). "Yah is mighty." He is the "mighty God" (Isa. 9:6), the "mighty One of Jacob" (Isa. 49:26).

Anaiah (Neh. 8:4). "Yah has answered." Speaks of divine communion with the Lord, or prayer.

Ananiah (Neh. 3:23). "Protected by Yah." Pertains to God as the Shield, Sanctuary, and Guardian of the righteous. (See also part 2: *Shield; Sanctuary.*)

Antothijah (1 Chr. 8:24). "Answers of Yah." (See also *Anaiah.*)

Asaiah (1 Chr. 4:36). "Yah has made." (See also *Asahel.*)

Athaiah (Neh. 11:4). "Yah has succored." He furnishes relief to those whose burdens are heavy.

Athaliah (2 Kgs. 8:26). "Yah is exalted." He dwells eternally upon the right hand of the Father.

Azaliah (2 Kgs. 22:3). "Helped by Yah." (See also part 2: *Help.*)

Azaniah (Neh. 10:9). "Heard by Yah." (See also *Anaiah.*)

Azariah (2 Chr. 15:1). "Yah has helped." (See also part 2: *Help.*)

Azaziah (1 Chr. 15:21). "Strengthened by Yah." (See also part 2: *Strength of Israel.*)

Baaseiah (1 Chr. 6:40). "Work of Yah." His work is the "immortality and eternal life of man" (Moses 1:39).

Bakbukiah (Neh. 11:17). "Pouring of Yah." Speaks of the issuing of heavenly blessings which are poured into the cup of the faithful.

Bealiah (1 Chr. 12:5). "Yah is Lord." (See also *Adonijah.*)

Bedeiah (Ezra 10:35). "Servant of Yah." (See also *Abdeel.*)

Benaiah (2 Sam. 8:18). "Yah has built." He is the master builder. (See also part 1: *Builder.*)

Beraiah (1 Chr. 8:21). "Yah has created." (See also *Asahel.*)

Berechiah (2 Chr. 28:12). "Blessed by Yah." (See also *Barachel.*)

Besodeiah (Neh. 3:6). "In the secret council of Yah." Pertains to the Great Council in Heaven.

Bukkiah (1 Chr. 25:4). "Proved by Yah." Like gold, tested in the fires of affliction and found to be pure.

Chenaniah (1 Chr. 15:22). "Yah is firm." As a foundation, God is firm and immovable as a rock.

Delaiah (Jer. 36:12). "Yah has drawn up." He lifts the righteous unto him.

Dodavah (2 Chr. 20:37). "Beloved by Yah." A play on words, as Jehovah is denominated Beloved (Matt. 3:17).

Elijah (1 Kgs. 17:1). "Yah is God." An affirmation that Jehovah is God.

Elioenai (1 Chr. 26:3). "Toward Yah are my eyes." My thoughts are continually upon the Lord.

Gedaliah (2 Kgs. 25:22). "Yah has magnified." He has enlarged, glorified, and exalted.

Gemariah (Jer. 29:3). "Yah has completed." He has completed his everlasting and eternal sacrifice on behalf of humanity.

Habaiah (Ezra 2:61). "Yah hides himself." From the wicked. On the contrary, the pure in heart have the promise of communion with God.

Haggiah (1 Chr. 6:30). "Yah is my festival." Many aspects of the Old Testament festivals pointed to the life and ministry of Jesus Christ. (See also part 1: *Day of Atonement.*)

Hananiah (Neh. 3:8). "Yah has shown favor." (See also *Elhanan.*)

Hasadiah (1 Chr. 3:20). "Yah is faithful." He is the quintessential example of faithfulness.

Hashabiah (Ezra 8:19). "Yah has taken into account." He weighs the heart of every soul, and then pronounces an eternal judgment.

Hazaiah (Neh. 11:5). "Yah has seen." (See also *Jahaziel.*)

Hezekiah (2 Kgs. 16:20). "My strength is Yah." (See also part 2: *Strength of Israel.*)

Hilkiah (1 Chr. 6:13). "My share is Yah." Saints of God receive an equal portion of the Father's inheritance.

Hodaviah (1 Chr. 5:24). "Celebrate Yah." (See also *Haggiah.*)

Hodiah (1 Chr. 4:19). "Yah is Majesty." (See also *Eliud.*)

Hoshaiah (Jer. 42:1). "Yah has saved." (See also *Meshezabel.*)

Hoshama (1 Chr. 3:18). "Yah hears." (See also *Anaiah.*)

Hoshea (Deut. 32:44). "Yah saves." (See also *Meshezabel.*)

Ibnijah (1 Chr. 9:8). "Yah builds." (See also *Benaiah.*)

Igdaliah (Jer. 35:4). "Yah is great." He is omniscient, omnipotent, and omnipresent.

Irijah (Jer. 37:13). "Yah sees." (See also *Jahaziel.*)

Isaiah (2 Kgs. 19:2). "Yah is salvation." (See also part 2: *Salvation.*)

Ishmaiah (1 Chr. 27:19). "Yah hears." (See also *Anaiah.*)

Izrahiah (1 Chr. 7:3). "Yah will arise." Speaks of the resurrection. (See also part 2: *Resurrection.*)

Jaazaniah (2 Kgs. 25:23). "Yah hears." (See also *Anaiah.*)

Jahaziah (Ezra 10:15). "Yah sees." (See also *Jahaziel.*)

Jahzeel (Gen. 46:24). "Yah divides." He divides the sheep from the goats.

Jecoliah (2 Chr. 26:3). "Yah can." There is nothing that is too difficult for the Lord to accomplish.

Jedaiah (Zech. 6:10). "Yah knows." (See also *Elyada.*)

Jedidiah (2 Sam. 12:25). "Loved by Yah." Jehovah is the personification of love.

Jehdeiah (1 Chr. 24:20). "May Yah rejoice." That is rejoice over those who choose righteousness and good works.

Jehiah (1 Chr. 15:24). "May Yah live." (See also *Izrahiah.*)

Jehoiachin (2 Kgs. 24:6). "Yah has established." (See also *Jekamiah.*)

Jehoiada (2 Sam. 8:18). "Yah knows." (See also *Elyada.*)

Jehoiakim (2 Kgs. 23:34). "Yah causes to stand upright." (See also *Eliakim.*)

Jehoram (1 Kgs. 22:50). "Yah is high." He is exalted and dwells in the highest heaven.

Jekamiah (1 Chr. 2:41). "May Yah establish." That is, establish his gospel, his prophets, the scriptures, and his Saints.

Jeremiah (Jer. 1:1). "Yah raises up." He is the Resurrection.

Jeriah (1 Chr. 23:19). "Foundation of Yah." An eternal foundation upon which the Saints build.

Joab (1 Sam. 26:6). "Yah is Father." True disciples are spiritually begotten of God.

Joah (1 Chr. 6:21). "Yah is brother." Jehovah shares the same Heavenly Father as do the children of men.

Joash (Judg. 6:11). "Yah has given." He has given us power over death, eternal life, and so on.

Jochebed (Ex. 6:20). "Yah is glory." (See also part 2: *Glorious Lord.*)

Joed (Neh. 11:7). "Yah is witness." (See also part 2: *Witness.*)

Joel (1 Sam. 8:2). "Yah is God." In contrast to the gods of the Canaanites, Hittites, Egyptians, and so on.

Joezer (1 Chr. 12:6). "Yah is help." (See also part 2: *Help.*)

Johanan (Ezra 8:12). "Yah has shown favor." (See also *Elhanan.*)

Joiarib (Ezra 8:16). "Yah renders justice." (See also part 2: *Judge.*)

Jonadab (2 Sam. 13:3). "Yah is generous." Mercy and grace emanate from him.

Jonathan (1 Sam. 13:2). "Yah has given." (See also *Joash.*)

Joshaphat (1 Chr. 11:43). "Yah judges." Pertains to the great Day of Judgment.

Joshua (Ex. 17:9). "Yah saves." (See also *Meshezabel.*)

Josiah (1 Kgs. 13:2). "Yah supports." He upholds, preserves, and sustains; he is the Staff of Life.

Josiphiah (Ezra 8:10). "May Yah add." Line upon line, grace for grace, glory for glory.

Jozabad (1 Chr. 12:20). "Yah has bestowed." Spiritual gifts, priesthood powers, and glorious honors.

Jozadak (Ezra 3:2). "Yah is just." His judgments are fair, his ways are righteous.

Kolaiah (Jer. 29:21). "Yah has spoken." That is, to his prophets, to his disciples, and to the nations of the world.

Kushaiah (1 Chr. 15:17). "Gift of Yah." The greatest gift of the Lord was the sacrifice of his own life.

Maaseiah (2 Chr. 23:1). "Work of Yah." (See also *Baaseiah.*)

Maaziah (Neh. 10:8). "Yah is a fortress." He is a shield, buckler, and refuge unto the righteous.

Malchijah (1 Chr. 9:12). "My king is Yah." In contrast to those who revere or glorify the kings of the world.

Mattithiah (1 Chr. 9:31). "Gift of Yah." (See also *Kushaiah.*)

Meraiah (Neh. 12:12). "Loved by Yah." (See also *Jedidiah.*)

Meshelemiah (1 Chr. 9:21). "Yah has replaced." Pertains to the Restoration.

Micaiah (1 Kgs. 22:8). "Who is like Yah." Speaks of those that have the image of Jehovah engraven upon their countenances.

Mikneiah (1 Chr. 15:18). "Possession of Yah." (See also *Lael.*)

Nedabiah (1 Chr. 3:18). "He whom Yah fills to overflowing." Speaks of the cup of the Lord's blessing. (See also part 1: *Cup.*)

Nehemiah (Ezra 2:2). "Yah consoles." He comforts his people in their afflictions, hardships, and trials.

Nethaniah (2 Kgs. 25:23). "Yah has given." (See also *Joash.*)

Noadiah (Neh. 6:14). "Encounter with Yah." Speaks of theophanic experiences, God's appearances unto mortal man.

Obadiah (1 Kgs. 18:3). "Servant of Yah." (See also *Abdeel.*)

Pedaiah (2 Kgs. 23:36). "Yah ransoms." Pertains to Jesus' mediation and atonement.

Pekahiah (2 Kgs. 15:22). "Yah has opened." The gate unto heaven, the way to eternal life. (See also part 1: *Gate; Door.*)

Pelaliah (Neh. 11:12). "Yah has mediated." (See also part 2: *Mediator.*)

Pelatiah (1 Chr. 3:21). "Survivor of Yah." The righteous endure the judgments of the Lord.

Reaiah (Neh. 7:50). "Yah has seen." (See also *Jahaziel.*)

Rehabiah (1 Chr. 23:17). "Yah has given room." Speaks of free agency.

Rephaiah (1 Chr. 3:21). "Yah has healed." He is the great Physician. (See also part 2: *Physician.*)

Semachiah (1 Chr. 26:7). "Yah has sustained." (See also *Ismachiah.*)

Seraiah (2 Sam. 8:17). "Yah has shown himself strong." (See also *Gabriel.*)

Shecaniah (1 Chr. 3:21). "Yah has taken up his abode." He dwells (*shakan*) in his temple (*Mishkan*).

Shelemiah (1 Chr. 26:14). "Yah has completed." (See also *Gemariah.*)

Shemariah (1 Chr. 12:5). "Yah has preserved." (See also *Josiah.*)

Shephatiah (2 Chr. 21:2). "Yah has judged." (See also part 2: *Judge.*)

Tobijah (Zech. 6:10). "Yah is good." (See also *Tabeel.*)

Uriah (2 Sam. 11:3). "My light is Yah." (See also *Uriel.*)

Urijah (2 Kgs. 16:10). "My light is Yahweh." (See also *Uriel.*)

Uzziah (2 Kgs. 15:13). "Yah is my strength." (See also part 2: *Strength of Israel.*)

Zebadiah (1 Chr. 8:15). "Gift of Yah." (See also *Kushaiah.*)

Zechariah (1 Chr. 5:7). "Yah remembers." He remembers his covenants.

Zedekiah (1 Kgs. 22:11). "Yah is righteous." He is denominated Righteous and Righteousness. (See also part 2: *Righteous; Righteousness.*)

Zephaniah (1 Chr. 6:36). "Yah protects." (See also *Ananiah.*)

Zerahiah (Ezra 7:4). "Yah has shone." He is the Sun of Righteousness. (See also part 2: *Sun of Righteousness.*)

Theophoric Names Containing the Name Adonai (Lord) or Shaddai (Almighty)

Adonijah (2 Sam. 3:4). "My Lord is Yahweh." (See also *Elijah.*)

Adonikam (Ezra 2:13). "My Lord has arisen." (See also *Izrahiah.*)

Adoniram (1 Kgs. 4:6). "My Lord is exalted." (See also *Jehoram.*)

Adoni-zedek (Josh. 10:1). "My Lord is righteous." (See also *Zedekiah.*)

Ammishaddai (Num. 1:12). "My kinsman is Almighty." (See also *Ammiel.*)

Names of Persons and Places Containing Theophoric Elements of Pagan Gods and Deities

Baal-Berith (Judg. 8:33). "Baal (lord) of the covenant."

Baal-Hanan (Gen. 36:38). "Baal (lord) has been gracious."

Baalzebub (2 Kgs. 1:2). "Ball (lord) of the fly." The god of Ekron.

Baal-Zephon (Ex. 14:2). "Baal (lord) of the North."

Bamoth-Baal (Josh. 13:17). "High places of Baal (lord)."

Beeliada (1 Chr. 14:7). "Baal (lord) knows."

Beelzebub (Matt. 10:25). "Lord of the fly." Prince of devils.

Belshazzar (Dan. 5:1). "Bel, protect the king." That is, the king of Babylon.

Beth-Anath (Josh. 19:38). "House (temple) of [the goddess] Anath."

Beth-Dagon (Josh. 15:41). "House (temple) of Dagon." The principal god of the Philistines.

Beth-Horon (1 Sam. 13:18). "House (temple) of [the god] Horon."

Beth-Shean (Josh. 17:11). "House (temple) of rest," or "house of [the goddess] Sha'an."

Esarhaddon (2 Kgs. 19:37). "[The god] Asshur has given a brother."

Ethbaal (1 Kgs. 16:31). "With Baal," or "living with Baal's favor."

Evil-Merodach (2 Kgs. 25:27). "Man of Marduk."

Meribbaal (1 Chr. 8:34). "Baal is champion," or "Baal is advocate."

Merodach-Baladan (Isa. 39:1). "Marduk has given a son."

Rameses (Gen. 47:11). "Begotten of Ra."

Sanballat (Neh. 2:10). "[The god] Sin gives life."

Sennacherib (2 Kgs. 18:13). "Sin has replaced the brothers."

Shalmaneser (2 Kgs. 17:3). "[The god] Shulman is superior."

Shenazar (1 Chr. 3:18). "Sin, protect."

Symbolic Names of Places

Abaddon (Rev. 9:11). "Destruction, lost, ruin." 1) Place of the lost or ruined, hence, a poetic name for the place of the dead. 2) A name for the devil, whose eternal station is destruction.

Aholah (Ezek. 23:4). See part 1: *Aholah.*

Aholibah (Ezek. 23:4). See part 1: *Aholibah.*

Ariel (Isa. 29:1). "Lioness of God." One of the many names of Jerusalem. (See also part 1: *Jerusalem.*)

Armaggedon (Rev. 16:16). "Mountains of Megiddo." (See also part 1: *Armegeddon.*)

Assyria (2 Kgs. 15:19). Named after the deity known as Asshur.

Babel (Gen. 11:9). "Confusion." A play on words. At one time the earth was of "one language, and of one speech," but due to the wickedness of mankind "the Lord did . . . confound the language of all the earth." (Gen. 11:1-9.) Thus the place was called Babel or "confusion."

Beersheba (Gen. 21:14). "Well of seven" or "well of oath." Speaks of sacred events which occurred at this place.

Bethel (Gen. 12:8). "House of God." So denominated because the Lord's sanctuary once stood at this location.

Bethlehem (Gen. 35:19). "House of bread." Prophetic name for the village in which Jesus, the Bread of Life, would enter the world in his mortal tabernacle.

Edom (Gen. 25:30). See part 1: *Edom*.

Garden of Eden (Gen. 2:15). See part 1: *Garden of Eden*.

Gethsemane (Matt. 26:36). "Olive press." (See also part 1: *Gethsemane*.)

Golgotha (John 19:17). "Place of the skull." Place of the Crucifixion.

Jeshurun (Deut. 32:15). "Upright." Poetic name for Israel.

Peniel (Gen. 32:30). "Face of God." The place where Jacob saw the face of God.

Sodom and Gomorrah (Gen. 10:19). See part 1: *Gomorrah*.

Symbolic Names of Persons

Abraham (Gen. 17:5). "Chief of a multitude." Pertains to Abraham as the father of the faithful. (See also part 1: *Abraham*.)

Abram (Gen. 11:26). "Exalted father." Abraham is a type of the Father. (See also part 1: *Abraham*.)

Adam (Gen. 2:19). See part 1: *Adam*.

Aholiab (Ex. 31:6). "Father's tent" or "Father's tabernacle." Perhaps so denominated because of his role as one of the chief builders of the Mosaic tabernacle.

Bathsheba (2 Sam. 11:3). "Daughter of oath." The irony of Bathsheba's sin with David is herein evident.

Benjamin (Num. 1:11). "Son at the right hand." Pertains to his chosenness (Gen. 35:18).

Dan (Ex. 1:4). "Judge." A shortened form of Daniel. (See also *Daniel*.)

David (1 Sam. 16:13). "Beloved." As a type of Jesus, the Beloved Son (Matt. 3:17). (See also part 1: *David*.)

Esau (Gen. 25:25). "Hairy." Called such because when he was born he "came out red, all over like an hairy garment" (Gen. 25:25; 27:11).

Eve (Gen. 3:20). "Living." Pertains to Eve as the mother of all living.

Gomer (Hosea 1:3). See part 1: *Hosea.*

Hosea (Hosea 1:1). "[Yah] saves." (See also part 1: *Hosea.*)

Isaac (Gen. 21:3). "May he laugh," or "may he rejoice." A play on words (Gen. 18:12-15; 17:17).

Jezreel (Josh. 15:56). See part 1: *Hosea.*
Jonah (Jonah 1:1). "Dove."

Lo-ammi (Hosea 1:9). "Not my people." (See also part 1: *Hosea.*)
Lo-ruhamah (Hosea 1:8). "Not having obtained mercy." (See also part 1: *Hosea.*)

Maher-shalal-hash-baz (Isa. 8:1). "To speed to the spoil, he hasteneth the prey." The second son of Isaiah was so named. The name served as both a prophecy and a type of Jesus (cf. Isa. 7:14-16).
Malachi (Mal. 1:1). "My messenger." Signifies Malachi's calling as a prophet-messenger.
Melchizedek (Ps. 110:4). "My king is righteous." In reference to the Lord, who is the righteous King of kings. (See also part 1: *Melchizedek*; part 2: *King of kings.*)

Peleg (Gen. 10:25). "Division." Perhaps so named in reference to the division of the lands, which division took place during Peleg's lifetime.
Peter (Matt. 4:18). "Rock." As a type of Christ, who is called a Rock. (See also part 2: *Rock.*)

Sarah (Gen. 17:15). "Princess." Pertains to her role as a queen and a priestess.
Satan (Job 1:6). "Accuser, adversary." Fittingly so named, descriptive of his demonic character.

Bibliography

Brown, Francis, S. R. Driver, Charles A. Briggs. *A Hebrew and English Lexicon of the Old Testament*. Translated by Edward Robinson. Oxford: Clarendon Press, 1977.

Bullinger, E. W. *Figures of Speech Used in the Bible*. Grand Rapids, MI: Baker Book House, 1987.

Caird, G. B. *The Language and Imagery of the Bible*. London: Duckworth Studies in Theology, 1980.

Clarke, Adam. *Clarke's Commentary*. 3 vols. Nashville: Abingdon Press, n.d.

Cooper, J. C. *An Illustrated Encyclopaedia of Traditional Symbols*. London: Thames and Hudson, 1982.

Eusebius. *The Ecclesiastical History and the Martyrs of Palestine*. 10 vols. Translated with introduction and notes by Hugh Jackson Lawlor and John Ernest Leonard Oulton. New York: Macmillan, 1927.

Girdlestone, Robert B. *Synonyms of the Old Testament*. Grand Rapids, MI: Wm. B. Eerdmans Publishing Co., 1978.

Harwood, Carl C. *Handbook of Bible Types and Symbols*. Denver: Denver Bible Institute Press, 1933.

Horton, George A. *Keys to Successful Scripture Study*. Salt Lake City: Bookcraft, 1989.

The Interpreter's Dictionary of the Bible. 5 vols. Nashville: Abingdon Press, 1962.

Jukes, Andrew. *The Law of Offerings*. Grand Rapids, MI: Kregal Publications, 1980.

Keel, Othmar. *The Symbolism of the Biblical World*. Translated by Timothy J. Hallett. New York: The Crossroad Publishing Company, 1985.

Lamsa, George M. *Idioms in the Bible Explained and a Key to the Original Gospels*. San Francisco: Harper and Row, 1985.

Leon-Dufour, Xavier. *Dictionary of the New Testament*. Translated by Terrence Prendergast. San Francisco: Harper & Row, 1980.

Lockyer, Herbert. *All the Divine Names and Titles in the Bible*. Grand Rapids, MI: Zondervan Publishing House, 1975.

Lund, Gerald N. "Understanding Scriptural Symbols." *Ensign*, Oct. 1986, pp. 23–27.

McConkie, Bruce R. *Doctrinal New Testament Commentary*. 3 vols. Salt Lake City: Bookcraft, 1965–73.

————. *The Millennial Messiah*. Salt Lake City: Deseret Book Co., 1982.

————. *Mormon Doctrine*. 2d ed. Salt Lake City: Bookcraft, 1966.

————. *The Promised Messiah*. Salt Lake City: Deseret Book Co., 1978.

McConkie, Joseph Fielding. *Gospel Symbolism*. Salt Lake City: Bookcraft, 1985.

————. *Prophets and Prophecy*. Salt Lake City: Bookcraft, 1988.

Metford, J. C. J. *Dictionary of Christian Lore and Legend*. London: Thames and Hudson, 1983.

Millet, Robert L., and Joseph Fielding McConkie. *In His Holy Name*. Salt Lake City: Bookcraft, 1988.

Murray, James A. H., H. Bradley, W. A. Craigie, C. T. Onions, eds., *The Oxford English Dictionary*. Oxford: Clarendon Press, 1989.

Odelain, O., and R. Seguineau. *Dictionary of Proper Names and Places in the Bible*. Translated and adapted by Matthew J. O'Connell. Garden City, NJ: Doubleday, 1981.

Parry, Donald W. "Hebrew Literary Patterns in the Book of Mormon." *Ensign*, October 1989, pp. 58–61.

————. "Sinai: Sanctuary and Temple." In *By Study and also by Faith: Essays in Honor of Hugh Nibley on Occasion of His Eightieth Birthday, 27 March 1990*, 2 vols., 1:451–69. Salt Lake City: Deseret Book Co., 1990.

————. "The Garden of Eden: Sacred Space, Sanctuary, Temple of God." *Explorations: A Journal for Adventurous Thought* 5 (Summer 1987): 83–107.

Partridge, Eric. *Origins: A Short Etymological Dictionary of Modern English*. New York: Greenwich House, 1983.

Richards, Lawrence O. *Expository Dictionary of Bible Words*. Grand Rapids, MI: Zondervan Publishing House, 1985.

Smith, Joseph. *History of The Church of Jesus Christ of Latter-day Saints*. Ed. B. H. Roberts. 7 vols. Salt Lake City: The Church of Jesus Christ of Latter-day Saints, 1932–51.

————. *Lectures on Faith*. Salt Lake City: Deseret Book Co., 1985.

————. *Teachings of the Prophet Joseph Smith.* Comp. Joseph Fielding Smith. Salt Lake City: Deseret Book Co., 1976.

Smith, Joseph Fielding. *Doctrines of Salvation.* Comp. Bruce R. McConkie. 3 vols. Salt Lake City: Bookcraft, 1954–56.

Taylor, John. *The Mediation and Atonement.* Salt Lake City: Deseret Book Co., 1970.

Thayer, Joseph Henry, D.D. *The New Thayer's Greek-English Lexicon of the New Testament.* Massachusetts: Hendrickson Publisher, 1981.

Times and Seasons. 6 vols. Nauvoo, Illinois: The Church of Jesus Christ of Latter-day Saints, 1839–46.

Webster's New World Dictionary of the American Language. 2d ed. Ed. David B. Guralnik. New York: World Publication Co., 1970.